THE BEST TV SHOWS THAT NEVER WERE

THE BEST TV SHOWS THAT NEVER WERE

LEE GOLDBERG

Text copyright © 2015 Adventures in Television, Inc.
All rights reserved.

ISBN: 1511590742
ISBN 13: 9781511590747

To Karen, Linda, and Tod…
and to Mom, who let me watch.
And to my wife, Valerie, for
putting up with me.

PREFACE TO THE NEW EDITION

This book was originally published back in 1991, following the enormous success of my big, fat hardcover *Unsold Television Pilots 1955-1989*. The original plan by Citadel Press was simply to release that book as a paperback. But when that proved too costly, the publisher decided they wanted a slim "Best Of" edition instead. I thought it was a mistake, but reluctantly went along with the idea, figuring it might be the first in a series of books. A pilot of its own, so-to-speak...

They gave the book the unwieldy and misleading title *Unsold TV Pilots: The Almost Complete Guide to Everything You Never Saw on TV, 1955-1990*. Even so, the book was a big success and established the format for the two, hour-long network TV specials that would follow: *The Greatest Shows You Never Saw* on CBS and *The Best TV Shows That Never Were* on ABC. I figured TV specials made much more sense than book sequels, and were also a lot more lucrative financially, so that was where I focused my energy (that said, the section in this book on TV series revivals did inspire me to write a spin-off book on the subject, which was published in 1993, and that I've re-released as *Television Fast Forward*).

There have been hundreds of great ... and truly terrible... unsold pilots in the years since this book was published, but I haven't added any of them to this edition, though I've added some new information here and there. Perhaps I'll do a new volume some day...or, more likely, another TV special. Until then, I hope you enjoy the 300 pilots in this book!

Lee Goldberg
June 2015

ACKNOWLEDGMENTS

This book would not have been possible without the help of Gloria Edwards of the Leo Burnett Agency—which has been reviewing pilots for its clients since 1955 and graciously made its files available to me.

I am indebted to Ms. Edwards, Leonard Reeg, and all the people who have worked in the TV Program Department of the Leo Burnett Agency over the years preparing those invaluable reports.

The information in this book is culled from the Leo Burnett reports, network press releases, personally conducted interviews, as well as listings, reviews, and articles from the entertainment industry publications *TV Guide*, *Variety*, *The Hollywood Reporter*, and *Electronic Media*.

All the information in this book was cross-referenced against previously published material whenever possible. A complete list of those books can be found in the bibliography. I'd like to thank authors Vincent Terrace, Alvin H. Marill, James Robert Parish, Jeb Perry, and Larry James Gianakos for their definitive works.

During the years it took to research and write the original, unabridged edition of this book, many people shared their time, experience, guidance, and patience with me—often more than I deserved. A special thanks to Burl Barer, William Rabkin, Adam Gold, Karen Bender, Stephen J. Cannell, Steven Bochco, Sherwood Schwartz, J. Bret Garwood, Roy Huggins, Harry Ackerman, David Gerber, Kelly Selvidge, Ron Givens, Janet Huck, Ron Alridge, David Klein, Richard Mahler, Morrie Gelman, David McDonnell, Lloyd Friedman, Elisa Williams, Megan Powell, Carol Fowler, Sean Hillier, Michael Carmack, Peter Biskind, and Bill Warren.

TABLE OF CONTENTS

HOW TO READ THIS BOOK

Here are the three hundred best, and worst, of what never was, the strangest and most unusual TV series ideas out of the thousands discarded by the networks over the years.

To qualify for the dubious honor of being included in this volume, the first criterion is failure. If a pilot sold and became a series, it is not included in this book. However, if the idea was for a prime-time network dramatic series or situation comedy, and it was given the thumbs-down, it could be included here.

The entries contained in these pages were culled from my book *Unsold Television Pilots 1955–1989*, a chronological listing of the 2,269 rejected ideas for prime-time series, as well as for the pilot ideas developed by the networks over the last three years.

The listings in this book, however, are arranged alphabetically within several sections—"High Concepts," "Sitcoms," "Big Screen to Small Screen," "The New Old," "Star Vehicles," "Real Dogs," "Johnny," and "Ghosts, Angels and Devils"—and were selected because, even among the failures, they were unique.

YOU KNOW IT'S A PILOT WHEN...

Pilots sneak onto the airwaves in many guises—TV movies, anthology stories, or even disguised as episodes of your favorite series.

Keep this checklist by your TV and you can quickly identify the pilots lurking on your airwaves.

You Know It's a Pilot When:
- the hero has been raised by animals.
- the hero is a robot created to be the perfect soldier, but decides he'd rather not kill.
- the hero, in a freak accident, becomes endowed with special powers and becomes either a secret agent, a private eye, or a wanderer helping people in need.
- the detective is blind, electric, or quadriplegic.
- you can hear a dog's or baby's thoughts.
- one of the stars is human, the other animated.
- the show is a television adaptation of last year's hit movie.
- the hero is pursued by an obsessed cop, scientist, reporter, or evil organization dedicated to his capture, dissection, or false imprisonment.
- a man hunts down the murderer of his best friend or immediate family and decides he likes it so much, he becomes a private eye.
- the stars are trapped in the past or future.
- the show focuses on a group of people wandering through space, either on a brave new mission, or just for the fun of it.
- the hero is an alien or a ghost, or was born in a petrie dish.
- it's a remake of an old series.
- the main character introduces his entire family and all his friends, and recites the story of his life in the first ten minutes.
- it stars Dale Robinette, Suzanne Somers, Art Hindle, or Stephanie Faracy.
- the *TV Guide* listing reads: PILOT.

INTRODUCTION

Do car companies share the new model designs they're thinking about? Does Yves St. Laurent pass out his sketches for everyone to see before unveiling his creations? Does Apple let IBM peek at its newest PC? Only television makes its developmental process available to competitors—and to us. And that's what's fun about unsold TV pilots.

By watching and studying flop pilots, we can feel like we "are in on the machinations of television," says producer David Gerber, president of MGM Television. "There's a curiosity factor, maybe even a true perversity, in watching these things and asking, 'Why the hell did it ever get made?'"

A television pilot is a sample episode of a proposed weekly series. An *unsold* pilot is much, much more.

A pilot is fresh faces and old favorites lining up for a one-night stand with the viewing public. It's producers, writers, directors, and network executives scrambling to keep up with the changing trends in American taste. It's the betting stub you're left with after your horse has lost the race.

"When pilots work, they work well," says Perry Simon, NBC's executive vice president of prime-time programs. "And when they flop, they thud pretty loudly. There are a thousand ways it can go wrong and only one way it will go right."

Pilots sneak onto the airwaves disguised as specials, TV movies, lavish mini-series, or even as an episode of your favorite show. Good or bad, pilots give viewers the rare opportunity to second-guess the networks at their own game—judging which ideas have the potential to become hit series.

But it's more than a game. It's a business that eats up more than $30 million a year—at *each* network. That doesn't count the $20 million or more a studio invests. Each year a network is bombarded with thousands of ideas—even many times commissioning its own. From these it may buy 125 scripts,

1

shoot thirty pilots, and pick up six or seven as fall series. Of those series, perhaps two will survive the season. One hundred and three pilots, for instance, were made for the 1986–87 schedule, only thirty-six became series, and of those, just thirteen survived to celebrate their first birthdays.

With odds like that, why bother? Because if a pilot sells, and if the series can make it through a few seasons, untold riches could await the producers in syndication—perhaps well over the hundreds of millions of dollars M*A*S*H, Magnum, P.I., and Cosby have made.

A pilot is a way for networks to hedge their bets before risking millions for twenty-two episodes of a show that may look great on paper and turn out rotten when made. For producers, pilot-making is a multimillion dollar gamble that offers no hedging. Although the networks pay a fee for making the pilot, producers invariably spend more because they want the show to look great—because they want it to sell.

But unless the pilot evolves into a series, "we've got to absorb substantial deficits," says Dean Hargrove, producer of Matlock. "It's a big gamble, and you'll probably never get your money back. Pilots are a waste of time and money. They don't make shows any more successful. At the end of every season, the streets are littered with canceled series."

Whether pilots are the best way to sell a series can be argued endlessly. The fact is, that's the way series have been sold since television began. What has changed is the buyer.

In its infancy, television was the bastard child of the entertainment industry. The new medium, modeled after radio, was shunned by the major Hollywood studios, which saw television as a threat to their bottom line. So, the programs came from aggressive, independent producers, and the networks, all of whom pitched their series concepts directly to the advertising agencies, whose clients footed a big chunk of the pilot-production costs and ultimately decided which series would get on the air. Network television became picture radio, adopting many of the same series and carrying on the practice of single-sponsor shows.

That all changed around 1960, when several powerful forces wrested control of television programming from the advertisers and gave it to the networks. The network chiefs had been anxious to change the power structure of commercial television for years. Sylvester "Pat" Weaver, then NBC's president and a former advertising agency executive, believed networks should control programming and that sponsors should buy advertising time the same way they bought space in a magazine. And like a magazine, which chooses what articles it will print, a network should decide what series it will air.

Financial realities forced the advertisers to consider Weaver's vision whether they liked it or not. The high cost of production was making it impossible for any one advertiser to bankroll a program. With Weaver's magazine concept, several advertisers could share the burden and the rewards of sponsoring a show.

Meanwhile, Mickey Mouse was changing the movie moguls' minds about television. The enormous success of ABC's 1954 series *Disneyland*, produced for television by Walt Disney's studio, convinced the majors there was money in the medium. The more established, deep-pocketed studios that earlier turned up their collective noses at this upstart medium called television started cranking out programming, and they weren't about to let a bunch of advertisers tell them how to do it.

But it wasn't the big network honchos, the big price tags, or the big studios that finally forced advertisers out of the programming business. It was the revelation that the advertisers had rigged popular, prime-time game shows, and the subsequent scandal that erupted, that dealt the final blow. The networks canceled the game shows and promised the American people they would control programming from now on.

The networks became the buyers, and frequently the originators, of series programming. Influential advertising agency executives like Lee Rich and Grant Tinker left their jobs to join the networks or create their own production companies. A new system emerged. Independent producers and studios developed pilots specifically to suit a particular network's needs and personality.

The key to making any sale is the right product, at the right time, at the right price. A producer with a series idea makes a sales pitch to the networks. Having a major star, a prestigious writer, or a well-known director already "attached" to the project can often turn an otherwise so-so concept into a quick sale. If the network likes the idea, it will commission a script, and if programming executives like what they read, they will order a pilot. For a sitcom, that usually means a thirty-minute sample episode. Dramatic series pilots are a different breed altogether.

By the early 1970s, most dramatic pilots were two-hour or ninety-minute television movies that cost a fortune and were designed to blow the network executives right out of their seats. The problem was, if the pilot sold, the studio had to "duplicate the pilot each week for a lot less money," says David Gerber. Often, the shows not only didn't but probably couldn't fulfill the promise of their multimillion-dollar pilots.

"If you dazzle 'em in your pilot with fancy footwork, spectacular car crashes, and European locales," says *Equalizer* producer James McAdams, "and then the first week that you're a series, the hero chases someone through the backlot and tackles him, that's not a pilot, that's deceit."

That's the major reason the networks currently are saving their pennies and ordering fewer movie-length pilots, opting instead for the so-called typical hour-long episode and other formats that don't cost as much. The networks feel that a sixty-minute pilot is more indicative of a typical episode of the proposed series. That's nice for the networks, but it makes pilots an even bigger risk for the studios. While a TV movie pilot can recoup its production deficits in syndication, foreign theatrical release, and home video sales, "what the hell can be done with a one-hour pilot that doesn't sell?" asks producer Stephanie Kowal, formerly Universal Television's dramatic development executive. "Nothing."

Producers also complain that the hour-long format forces them to cram too much information into the show, usually at the expense of character. And if the characters don't come across well, the pilot is dead. Greg Maday, formerly CBS's vice president of dramatic development, believes that a sixty-minute pilot can still be "good entertainment if it's done correctly. We don't want the pilots to feel like a piece of engineering with no dramatic values, and they don't have to be." But they almost always are.

The pilot has to get across the series concept, the backgrounds and relationships of the characters and tell a compelling story, all in one show. That fact alone guarantees the pilot can never be like a typical episode of the proposed series, where the concept is a given and the characters are already accepted by the viewers.

"The problem with one-hour pilots is you have to tell such a simple story that it's not interesting," says producer Stephen J. Cannell, the man behind such hits as *The Rockford Files* and *Hunter*. "The network says, 'Make it like episode five.' Well, I'm sorry, you can't do that."

One way to avoid that problem has been to shoot the pilot as an episode of an existing series. It's also a lot cheaper, because if the pilot doesn't sell, the costs can be recouped when the host series goes into syndication. *Star Trek, Who's the Boss?, Spenser: For Hire, Kojak, Cosby, Golden Girls, Magnum, P.I.,* and *The Untouchables* are just a few of the many series that count unsold pilots among their episodes. Ann Daniel, ABC's vice president of dramatic development, thinks episodes-as-pilots are "a terrific way to do a pilot. It's more economically responsible." But episodes-as-pilots have their own artistic and financial pitfalls.

"You have to minimize your own protagonists to give the show to the pilot star. It makes for a bad episode of the show," says James McAdams. "A good episode is where the hero of the series is the star, not the guest star. The hero is reduced to a bookend or a bystander." Some feel it's not worth the effort.

"They hardly ever work out. It's just a cheap way of knocking off a pilot," says Jeff Sagansky, president of CBS Entertainment.

And what do the viewers think? "They probably hate it," Sagansky says. "The reason they watch the show is not to see pilots. But, if you do it once a year, I guess it's okay."

Producers can get away with episodes-as-pilots much more often, and with a lot less grief, in anthology series. On shows like *Kraft Suspense Theatre, The Dick Powell Theatre,* and more recently with *Disney Sunday Movie* and *The Magical World of Disney,* nearly all the self-contained episodes were pilots.

With program costs and studio deficits skyrocketing, many producers believe the networks should junk pilots altogether and make series commitments to proven talent instead. "We are great believers that the best way to make the best series is to make commitments with the best possible people," says Stu Erwin, former president of MTM Enterprises, which sold several shows, including *St. Elsewhere* and *Mary,* that way.

"I understand networks wanting to see what the new guys can do," says Stephanie Kowal, "but when you're dealing with an established group, you don't need a pilot."

That philosophy worked with *Cheers, L.A. Law,* and *Hooperman,* but it can backfire, too. When *Hill Street Blues* producer Steven Bochco pitched NBC on the serialized adventures of a baseball team, it sounded like a great idea. In 1983, the network bought thirteen episodes of *Bay City Blues* sight unseen but canceled the series with half the episodes unaired. *Life With Lucy*, *AfterMASH*, *Jessie*, *Mr. Smith*, *Private Eye*, *Cassie and Company*, and *Partners in Crime* were also commitments—and disasters.

"It's the kind of deal everyone wants, but it has its flaws," says producer Tom Mankiewicz, who sold *Gavilan* to NBC in 1982 without a pilot. It was canceled so fast even he has trouble remembering it. "You go on the air right away, and everything that does and doesn't work about your character is rehearsed in front of the audience. But when you do a pilot, you can look at it and say, 'It works great when he does X, but it doesn't when he does Y.' You can fix it before the audience sees it."

Networks want pilots, but producers gripe about the high cost. Producers want commitments, but the networks want to see what they are buying. There's a possible compromise. Both networks and producers have long been experimenting with brief, ten-to twenty-minute demonstration films rather than shooting a pilot. The practice has yet to take hold, and only a few series, like *Knightrider* and *Emerald Point, NAS*, have sold that way.

"To get the point across, it works well," says Richard Chapman, who produced a demo film for CBS about a Ninja-trained female spy. "The twenty-minute presentation is more eye-catching and gets the best of a shorter attention span." Chapman wrote an hour-long pilot script and from that culled the demo film, which was made up of three character scenes—one funny, one tense, and one showing warmth—and some Ninja combat. The series didn't sell.

Greg Maday, now developing programs for Warner Bros., thinks demos are useless. "They simply aren't indicative of what the series will be."

"It's a vicious circle," says veteran producer William Blinn, whose credits include *Our House*, *Fame*, and *Roots*. "You can't say demos are wrong because they have highlights and that two hours are wrong because the series won't deliver what the pilot did."

Selling the pilot, in whatever form, as a series is a feat every producer tries to achieve in April, when the networks huddle in New York in boardrooms, restaurants, hotel suites, and limousines to devise their fall season programming strategy. And the producers are there to help them along—they are there for questions, drinks, dinners, plays, and schmoozing, especially schmoozing. That ritual, too, is questioned by producers.

"It's all a nice convention, part of salesmanship, but I don't think wining and dining the executives is a decisive factor," says McAdams. "There might be a few borderline cliffhanger situations where it might help. But if I were a network executive, I would look at the producer's abilities and the pilot and not be influenced by a filet mignon."

"A producer's enthusiasm for his product is infectious, that's something the networks listen to," Jeff Sagansky admits. "Is it a deciding factor? In the end, the program has to speak for itself." Yet most pilots die, whether it's in a scheduling meeting or over lobster at Sardi's.

"A lot of good scripts and pilots die because New York didn't understand them," laments David Gerber. "Or everybody on the West Coast loved it, but somewhere over the Rockies somebody with a death ray beam hit the plane, and the pilot show landed as dust in New York. You just sit there and wonder 'What happened to my film?'"

What happens to the flop pilot? Occasionally another network will pick one up. A few, like the disastrous *Marblehead Manor* and *She's the Sheriff*, get a second chance in first-run syndication. And still others end up gathering dust at your local video store.

Those are the exceptions. Unsold pilots are rarely exhumed by anyone.

"It's dead, on my shelf, and late some night I might get stoned and look at it," says *Family Ties* producer Gary David Goldberg. "Or it will show up in one of those 'Shame Theatres,' 'Failure Playhouses,' or four-in-a-row specials when America doesn't know what hit 'em late one night."

The networks are in the entertainment business and, lucky for us consumers, even the business-behind-the-business is entertainment. Pilots may be lunacy, but as long as they make them, as long as they sneak them into prime time, we can all pretend we can run a network.

HIGH CONCEPTS

The Flying Nun. Fantasy Island. My Mother, the Car. Supertrain. Me and the Chimp. The Six Million Dollar Man.

The titles say it all.

These shows were "high concepts," outlandish ideas designed to grab network executives and captivate viewers. Some work, like *The Flying Nun*, while others, like *My Mother, the Car*, are ridiculed and forever epitomize network insanity.

Despite the risks, "high concepts" are coveted. No idea is too wild, too offensive, or too crazy to be considered. CBS once contemplated the story of an unjustly disgraced policeman who is fired from the force, secretly undergoes a sex change operation and reenlists as a policewoman to clear his/her name.

Inane? Laughable? Unthinkable?

Maybe.

But is it any crazier than a man who fights crime with his talking car? A half-man, half-robot secret agent who runs in slow motion? An astronaut who marries a genie-from-a-bottle? A sewer-dwelling beast who battles evil with his above-ground lover, an attractive big-city district attorney?

As absurd as they sounded, *Knightrider, The Six Million Dollar Man, I Dream of Jeannie,* and *Beauty and the Beast* were still hits.

Most high concepts simply take a new twist on a typical television format (two cops—and one is an alien!) or exploit a familiar character (Merlin the Magician is a San Francisco auto mechanic!) or are built around a unique, audience-pleasing special effect (his truck becomes a laser-firing helicopter!).

The execution of the idea is everything. Can it be done with credibility? Will the viewers suspend their disbelief? Do the creators take their own idea seriously? What sounds really stupid on paper could look great on film and demolish the competition—or it could become an infamous, costly, and embarrassing, career-damaging failure.

Here are some that didn't make it. How would these proposed series have been remembered? You be the judge. And while you're deciding, ask yourself if *you* would have bought *The Flying Nun*....

DRAMAS

1. **The Annihilator.** NBC 4/6/86. 2 hours. Universal Television. Director: Michael Chapman. Executive Producer: Roderick Taylor. Producer: Alex Beaton. Writers: Roderick Taylor and Bruce Taylor. Music: Sylvester Levay.

   Newspaper publisher Richard Armour discovers that Angela Taylor, his reporter girlfriend, and all passengers of a commercial jetliner on which she was flying, have been eliminated and replaced by alien-created robots. He kills "her" in self-defense and is hunted both by the police (who want him for murder) and the aliens (who don't want him ruining their plans for world domination). Mark Chapman, star of the pilot and prospective star of the series, was to have portrayed John Lennon in the 1985 TV movie *John and Yoko: A Love Story* but was persuaded to give up the role because he had the misfortune of having the same name as Lennon's killer.

   Cast: Mark Lindsay Chapman (as Richard Armour), Catherine Mary Stewart (Angela Taylor), Susan Blakely (Layla), Lisa Blount (Cindy), Earl Boen (Sid), Geoffrey Lewis (Alan Jeffries), Nicole Eggert (Elyse), Brion James (Alien), Barry Pearl (Eddie), Paul Brinager (Pops), Channing Chase (Susan Weiss), Barbara Townsend (Celia Evans), Glen Vernon (Henry Evans), Biff Yeager (FBI Agent), Richard Partlow (FBI Agent #2), Toni Attell (Patti), James Parks (Policeman), Roger LaRue (Man in Coat), Stanley Bennett Clay (Cammie), Gregg Collins (Policeman).

2. **Assignment: Earth.** NBC 3/29/68. 60 minutes. Desilu. Director: Marc Daniels. Producer: Gene Roddenberry. Associate Producer: Robert H.

Justman. Writer: Art Wallace, from a story by Art Wallace and Gene Roddenberry. Music: Alexander Courage.

Aired as an episode of *Star Trek*. Robert Lansing plays a benevolent alien who comes to earth to protect us from destroying ourselves. He's aided by a scatterbrain (Teri Garr) and a magical cat named Isis. He also brings with him a wide array of strange devices and his own version of a "transporter room." In the pilot, he tries to stop the launching of a satellite-come-nuclear bomb and clashes with the crew of the *U.S.S. Enterprise*, which has journeyed into the past on a routine historic research mission. At the end of the episode, Captain Kirk (William Shatner) and Mr. Spock (Leonard Nimoy) examine their computer's history banks and tell the two that they have "some interesting experiences" awaiting them. Unfortunately, TV viewers never got a chance to see them.

Cast: Robert Lansing (as Gary Seven), Teri Garr (Roberta Lincoln), James Keefer (Cromwell), Morgan Jones (Col. Nesvig), Paul Baxley (Security Chief), Bruce Mars (First Policewoman), Ted Gehring (Second Policeman).

3. **Badlands 2005.** ABC 8/29/88. 60 minutes. Lizard Productions, Hoyts Productions, and Columbia Pictures Television. Director: George Miller. Executive Producer/Writer/Creator: Reuben Leder. Music: Bruce Rowland.

    The story of a U.S. marshal (Lewis Smith) and his Cyborg partner (Miguel Ferrer) who patrol the now-barren American West in a high-tech car for a tough female boss (Sharon Stone). The pilot opened with the crawl: "In 1995, a severe drought forced Americans to flee the West for the cities. Water became more precious than gold. Now, in 2005, settlers are coming back, meeting new challenges and age-old adversaries." And age-old plots—in the pilot, titled "Brides of Lizard Gulch," the hero must escort mail-order brides through dangerous territory.

    Cast: Lewis Smith (as Garson MacBeth), Miguel Ferrer (Rex), Sharon Stone (Alex Neil), Debra Engle (Joanie Valentine), Caitlin O'Heaney (Sara Gwynne), Lloyd Alan (Johnny Cantrell), Hugh Keays-Byrne (Moondance), Gus Mercurio (Stubbs), Robyn Douglass (Sue

Cantrell), Marc Cales (Engineer), Steven Kuhn (Delaney), Justin Mongo (Braggo), Dave Arnett (Technician).

4. **Baffled.** NBC 1/30/73. 2 hours. Arena Productions and ITC Entertainment. Director: Philip Leacock. Executive Producer: Norman Felton. Producers: Philip Leacock and John Oldknow. Writer: Theodore Apstein. Music: Richard Hill.

    Leonard Nimoy stars as a race car driver who, after being injured in a crash, acquires amazing psychic abilities and is called upon to help police and government agencies. He's aided by a female psychiatrist (Susan Hampshire) who specializes in the occult, and, by his chauffeur (Ewan Roberts). Although shot in England, had this gone to series, it would have been produced in Hollywood.

    Cast: Leonard Nimoy (as Tom Kovack), Susan Hampshire (Michelle Brent), Ewan Roberts (Hopkins), Rachel Roberts (Mrs. Farraday), Vera Miles (Andrea Glenn), Jewel Branch (Jennifer Glenn), Valeria Taylor (Louise Sanford), Ray Brookes (George Tracewell), Angharad Rees (Peggy Tracewell), Christopher Benjamin (Verelli), Mike Murray (Parrish), Milton Johns (Dr. Reed), A1 Mancini (TV Interviewer), John Rae (Theater Doorman), Patsy Smart (Cleaning Woman), Shane Rimmer (Track Announcer), Roland Brand (Track Mechanic), Bill Hutchinson (Doctor), Michael Sloan (Ambulance Man), Dan Meaden (Policeman).

5. **The Bakery.** CBS 7/20/90. 60 minutes. GTG Entertainment. Director: Peter Levin. Executive Producers/Writers/Creators: Brad Kern and John Wirth. Producer: Mel Efros.

    An exceptionally well-made, innovative twist on the conventional cop show, developed for CBS for the 1989–90 season. Each episode of the proposed series would frequently time-shift between decades while following a core group of police officers through the 1960s, the 1990s, and the early part of the twenty-first century. In the mid-sixties, the precinct where Officer Mike Kelly works has been relocated temporarily to an abandoned bakery. The city's racial tension has seeped into the precinct cops, who are rebelling against the arrival of Charles Slater, a black officer who is teamed with a draft-dodging rookie, Buck Bradford. In the nineties, the precinct still is "temporarily" housed in the bakery, Kelly is now the captain, and Slater has risen to detective and is teamed with his long-dead partner's daughter Dana Bradford. But by the year 2000, whites are in the minority in L.A., Kelly has been demoted to sergeant and has a partner named Hotshot Williams, a cowboy-ish cop who flaunts the rules—to the consternation of the new captain, Dana Bradford, who is having a secret affair with Kelly. This remarkable pilot, in the *Hill Street Blues/St. Elsewhere* mold, was passed over by the network, which didn't have a late-night slot for it. CBS should have made room.

Cast: David Dukes (as Mike Kelly), Clevant Derricks (Charles Slater), Stephen Eckholdt (Buck Bradford), Kate McNeil (Dana Bradford), Perry Lang (Hotshot Williams), also David Kagan, Kim McArthur.

6. **Band of Gold.** CBS 3/19/61. 30 minutes. MCA. Director: Bud Yorkin. Producers: Norman Lear and Bud Yorkin. Writers: Dale and Katherine Eunson.

Aired as an episode of *G.E. Theatre.* This was a pilot for a series of unrelated, thirty-minute stories dealing with marriage and all starring James Franciscus and Suzanne Pleshette as a different couple each week.

Cast: Suzanne Pleshette (as Renee Fontaine), James Franciscus (Bill Taylor), Jack Weston (Freddie Pringle), Fifi D'Orsay (Simone), J. Pat O'Malley (Cabbie), Mary Ellen Smith (Girl).

7. **Battles: The Murder That Wouldn't Die (aka Battles).** NBC 3/9/80. 2 hours. Universal Television and Glen Larson Productions. Director: Ron Satlof. Executive Producer: Glen A. Larson. Producer: Ben Kadish. Writers: Glen A. Larson and Michael Sloan. Music: Stu Phillips and Glen A. Larson.

William Conrad as a cop-turned-college-security-chief and part-time football coach at a Hawaii university who also dabbles in crime-solving. The concept was designed to both provide room for young storylines (and engender youth appeal) and more traditional action / adventure plots (and appeal to adults). Six episodes were written, but the series never materialized.

Cast: William Conrad (as William Battles), Lane Caudell (Joe Jackson), Robin Mattson (Shelby Battles), Marj Dusay (Dean Mary Phillips), Tommy Aguilar (Tuliosis), Roger Bowen (Jack Spaulding), Edward Binns (Alan Battles), Don Porter (Rocky Jenson), John Hillerman (Paul Harrison), Kenneth Tobey (Chuck Parks), Ben Piazza (Dr. John Spencer), Sharon Acker (Jill Spencer), Mike Kellin (Capt. Ames), Jose Ferrer (Jeff Briggs).

8. **Beach Patrol.** ABC 4/30/79. 90 minutes. Spelling/Goldberg Productions. Director: Bob Kelljan. Executive Producers: Aaron Spelling and Leonard Goldberg. Producer: Philip Fehrle. Writers: James David Buchanan and Ronald Austin. Music: Barry DeVorzon.

A female narcotics cop (Robin Strand) is transferred to an elite police squad of three (Christine DeLisle, Richard Hill, and Jonathan Frakes) that patrols the California beaches. In the pilot, she is targeted for assassination after spotting a fugitive mafioso.

Cast: Robin Strand (as Russ Patrick), Jonathan Frakes (Marty Green), Christine DeLisle (Jan Plummer), Richard Hill (Earl "Hack" Hackman), Michael Gregory (Sgt. Lou Markowski), Paul Burke (Wes Dobbs), Michael V. Gazzo (Banker), Panchito Gomez (Wild Boy), Mimi Maynard (Wanda), Princess O'Malley (Tall Girl).

9. **Braddock.** CBS 7/22/68. 60 minutes. Twentieth Century Fox Television. Director: Walter Doniger. Producer/Writer: Paul Monash.

A science-fiction adventure about a private eye, played by Tom Simcox, who works in Los Angeles in 1977 and uses such futuristic devices as a Viewphone. It was shot on location at U.C.L.A.

Cast: Tom Simcox (as Braddock), Stephen McNally (Tratner), Karen Steele (Louise Tratner), Lloyd Bochner (Lawrence), Kathy Kersh (Marie), Tom Reese (Mongol), John Doucette (Lt. McMillan), Colette Jackson (Beverly), Arthur Adams (Hitchess), Don Marshall (Gilmore), Laura Lindsay (Victoria), Robert Sampson (Policeman), Charles Macauley (Man).

10. Chain Letter. ABC 8/5/89. 60 minutes. Indie Production Company and Phoenix Entertainment. Director: Thomas J. Wright. Executive Producers: Bruce J. Sallan and Daniel Melnick. Producer: Irv Zavada. Writer: Bill Bleich. Music: Brad Fiedel.

Ian McShane is The Messenger of Death who sends out chain letters to mortals that offer temptation—and those who give in could die. His adversary is Miss Smith (played by Leslie Bevis), who believes that people are basically good, and who tries to steer people away from temptation—and doom. The critics were not kind. *Variety* called it "utter hokum...this is one of those dumb pilots that should never have been made."

Cast: Ian McShane (as Messenger of Death), Leslie Bevis (Miss Smith), Mary Page Keller (Janet Coulter), Merritt Butrick (Raymond Maston), Granville Van Deusen (John Hastings), Nancy Cartwright (Margo), John Hostetter (Lt. Harris), Sam Melville (Tom), Mike Tino (Nick), Bruce Newbold (Cop), Margot Rose (Lois), Tom Spackman (Patrolman), Edgar Small (Sammy Cofwin), Mark Phelan (Lt. Miller).

11. Clone Master. NBC 9/14/78. 2 hours. Mel Ferber Productions and Paramount Television. Director: Don Medford. Executive Producer: Mel Ferber. Producer/Writer: John D.F. Black. Music: Glen Paxton.

Art Hindle is a government scientist who makes thirteen clones of himself, each sent out to fight evil and each of whom would become the focus of a different episode of the proposed series. If the series had continued past thirteen weeks, presumably the scientist would clone thirteen more of himself.

Cast: Art Hindle (as Dr. Simon Shane), Robyn Douglass (Gussie), John Van Dreelen (Salt), Ed Lauter (Bender), Mario Roccuzzo (Harry Tiezer), Ralph Bellamy (Ezra Louthin), Stacey Keach, Sr. (Admiral Millus), Lew Brown (Fire Chief), Bill Sorrells (Reporter), Robert Karnes (Trankus), Betty Lou Robinson (Alba Toussaint), Vernon Weddle (Pine), Steve Eastin (Huberman), Philip Pine (Commander Tiller), Kirk Duncan (General), Ian Sullivan (Pat Singer), Trent Dolan (Schnerlich), James O'Connell (Sands).

12. Condor (aka Cobra). ABC 8/10/86. 90 minutes. Orion Television and Jay gee Productions. Director: Virgil Vogel. Executive Producer: Jerry Golod. Producers: Peter Nelson, Arnold Oroglini, Len Janson, and Chuck Menville. Writers: Len Janson and Chuck Menville. Music: Ken Heller.

Set in the 1990s, this action pilot followed the exploits of an ace secret agent (Ray Wise) and his robot partner (Wendy Kilbourne), working for an elite, high-tech espionage agency run by Craig Stevens.

Cast: Ray Wise (as Chris Proctor), Wendy Kilbourne (Lisa Hampton), Craig Stevens (Cyrus Hampton), Vic Polizos (Commissioner Ward), James Avery (Cass), Cassandra Gava (Sumiko), Carolyn Seymour (Rachel Hawkins), Shawn Michaels (Watch Commander), Mario Roccuzzo (Manny), Catherine Battistone (Lieutenant), Barbara Beckley (Water Controller), Diane Bellamy (Opera Singer), Gene Ricknell (Bartender), Myra Chason (Pirate Pete Waitress), Tony Epper (Cop), Brad Fisher (Man), Phil Fondacaro (Quaid), Mike Freeman (Technician), Karen Montgomery (Monique).

13. Cover Girls. NBC 5/18/77. 90 minutes. Columbia Pictures Television. Director: Jerry London. Executive Producer: David Gerber. Producers: Charles B. FitzSimons and Mark Rodgers. Writer: Mark Rodgers. Music: Richard Shores.

Cornelia Sharpe and Jayne Kennedy are globetrotting fashion models who are actually secret agents working for stone-faced Don Galloway. George Lazenby, who once played James Bond, and Vince Edwards, Ben Casey of yore, guest star.

Cast: Cornelia Sharpe (as Linda Allen), Jayne Kennedy (Monique Lawrence), Don Galloway (James Andrews), George Lazenby (Michael), Vince Edwards (Russell Bradner), Jerry Douglas (Fritz Porter), Michael Baselson (Paul Reynolds), Don Johnson (Johnny Wilson), Ellen Travolta (Ziggy), Sean Garrison (Sven), Bill Overton (Football Player).

14. Crash Island. NBC 4/11/81. 60 minutes. Universal Television. Director: Hollingsworth Morse. Producers: Don Nelson and Gino Grimaldi. Writers: Don Nelson and Arthur Alsberg. Music: Jimmy Haskell.

Yet another in Universal's endless stream of "stranded-on-an-uncharted-island" pilots and, by far, the worst of the lot. Greg Mullavey and Meadowlark Lemon are charter airline pilots flying a fifteen-member Y.M.C.A. coed swim team to Hawaii when, suddenly, the weather started getting rough, the tiny plane was tossed…you get the idea. Stranded on an uncharted isle, and aided by a Japanese soldier (Pat Morita) who has been a castaway there for thirty years, they form their own society and try to cope with their plight. *Variety* called it a cross between *Gilligan's Island* and *The Bad News Bears*, and "the resultant silliness was highly unpromising."

Cast: Greg Mullavey (as Happy Burleson), Meadowlark Lemon (Meadowlark), Jenny Sherman (Ceci), Warren Berlinger (Coach Bundy), Sheila DeWindt (Tina), Pat Morita (Kazi Yamamora), Penelope Sudrow (Sandy), Lisa Lindren (Kris), Heather Hobbs (Heather), Elizabeth Ringwald (Susan), Paul Jarnagin, Jr. (Chubby), Jeffrey Knootz (Harry), Gregory Knootz (Larry), Bradley Liberman (Brett), Rusty Gilligan (Fred), Danie Wade Dalton (Mark), Cjon Damitri Patterson (Angie), Jeff Kirkland (Jeff).

15. **Cro-Magnon (aka The Tribe).** ABC 12/11/74. 90 minutes. Universal Television. Director: Richard A. Colla. Producer: George Eckstein. Writer/Creator: Lane Slate. Music: Hal Mooney.

The adventures of a Cro-Magnon family fighting for survival—and against Neanderthals—in Europe at the end of the last Ice Age. Victor French played the leader of the family, Adriana Shaw was his wife, Mark Gruner his son, and Henry Wilcoxon was the wise elder. Shot in Beaumont, California.

Cast: Victor French (as Mathis), Adriana Shaw (Jen), Henry Wilcoxon (Gana), Warren Vanders (Gorin), Stewart Moss (Gato), Sam Gilman (Rouse), Tani Phelps Guthrie (Sarish), Mark Gruner (Perron), Meg Wyllie (Hertha), Nancy Elliot (Ardis), Jeannine Brown (Orda), Dominique Pinassi (Kiska), Jack Scalici (The Neanderthal), Paul Richards (Narrator).

16. **Danger Team.** ABC 1990. 30 minutes. Lorimar Television. Director: Helaine Head. Executive Producer: Tom Greene. Producers: David

Bleiman and Ken Pontac. Writers: Michael Wagner, Harley Peyton, and Tom Greene.

Kathleen Beller plays a bookkeeper-turned-private-eye who solves crimes with the help of three animated clay figures and the latest high-tech equipment.

Cast: Kathleen Beller (as Cheryl Stinger), Steve Levitt (Chris), Steven Gilborn (Mr. Weidner).

17. **D5B—Steel Collar Man.** CBS 8/7/85. 60 minutes. Columbia Pictures Television and Cypress Point Productions. Director: James Frawley. Executive Producers: Gerald Abrams and Dave Thomas. Producer: David Latt. Writer/Creator: Dave Thomas. Music: Tom Scott.

Like ABC's *J.O.E. and the Colonel*, this is the story of a government-created robot soldier (Charles Rocket) that can think for itself—which isn't exactly what the government ordered when it financed the experiments. The government wants it destroyed. The scientist (Dorian LoPinto) who created D5B helps the robot escape, and they team up with a truck driver (Hoyt Axton). Together, the robot, trucker, and scientist roam the country, helping people and running from an obsessed government agent (Chuck Connors). The proposed series would mix adventure with comedy.

Cast: Charles Rocket (as D5B), Dorian LoPinto (Dr. Constance Fletcher), Hoyt Axton (Red), Chuck Connors (J.G. Willis), Paul Dooley (Don Liddle), Chuck Mitchell (Big Jake), David Wohl (Weasel), Robert O'Reilly (Johnny), Jeffrey Josephson (Tino), John Brandon (General), Kevin Scannell (Trooper), John Lystine (Trooper #2), John Furlong (Security Guard), Biff Yeager (Truck Driver #1), Scott Perry (Truck Driver #2), John C. Reade (Truck Driver #3), Ebbe Roe Smith (Salesman), John Solari (Cashier), David Dunard (Bob), Kelly Jean Peters (Bob's Wife), Barry Kivel (Attendant), Dan Barrows (Al).

18. **The Disciple.** CBS 3/16/79. 60 minutes. Universal Television. Director: Reza Badiyi. Executive Producer: Kenneth Johnson. Producers/ Writers: Nicholas Corea and James G. Hirsch. Music: Joe Harnell.

Aired as an episode of *The Incredible Hulk*. An Irish cop (Rick Springfield) resigns from the force after his father is killed and studies with an ancient Chinese philosopher. The ex-cop uses these new skills of self-discipline as a private eye whose cases often bring him into conflict with his brother (Gerald McRaney), who is still on the force. Guest stars include Mako, Stacy Keach, Sr., and George Loros.

19. **Divided We Stand.** ABC 7/21/88. 60 minutes. Don Brinkley Productions and Aaron Spelling Productions. Director: Michael Tuchner. Executive Producer: Aaron Spelling. Producer/Writer: Don Brinkley. Music: Artie Kane.

This pilot offers an unusual format for telling a traditional story. The proposed series would focus on Cody (Seth Green), a ten-year-old boy whose parents (Michael Brandon and Kerrie Keane) are divorced but share joint custody. In television land, that means Daddy gets Cody for the first half of the show, and Mommy gets him for the second half. In the pilot, Cody tries to reunite his parents on what would have been their fourteenth wedding anniversary. The "Gibbs" became the "Dobbs" in the final pilot.

Cast: Michael Brandon (as Bryan Gibbs), Kerrie Keane (Katie Gibbs), Seth Green (Cody Gibbs), Madge Sinclair (Hattie Wickwire), Irena Ferris (Topaze), Diane Stilwell (Rachel).

20. **Doctor Franken.** NBC 1/13/80. 2 hours. Titus Productions, Janus Productions, and NBC Productions. Directors: Jeff Lieberman and Marvin J. Chomsky. Executive Producer: Herbert Brodkin. Producer: Robert Berger. Writer: Lee Thomas, from a story by Jeff Lieberman and Lee Thomas, from the book *Frankenstein* by Mary Shelley. Music: John Morris.

In the television world, a man with special powers either becomes a secret agent or a fugitive. The latter is the case in this pilot, a weird rehash of *Frankenstein*, set in modern-day Manhattan. Dr. Victor Franken (Robert Vaughn) is a descendant of the infamous Dr. Frankenstein and creates a creature of his own when he revives a dead accident victim by rebuilding him with organs and limbs from the hospital medical bank. The result is a creature (Robert Perrault) with a mind of his own—but also with the memories, convictions, and emotions of the people whose "parts" he now has. In the proposed series, he'd seek out those associated with the people who gave him organs to learn more about himself and would inevitably get involved in their lives. He is pursued by police and scientists out to destroy him, but he stays one step ahead of them, thanks to Dr. Franken. Composer John Morris, coincidentally, did the score for Mel Brooks's spoof *Young Frankenstein*, which costarred Teri Garr, a guest star in this pilot.

Cast: Robert Vaughn (as Dr. Franken), Robert Perrault (John Doe), David Selby (Dr. Mike Foster), Teri Garr (Kelly Fisher), Josef Sommer (Mr. Parker), Cynthia Harris (Anita Franken), Addison Powell (Dr. Eric Kerwin), Takayo Doran (Claire), Claiborne Carey (Jenny), Nicolas Surovy (Martin Elson), Rudolph Willrich (Arthur Gurnesy), Sam Schracht (Lt. Pearson), Conchetta Tolman (Reporter), Theodore Sorel (Gerald Blake), Sylvia Loew (Mrs. Parker), Penelope Paley (Technician), Roger Til (Anesthesiologist), Myra Stennett (Hello Woman), Ed Van Nuys (Bartender), William Huston (Cop), Ralph Driscoll (Doorman), Norman Parker (Morgue Attendant), Florence Rupert (Woman).

21. **Dracula.** NBC 1979. 60 minutes. Universal Television. Executive Producer/Writer/Creator: Kenneth Johnson. Music: Joe Harnell.

A spin-off from *Cliffhangers*, a short-lived series made up of three continuing twenty-minute serials each week, one of which was *Curse of Dracula*. Michael Nouri is Dracula who, in this reworking, teaches a night course in history at a San Francisco college so he can meet chicks. He was a bad guy, and was killed off in the serial, but in the proposed series, he's alive and well and wants to be cured. He has fallen in love with a woman (Carol Baxter) whose mother he also loved—and killed—decades ago. The series would follow his efforts to find a cure, withstand the urge to kill his beloved, and avoid those who are chasing him. Three one-hour pilots were being developed but apparently never came to fruition.

22. **Dusty.** CBS 7/24/83. 60 minutes. Lorimar Productions. Director: Don Medford. Executive Producers: Lee Rich and Marc Merson. Producer: Stuart Cohen. Writers: Ron Leibman and Marc Merson. Creator: Ron Leibman. Music: Jerry Goldsmith.

Saul Rubinek is a Los Angeles cabbie who dreams of being a private eye—and gets his chance when he picks up a legendary detective (Gerald

S. O'Loughlin) and is ordered to "follow that car." An uneasy alliance develops, and the cabbie finds himself moonlighting as a P.I.

Cast: Saul Rubinek (as Dusty), Gerald S. O'Loughlin (Tim Halloran), Nancy McKeon (Slugger), Hank Garrett (Lt. Harry Beathoven).

23. **Earthbound.** NBC 1979. 90 minutes. Schick Sunn Classic Films. Director: James L. Conway. Executive Producer: Charles E. Sellier, Jr. Producer/Writer: Michael Fisher.

The adventures of a kindly old man and his orphaned grandson (Todd Porter) who befriend an extraterrestrial family (Christopher Connelly, Meredith MacRae, Marc Gilpin, and Elissa Leeds) when the aliens' flying saucer crashlands in a nearby lake. The alien family does its best to fit into American society, but their super-strength and psychic powers cause problems, and could betray them to the military man (Joseph Campanella) who is searching for them. Burl Ives replaced Ken Curtis as the star early in the making of this pilot, which Leonard Matlin, in his *TV Movies and Video Guide*, lambasted as "trite, dumb, (and) idiotic." This was released as a feature film before it was broadcast on television.

24. **Ebony, Ivory and Jade.** CBS 8/3/79. 90 minutes. Frankel Films. Director: John Llewellyn Moxey. Executive Producer: Ernie Frankel. Producer/Writer: Jimmy Sangster, from a story by Ann Beckett and Mike (*M*A*S*H*) Farrell. Music: Earle Hagen.

A *Charlie's Angels* rip-off. On the surface, Ebony Bryant (Debbie Allen) and Ivory David (Martha Smith) are a Las Vegas song-and-dance team, managed by slick guy Nick Jade (Bert Convy)—but they are actually three crack secret agents.

Cast: Bert Convy (as Nick Jade), Debbie Allen (Claire "Ebony" Bryant), Martha Smith (Maggie "Ivory" David), Claude Akins (Joe Blair), Donald Moffat (Ian Cabot), Nina Foch (Dr. Adela Teba), Clifford David (Grady), Nicolas Coster (Linderman), Lucille Benson (Mrs. Stone), Ji-Tu Cumbuka (Thurston), David Brenner (Himself), Frankie Valli (Himself), Ted Shackelford (Barnes), Bill Lane (Heyman), Ray Guth (Conductor), Cletus Young (Plant Cop).

25. Escape. ABC 4/6/71. 90 minutes. Paramount Television. Director: John Llewellyn Moxey. Producer: Bruce Lansbury. Writer/Creator: Paul Playdon. Music: Lalo Schifrin.

Christopher George is an escape artist who, with his faithful sidekick Avery Schreiber, helps those who are wrongly imprisoned to escape their captors. In the pilot, he rescues a kidnapped scientist from a megalomaniac and saves the world.

Cast: Christopher George (as Cameron Steele), Avery Schreiber (Nicholas Slye), William Windom (Dr. Henry Walding), Marlyn Mason (Susan Walding), John Vernon (Charles Walding), Gloria Grahame (Evelyn Harrison), William Schallert (Lewis Harrison), Huntz Hall (Gilbert), Mark Tapscott (Dan), George Clifton (Roger), Lucille Benson (Trudy), Lisa Moore (Vicki), Chuck Hicks (Carter), Ed Gail (Customer), Lester Fletcher (Designer), Merriana Henrig (Model), Caroline Ross (Photographer).

26. The Exo-Man. NBC 6/18/77. 2 hours. Universal Television. Director: Richard Irving. Executive Producer: Richard Irving. Producer: Lionel E. Siegel. Writers: Martin Caiden, Howard Rodman, and Lionel E. Siegel, from a story by Martin Caiden and Henri Simoun (aka Howard Rodman). Creator: Martin Caiden. Music: Dana Kaproff.

Created by the man who devised *The Six Million Dollar Man*. David Ackroyd is a psychics professor who, after apprehending a bank robber, is gunned down by hit men. Crippled, he creates a super "exo" suit that revitalizes his limbs and gives him superhuman strength—and enables him to not only catch the hit man, but wage a continuing battle against crime. Caiden says the pilot "was destroyed by the marketing people at Universal. They said, 'You have to build the suit this way, so it'll be easier to mass-produce toys.' They killed the damn thing, turned it into cardboard. We had a great show planned, but execution was *pffft*."

Cast: David Ackroyd (as Nick Conrad), Anne Schedeen (Emily Frost), A Martinez (Raphael), José Ferrer (Kermit Haas), Harry Morgan (Travis), Kevin McCarthy (Kamensky), Jack Colvin (Martin), Jonathan Segal (Rubenstein), Richard Narita (Yamaguchi), John Moio (Dominic Leandro).

27. The Eyes of Charles Sand. ABC 2/29/72. 90 minutes. Warner Bros. Television. Director: Reza S. Badiyi. Producer: Hugh Benson. Writers: Henry Farrell and Stanford Whitmore, from a story by Farrell. Creator: Henry Farrell. Music (Uncredited): Henry Mancini.

Charles Sand is a man who can see, very unclearly, the future. In the pilot, he helps a woman prove her brother was murdered. A composer's strike prevented Warner Bros. from commissioning an original score, and instead, it pirated Mancini's soundtrack for *Wait Until Dark*.

Cast: Peter Haskell (as Charles Sand), Joan Bennett (Aunt Alexandra), Barbara Rush (Katherine Winslow), Sharon Farrell (Emily Parkhurst), Bradford Dillman (Jeffrey Winslow), Adam West (Dr. Paul Scott), Gary Clarke (Raymond), Ivor Francis (Dr. Ballard), Owen Bush (Gardner), Donald Barry (Trainer), Larry Levine (Groom).

28. Generation. ABC 5/24/85. 2 hours. Embassy Television. Director: Michael Tuchner. Executive Producer/Writer: Gerald DiPego. Producers: Bill Finnegan and Pat Finnegan. Music: Charles Bernstein.

The adventures of a typical American family, the Breeds, in the year 2000. Alan Breed (Richard Beymer) is an inventor for a large corporation, which frequently alters his creations for its own profit. His brother (Drake Hogestyn) is a gladiator in a national sport not unlike *Rollerball*. Alan's wife (Marta Dubois) is the host of a self-help television show. Hanna Cutrona is Kate and Alan Breed's daughter. Bert Remsen and Priscilla Pointer are the grandparents, who fight to retain the values of the 1900s.

Cast: Richard Beymer (as Alan Breed), Marta Dubois (Kate Breed), Drake Hogestyn (Jack Breed), Cristina Raines (Roma Breed), Hanna Cutrona (Bel Breed), Bert Remsen (Tom Breed), Priscilla Pointer (Ellen Breed), Kim Miyori (Teri Tanaka), Reid Sheldon (Raymond Wilke), Lorene Yarnell (Pal), Scott Paulin (Graff), Harrison Page (George Link), Liz Sheridan (Clara), Michael Young (Rick Tolmer), Grand L. Bush (Catt), Nick Corri (Scrad), Beau Richards (Edna), Stephen Lee (Mark Stein), Leigh Lombardi (Ann), Michael Lemon (Henderson), Paige Price (Gila), Bill Erwin (John), Kevin Sifuentes (Gang Boy), Dean Dittman (Taxi Driver).

29. Genesis II. CBS 3/23/73. 90 minutes. Warner Bros. Television. Director: John Llewellyn Moxey. Producer/Writer/Creator: Gene Roddenberry. Music: Harry Sukman.

Alex Cord is Dylan Hunt, a modern-day scientist experimenting with suspended animation in a secret base in Carlsbad Caverns when an earthquake buries him—and leaves him trapped in suspended animation. He is found—and revived—one hundred fifty years later by the few civilized people left in our post-apocalypse world. Together with Isiah (Ted Cassidy), Isaac Kimbridge (Percy Rodrigues), Primus Dominic (Majel Barrett) and Harper-Smythe (Lynne Marta), Dylan Hunt travels on a subterranean bullet train bringing peace, knowledge, and order to this futuristic world. The pilot lost out to *Planet of the Apes* at CBS and was abandoned, although several scripts were commissioned. One became the pilot *Planet Earth* for ABC the following season, with John Saxon replacing Cord. When that failed, Warner Bros, developed, without Roddenberry's participation, *Strange New World* for ABC. Saxon starred as one of a team of astronauts who, after floating through space in suspended animation, return to earth one hundred fifty years later and find a—you guessed it—*Strange New World*. It flopped, too.

Cast: Alex Cord (as Dylan Hunt), Ted Cassidy (Isiah), Lynne Marta (Harper-Smythe), Linda Grant (Astrid), Percy Rodrigues (Primus Isaac Kimbridge), Majel Barrett (Primus Dominic), Mariette Hartley (Lyra-a), Harvey Jason (Singh), Titos Vandis (Yuloff), Tom Pace (Brian), Leon Askin (Overseer), Liam Dunn (Janus), Harry Raybould (Slan-u), Beulah Quo (Lu-Chan), Ray Young (Tyranian Teacher), Ed Ashley (Weh-r), Dennis Young (General), Robert Hathaway (Shuttle Dispatcher), Bill Striglos (Dr. Kellum), David Westburg (Station Operator), Tammi Bula (Teenager), Terry Wills (Cardiologist), Didi Conn (TV Actress).

30. Gladiator. ABC 2/3/86. 2 hours. Walker Bros. Productions and New World Television. Director: Abel Ferrara. Executive Producers: Jeffrey Walker, Michael Chase Walker, and Tom Schulman. Producers: Robert Lovenheim and Bill Bleich. Writer: Bill Bleich, from a story by Tom Schulman and Jeffrey Walker. Creators: Jeffrey Walker and Tom Schulman. Music: David Frank.

Ken Wahl plays a secret vigilante who roams the roads of southern California fighting all sorts of vehicular crimes (reckless driving, drunk drivers, etc.) with his souped-up tow truck after his brother is killed by a psychopathic, hit-and-run driver. Nancy Allen is a radio talk show host who becomes romantically involved with the hero.

Cast: Ken Wahl (as Rick Benson), Nancy Allen (Susan Neville), Robert Culp (Lt. Frank Mason), Stan Shaw (Joe), Rosemary Forsyth (Dr. Loretta Simpson), Bart Braverman (Man), Brian Robbins (Jeff Benton), Rick Dees (Garth), Michael Young (Reporter), Harry Beer (Franklin), Garry Goodrow (Cadillac Drunk), Gary Lev (Fast Food Manager), Georgie Paul (Elderly Woman), Mort Sertner (Elderly Man), Jose Flores (Policeman), Royce D. Applegate (Phil), Robert Phalen (Dr. Maxwell), Linda Thorson (Woman in Class), Stephen Anthony Harry (Man in Class), Jim Wilkey (Death Car Driver).

31. **Good Against Evil (aka Time of the Devil).** ABC 5/22/77. 90 minutes. Twentieth Century Fox Television and Frankel-Bolen Productions. Director: Paul Wendkos. Executive Producers: Ernie Frankel and Lin Bolen. Writer: Jimmy Sangster. Music: Lalo Schifrin.

     Dack Rambo is a writer with the great misfortune of falling in love with Satan's girlfriend (Elyssa Davalos). When she is unceremoniously spirited away from him by a group of devil-worshippers, led by the evil Rimmin (Richard Lynch), he enlists the aid of an exorcist (Dan O'Herlihy) to help search for her and rid the world of evil as they go.

     Cast: Dack Rambo (as Andy Stuart), Elyssa Davalos (Jessica Gordon), Dan O'Herlihy (Father Kemschler), Richard Lynch (Rimmin), John Harkins (Father Wheatley), Jenny O'Hara (The Woman), Lelia Goldoni (Sister Monica), Peggy McCay (Irene), Peter Brandon (Dr. Price), Kim Cattrall (Lindsay Isley), Natasha Ryan (Cindy Isley), Richard Sanders (The Doctor), Lillian Adams (Beatrice), Erica Yohn (Agnes), Richard Stahl (Brown), Sandy Ward (Lt. Taggert), Isaac Goz (Merlin).

32. **Hear No Evil.** CBS 11/10/82. 2 hours. Paul Pompian Productions and MGM Television. Director: Harry Falk. Producer: Paul Pompian. Writer: Tom Lazarus. Music: Lance Rubin.

Gil Gerard is a cop who is left deaf by a car bomb and adapts to his new disability with the help of his partner (Bernie Casey), a therapist (Mimi Rogers), and a "hearing" dog. In the pilot, he tracks the PCP-producing motorcycle gang that tried to kill him.

Cast: Gil Gerard (as Inspector Bill Dragon), Bernie Casey (Inspector Monday), Mimi Rogers (Meg), Ron Karabatsos (Lt. Lew Haley), Robert Dryer (Vinnie Holzer), Christina Hart (Sheila Green), Brion James (Bobby Roy Burns), Wings Hauser (Don Garrard), Emily Heebner (Vicki), Bruce McKay (Capt. Shelhart), Parker Whitman (Riles), Joe Bellan (Cabbie), Mickey Jones (Blackman), Raven De La Croix (Candy Burns), William Paterson (Minister), John G. Scanlon (Summers), Jana Winters (Hooker), Charles Bouvier (Wilkes), Steve Burton (Cop), Sam Conti (Sonny), W. Scott Devenney (Rachmil), Chuck Dorsett (Dr. Larsen), Paul Drake (T.D.), Julianna Fjeld (Rico), Cab Covay (Hit Man), Gary Pettinger (Wrigley), Janet Raney (Terri).

33. **High Risk (aka The Troubleshooters).** ABC 5/15/76. 90 minutes. Danny Thomas Productions and MGM Television. Director: Sam O'Steen. Executive Producer: Paul Junger Witt. Producer: Robert E. Relyea. Writer: Robert Carrington. Music: Billy Goldenberg.

Six former circus performers team up to solve crimes and help people in need. They aren't altruistic, they just love the sheer challenge of it—and the money. In the pilot, they use all their Big Top experience to steal a priceless golden mask. Proposed series regular JoAnna Cameron at the time was starring as the superheroine *Isis* in the CBS Saturday morning show.

Cast: Victor Buono (as Sebastian), Joseph Sirola (Guthrie), Don Stroud (Walter-T), JoAnna Cameron (Sandra), Ronne Troup (Daisy), Wolf Roth (Erik), René Enriquez (Ambassador Henriques), John Fink (Quincy), George Skaff (Aide), William Beckley (Butler).

34. **Huggy Bear and the Turkey.** ABC 2/19/77. 60 minutes. Spelling-Goldberg Productions. Director: Claude Ennis Starrett, Jr. Executive Producers: Aaron Spelling and Leonard Goldberg. Producers: Joseph T. Naar and Michael Hiatt. Writer/Creator: Ron Friedman, from characters created by William Blinn. Music: Tom Scott.

Aired as an episode of *Starsky and Hutch*. Loosey-goosey snitch Huggy Bear (Antonio Fargas) teams up with strait-laced J.D. "Turkey" Turquet (Dale Robinette) and opens his own detective agency. In the pilot, Foxy Baker (Emily Yancy) asks Starsky (Paul Michael Glaser) and Hutch (David Soul) to find her missing husband, and they refer her to the private eyes. This pilot went nowhere, and the situation it set up was ignored in subsequent episodes of *Starsky and Hutch*—Huggy Bear showed up as a snitch again (as if nothing ever happened), and J.D. disappeared for good.

Cast: Antonio Fargas (as Huggy Bear), Dale Robinette (J.D. "Turkey" Turquet), Emily Yancy (Foxy Baker), Richard Romanus (Sonny), Carole Cook (Scorchy), Blackie Dammett (Sugar), Mickey Morton (Moon), Stan Shaw (Leotis), La Wanda Page (Lady Bessie), R.G. Armstrong (Dad Watson), Fuddie Bagley (Walter T. Baker), Joe La Due (Yank), Darryl Zwerling (Man), Titus Napolean (Milo), Eddie Lo Russo (Doc Rafferty), Robyn Hilton (Miss O'Toole).

35. Hurricane Island. CBS 1961. Producer: Sam Rolfe. Special Effects: Jack Harris.

A group of travelers are shipwrecked on an island that is populated by dinosaurs and other prehistoric terrors.

36. The Impostor. NBC 3/18/75. 90 minutes. Warner Bros. Television. Director: Edward Abroms. Executive Producer: Richard Bluel. Producer: Robert Stambler. Writers/Creators: Jerome Coopersmith and Jon Sevorg. Music: Gil Melle.

Paul Hecht is a retired spy for the U.S. military who works as an actor Off-Broadway to hide his real vocation—a professional impostor used to ferret out crime.

Cast: Paul Hecht (as Joe Tyler), Nancy Kelly (Victoria Kent), Meredith Baxter (Julie Watson), Jack Ging (Carl Rennick), Barbara Baxley (Margaret Elliot), John Vernon (Sheriff Turner), Edward Asner (Barney West), Paul Jenkins (Teddy Durham), Joseph Gallison (Dwight Elliot), Victor Campos (Del Gazzo), Brace Glover (Jennings), Sherwood Price (Reager), Charlotte Stewart (Jean Durham), Suzanne Denor (April), Ronnie Schell (Dance Director), George Murdock (Glover).

37. **I-Man.** ABC 4/6/86. 2 hours. Mark Ovitz Productions and Walt Disney Television. Director: Corey Allen. Executive Producer: Mark Ovitz. Producers: Richard Briggs, Howard Friedlander, and Ken Peragine. Writers: Howard Friedlander and Ken Peragine. Music: Craig Safan.

Aired as an episode of the *Disney Sunday Movie*. A single father working as a cabbie (Scott Bakula) is accidentally exposed to a strange gas—while rescuing a truck driver from a wreck—that makes him an "indestructible man." He, of course, becomes a secret agent and, in the pilot, teams up with a sexy female spy (Ellen Bry) to retrieve a stolen laser from an evil madman (John Anderson). The late Herschel Bernardi plays I-Man's boss.

Cast: Scott Bakula (as Jeffrey Wilder), Joey Cramer (Eric Wilder), John Anderson (Oliver Holbrook), Ellen Bry (Karen McCorder), Herschel Bernardi (Internal Security Agency Chief), John Bloom (Harry), Dale Wilson (Rudy), Cindy Higgins (Allison), Charles E. Siegel (Cannoe), Joseph Golland (Meek Man), Jan Tracey (Robbery Suspect), Ted Stidder (Dr. Allen), George Josef (Guide Guard), Campbell Lane (General), Terry Moore (Distinguished Man), Lillian Carlson (Emergency Room Nurse), Roger Allford (ISA Agent), Anthony Harrison (Curtain Guard), Don Davis (Surgeon), Rebecca Bush (Sara), Garwin Sanford (Van Driver), Doug Tuck (Paramedic), Brian Arnold (Newscaster), Raimund Stamm (Norman), Janne MacDougall (Station Nurse), Nicolas Von Zill (Party Guard).

38. **Infiltrator.** CBS 8/14/87. 60 minutes. Ron Samuels Productions and TriStar Television. Director: Corey Allen. Executive Producer: Ron Samuels. Producer: Terry Morris. Writers: Kerry Lenhart and John Sakmar. Music: Barry Goldberg.

Aired as a segment of *CBS Summer Playhouse*. Scott Bakula, an irreverent scientist working on a transporter device in the same complex where Deborah Mullowney is working on an ultra-high-tech space satellite, accidentally beams himself into the satellite, which is then absorbed into his molecules. Now, whenever he gets angry, he becomes a neon-and-metal Gobot with an array of deadly weapons. Of course, like most guys who gain an uncontrollable and unpredictable power in a freak accident, he becomes a secret agent. The cute female colleague tags along to keep a watchful eye on her satellite—and on him, though she'd never admit she's got the hots for him. Charles Keating is the boss who sends them on their missions.

Cast: Scott Bakula (as Paul Sanderson), Deborah Mullowney (Kerry Langdon), Charles Keating (John J. Stewart), Michael Bell (Markus), Peter Palmer (Minion).

39. J.O.E. and the Colonel (aka J.O.E. and Michael). CBS 9/13/85. 2 hours. Production Companies: Mad Dog Productions and Universal Television. Director: Ron Satlof. Executive Producer/Writer/Creator: Nicholas Corea. Producer: Stephen P. Caldwell. Music: Joseph Conlan.

The title change reflects a change in concept. Originally, this was the ninety-minute story of liberal, idealistic scientist Michael Moran (Terence Knox), whose genes are used by the government to create a "superhuman" soldier (Gary Kasper) named Joe that's designed to be the ultimate killer. Unfortunately, because Joe won't just obey orders—he has to make up his own mind whether to kill or not—the government decides to destroy him. Michael fakes his demise, as well as Joe's, and they hit the road to help people in need. In the two-hour version that aired, Michael is killed off and Joe is teamed up with a tough army man (William Lucking). The J.O.E. of the title, incidentally, is an acronym for something called—but never explained—J-Type Omega Elemental. This pilot was rechristened yet again, as *Humanoid Defender*, when it was released on video cassette in 1987.

Cast: Gary Kasper (as J.O.E.), Terence Knox (Michael Moran), William Lucking (Col. Fleming), Gail Edwards (Dr. Lena Grant), Allan Miller (Lyle), Christie Houser (Pam), Allan Rich (Pop Roth), Aimee Eccles (Miss Kai), William Riley (Travis), Michael Swan (Pike), Don Swayze (Max Carney), Douglas Alan Shanklin (Alpha), Robert Feero (Mueller), Bruce Corvi (Technician), Frankie Hill (Technician), John Davey (Wilson), Joe Borgese (Agent), Leigh Lombardi (Angelina).

40. Judge Dee (aka Judge Dee and the Monastery Murders). ABC 12/29/74. 2 hours. ABC Circle Films. Director: Jeremy Paul Kagan.

Producer: Gerald I. Isenberg. Writer: Nicholas Meyer, from the novel *Judge Dee and the Haunted Monastery* by Robert Van Gulick. Music: Leonard Rosenman.

In this truly offbeat, highly entertaining pilot with an all Oriental cast, Khigh Dhiegh is a roving judge in seventh century China, deciding right and wrong and solving crimes. The series, had it materialized, would have focused both on the judge's home life as well as the crimes he was involved with.

Cast: Khigh Dhiegh (as Judge Dee), Mako (Tao Gan), Soon-Teck Oh (Kang I-Te), Miiko Taka (Jade Mirror), Irene Tsu (Celestial Wife), Susie Elene (Miss Ting), James Hong (Prior), Beverly Kushida (Bright Flower), Ching Hocson (White Rose), Yuki Shimoda (Pure Faith), Robert Sadang (Tsung Lee), Keye Luke (Lord Sun Ming), Frances Fong (Mrs. Pao), Tommy Lee (True Wisdom), Richard Lee-Sung (Driver), Tadashi Yamashita (Motai).

41. **The Letters.** [Pilot #1]. ABC 3/6/73. 90 minutes. Spelling/Goldberg Productions. Directors: Gene Nelson and Paul Krasny. Executive Producers: Aaron Spelling and Leonard Goldberg. Producers: Paul Junger Witt and Tony Thomas. Writers: Ellis Marcus, Hal Sitowitz, and James G. Hirsch. Creator: Paul Junger Witt. Music: Pete Rugolo.

A precursor to Spelling's subsequent "Love Boat"-brand of anthology series and pilots (*Fantasy Island, Hotel, Airport, Finder of Lost Loves,* etc.) and the first of two pilots about what happens to people when they receive letters that have been delayed by one year (lost in a plane crash and recently recovered). Henry Jones stars as the postman, bringer of sadness, happiness, and danger.

"The Andersons: Dear Elaine." Cast: John Forsythe (as Paul Anderson), Jane Powell (Elaine Anderson), Lesley Ann Warren (Laura Reynolds), Trish Mahoney (Stewardess), Gary Dubin (Paul Anderson, Jr.), Mia Bendixsen (Lisa).

"The Parkingtons: Dear Penelope." Cast: Dina Merrill (as Penelope Parkington), Leslie Nielsen (Derek Childs), Barbara Stanwyck (Geraldine Parkington), Gil Stuart (Michael), Orville Sherman (Minister).

"The Forresters: Dear Karen." Cast: Pamela Franklin (as Karen Forrester), Ida Lupino (Mrs. Forrester), Ben Murphy (Joe Randolph),

Shelly Novack (Sonny), Frederick Herrick (Billy), Ann Noland (Sally), Brick Huston (Officer), Charles Picerni (First Man).

41a. Letters From Three Lovers (aka The Letters II). [Pilot #2]. ABC 10/3/73. 90 minutes. Spelling/Goldberg Productions. Director: John Erman. Executive Producers: Aaron Spelling and Leonard Goldberg. Producer: Parke Perine. Writers: Ann Marcus ("Dear Vincent" and "Dear Maggie") and Jerome Kass ("Dear Monica"). Creator: Paul Junger Witt. Music: Pete Rugolo.

The same concept as the previous pilot, with one slight alteration— the long-delayed letters are from lovers. Henry Jones again plays the postman.

"Dear Vincent." *Cast:* Belinda J. Montgomery (as Angie), Martin Sheen (Vincent), Logan Ramsey (Wilson), Lou Frizzell (Eddie), James McCallion (Al), Claudia Bryar (Manager), J. Duke Russo (Harry), Frank Whiteman (Officer).

"Dear Monica." *Cast:* June Allyson (as Monica), Robert Sterling (Bob), Barry Sullivan (Joshua), June Dayton (Jeanne), Roger Til (Maitre d'), Amaentha Dymally (Maid), Howard Morton (Desk Clerk).

"Dear Maggie." *Cast:* Ken Berry (as Jack), Juliet Mills (Maggie), Lyle Waggoner (Sam), Dan Tobin (Thompson), Ellen Weston (Donna), Kathy Baumann (Girl), Navis Neal (Jewelry Clerk), Bill McClean (Irate Man), Ed Fury (Man at Pool).

42. The Little Green Book. CBS 1960. Producers: Richard Sale and Al Scalpone.

The series would follow the adventures of a boy whose father is killed by the FBI. When the boy becomes a man, he inherits his father's diary and discovers his dad was a mobster. The hero then sets out to right his father's wrongs.

43. Lost Flight. CBS 1970. 105 minutes. Universal Television. Director: Leonard Horn. Executive Producer: Frank Price. Producer: Paul Donnelly. Writer/Creator: Dean Riesner. Music: Dominic Frontiere.

Price's second attempt to sell the "people-lost-on-uncharted-island-and-must-create-own-civilization" concept. This time, it's an airliner that crashlands on a mid-Pacific island with Lloyd Bridges as the captain and the leader of the survivors and Bobby Van as the troublemaker. This pilot was diverted to theatrical release. Shot on location in Hawaii.

Cast: Lloyd Bridges (as Steve Bannerman), Anne Francis (Gina Talbot), Ralph Meeker (Glenn Walkup), Andrew Prince (Jonesy), Billy Dee Williams (Merle Barnaby), Jennifer Leak (Beejay Caldwell), Bobby Van (Eddie Randolph), Linden Chiles (Allen Bedecker).

44. **Madame Sin.** ABC 1/15/72. 2 hours. ITC Entertainment. Director: David Greene. Executive Producer: Robert Wagner. Producers: Lou Morheim and Julian Wintle. Writer: Barry Oringer. Creators: Barry Shear and Lou Morheim. Music: Michael Gibbs.

A strange pilot distinguished by having Bette Davis as an all-powerful dragon lady who kidnaps a former C.I.A. agent (Robert Wagner), brainwashes him with a special ray gun, and enlists him in her high-tech global intelligence agency that operates out of her Scottish castle. In the pilot, she uses him to steal a Polaris submarine. Shot in England, had it gone to series, it would have been produced in Hollywood.

Cast: Bette Davis (as Madame Sin), Robert Wagner (Tony Lawrence), Denholm Elliott (Sin's Aide), Gordon Jackson (Commander Ted Cavendish), Dudley Sutton (Monk), Catherine Schell (Barbara), Paul Maxwell (Connors), Pik-Sen Lim (Nikko), David Healy (Braden), Alan Dobie (White), Roy Kinnear (Holidaymaker), Al Mancini (Fisherman), Charles Lloyd Park (Willoughby), Arnold Diamond (Lengett), Frank Middlemass (Dr. Henriquez), Burt Kwouk (Scarred Operator), Paul Young (Naval Officer), Jack Weir (Chief Petty Officer), Gerard Norman (Lt. Brady), Stuart Hoyle (Naval Officer), Stuart McGugan (Sailor), Gabriella Ligudi (Nun), Vanessa Kempeter (Nun), John Orchard (Revolutionary), John Slavid (Revolutionary), Barry Moreland (Musician).

45. **Man From the 25th Century.** CBS 1968. 20 minutes. Twentieth Century Fox Television. Producer: Irwin Allen.

A demonstration film (completed 2/15/68) inspired by *The Day the Earth Stood Still* and starring James Darren as an alien who, for reasons unknown, Irwin Allen chose to call "The Man from the 25th Century." Costars included John Napier, John Crawford, and Ford Rainey. From John Gregory Dunne's book *The Studio* comes this description, by Irwin Allen, of the series: "A one-hour weekly television series of science fiction, high adventure and action. It is the eerily horrifying tale of Andro, our nearest planetary neighbor, whose source of power is being used far more quickly than it can be created and whose need to attack earth and replenish such power is of the highest priority. An earthling, kidnapped in infancy and transported to Andro for indoctrination, is returned to earth to start its downfall. He is repelled by his assignment and defects to the earthlings. Each week the non-humans from Andro arrive in flying saucers and create havoc on earth. Each week the earthlings, aided by The Man from the 25th Century and his weaponry, succeed in dissuading the enemy."

Allen, in Dunne's book, also went on to describe the leading character as "twenty-four, dark, handsome, six feet, three inches tall...he is the most unusual of men. Graduate of the sciences of Nali, the great technological studies offered by the scientists of the planet Andro. Brilliant, trained to kill, and a master in the art of self defense. Hidden deep within is a warm, friendly nature. But, so penetrating was his indoctrination, even he is unaware of his second personality." Originally planned as a spin-off of *Lost in Space*, this presentation film never aired.

46. The Man With the Power. NBC 5/24/77. 90 minutes. Universal Television. Director: Nicholas Sgarro. Producer/Writer: Alan Baiter. Music: Patrick Williams.

Bob Neill is a high school teacher, but not an ordinary high school teacher. He's actually the child of an alien being and an earth woman—and he uses his incredible psychic powers as a part-time secret agent who, on this mission, protects a visiting princess from killers.

Cast: Bob Neill (as Eric Smith), Persis Khambatta (Princess Siri), Vic Morrow (Paul), Noel DeSouza (Shanda), Rene Assa (Sajid), Tim

O'Connor (Agent Bloom), Roger Perry (Farnsworth), Jason Wingreen (Klein).

47. **McClone.** NBC 4/8/88. 60 minutes. New West Productions. Director: Allan Holzman. Executive Producer: Glen A. Larson. Producers: Donald C. Klune, Scott Levita, J.C. Larson, David Garber, and Bruce Kalish. Writers: Glen A. Larson, David Garber, and Bruce Kalish. Creator: Glen A. Larson. Music: Dave Fisher and Rocky Davis.

Aired as the "Send in the Clones" episode of *The Highwayman*. The adventures of a genetically engineered soldier (Howie Long) who escapes from the secret military research base where he was created and now roams America, pursued by evil clones and government scientists. The episode doubled as a sendup of producer Glen Larson's *McCloud* series, with J.D. Cannon and Terry Carter returning in thinly disguised reprises of their former roles. Cannon has just been released from the loony bin when he encounters McClone, a fish-out-of-water who makes working with McCloud seem positively tranquil. The city of Phoenix badly, and obviously, stood in for New York locations (with palm trees in Central Park!) in this sloppily shot pilot.

Cast: Howie Long (as Mac), J.D. Cannon (Cmdr. Briggs), Terry Carter (Lieutenant), Pamela Shoop (Dr. Chadway), Gary Lockwood (Col. Westcourt), Greta Blackburn (Prostitute), Michael Pataki (Detective), Mel Young (Reporter), John Wade (Clone), Perry D'Marco (Hood), Sam Jones (Highwayman), Jacko (Jetto), Jane Badler (Miss Winthrop), Tim Russ (D.C. Montana).

48. **Men of the Dragon.** ABC 3/20/74. 90 minutes. David Wolper Productions. Director: Harry Falk. Executive Producer: Stan Margulies. Producer: Barney Rosenzweig. Writer /Creator: Denne Bart Petitclerc. Music: Elmer Bernstein.

Jared Martin and Katie Saylor star as an American brother and sister who are experts in the martial arts and, with an Asian friend (Robert Ito), open a self-defense school in Hong Kong—where this pilot was shot on location. Inevitably, they are called on to use their special skills to help people in trouble. Martin and Saylor would later costar in the short-lived NBC series *Fantastic Journey*.

Cast: Jared Martin (as Jan Kimbro), Katie Saylor (Lisa Kimbro), Robert Ito (Li-Teh), Joseph Wiseman (Balashev), Lee Tit War (Sato), Hsai Ho Lan (Madame Wu), Nang Sheen Chiou (O-Lan), Bill Jarvis (Inspector Endicott), Bobby To (K'Ang), Victor Kan (Chok), Herman Chan (Bellboy), David Chow (Tao).

49. **Microcops (aka Micronauts; aka Meganauts).** CBS 6/20/89. 60 minutes. MGM/UA Television and Moonglow Productions. Director: David Jackson. Executive Producer: Lewis Chesler. Producers: Charles "Chip" Proser, Rachel Singer, Terry Carr, and Alan Levy. Writers: Charles "Chip" Proser and Rachel Singer. Music: Tim Truman.

The adventures of microscopic, alien cops (William Bumiller and Shanti Owen) who come to earth pursuing an intergalactic criminal (Page Moseley). The aliens, because of their size, attach their tiny spaceships to people, dogs, birds, or whatever creature is convenient, and communicate to their human hosts through holograms or by appearing in any electronic monitors that are around. Special effects by Industrial Light and Magic.

Cast: William Bumiller (as Nardo), Shanti Owen (Bidra), Page Moseley (Cloyd), Peter Scolari (Morgan), Tony Bill (Travis), Lucinda Jenney (Lucy), also Lois Bromfield, Rex Ryan, Brian George.

50. **Momma the Detective.** CBS 11/12/81. 60 minutes. Big Hit Productions. Director/Writer/Creator: Larry Cohen. Producers: Larry Cohen and Hal Schaffel. Music: Joey Levine and Chris Palmaro.

Esther Rolle is a maid who solves mysteries, and, in the pilot, she unravels the stabbing death of her boss, to the consternation of her son (Kene Holliday), a homicide detective. Shot on location in New York in 1979.

Cast: Esther Rolle (as Momma Sykes), Kene Holliday (Sgt. Alvin Sykes), Paul Dooley (Ames Prescott), Andrew Duggan (Edward Forbes), Jean Marsh (Sally Hackman), Frank Converse (Tom Hackman), Laurence Luckinbill (Dr. Glickman), Fritz Weaver (Mr. Foster), Claude Brooks

(Jessie Sykes), William Walker, II (Andy Sykes), Jack Straw (Norman), Arthur French (Ribman), Colin Evans (Butler), James Dickson (Sweeney), Gordon Gould (DeSantos), also Jane Hitchcock and Miguel Pinero.

51. **The Mysterious Two (aka Follow Me If You Dare).** NBC 5/31/82. 2 hours. Alan Lansburg Productions. Director: Gary Sherman. Executive Producer: Alan Landsburg. Producers: Sonny Fox and Gary Credle. Writer: Gary Sherman. Music: Joe Renzetti.

James Stephens is the only one who knows that two evangelists (John Forsythe and Priscilla Pointer) are actually alien invaders out to brainwash earthlings as the first step toward invasion. They snatch his girlfriend, and he vows to save her, warn society, and thwart the aliens' evil plot. This pilot sat on the shelf for more than two years before being aired.

Cast: James Stephens (as Tim Armstrong), John Forsythe (He), Priscilla Pointer (She), Vic Tayback (Ted Randall), Noah Beery, Jr. (Sheriff Virgil Malloy), Robert Pine (Arnold Brown), Karen Werner (Natalie), Kenny Roker (William), Robert Englund (Boone), Mo Malone (Martha), Candy Mobley (Amanda), Dale Reynolds (Reporter), Georgia Paul (Woman).

52. **Nick Knight.** CBS 8/30/89. 2 hours. New World Television, Barry Weitz Films, and Robirdie Pictures Inc. Director: Farhad Mann. Executive Producers: James Parriott, Barry Weitz, and Roberta Becker Ziegel. Producer: S. Michael Formica. Writer: James Parriott. Story: Barney Cohen and James Parriott. Music: Joseph Conlan.

Rick Springfield is Nick Knight, a crimefighting vampire on the San Francisco police force. He drives a '59 Caddy, lives in a spiffy loft, and has a refrigerator stocked with blood. The only one who knows his secret is... the police coroner (Robert Harper). Not even his loudmouth partner (John Kapelos) knows that Nick Knight can turn into a bat—and that the nocturnal detective, in the pilot, is pursuing an evil vampire named LaCroix, responsible for the gruesome murders of some transients. After the publication of the original edition of this book, this pilot became the 1992-1996 Canadian TV series *Forever Knight* starring Geraint Wyn Davies in the lead role.

Cast. Rick Springfield (as Nick Knight), John Kapelos (Don Schanke), Laura Johnson (Alyce Hunter), Robert Harper (Dr. Jack

Brittington), Michael Nader (LaCroix), Cec Verrell (Janette), Craig Richard Nelson (Jack Fenner), Fran Ryan (Jeannie), Jack Murdock (Topper), also Al Fann, Al Berry, Robert Neckes, Gregory Wagrowski, Davis Roberts, Irene Miracle, David Correia.

53. **Night Vision.** NBC 11/30/90. 2 hours. Wes Craven Films and MGM/UA Television. Director: Wes Craven. Executive Producer: Wes Craven. Producers: Rick Nathanson, Thomas Baum and Marianna Maddelena. Writers: Wes Craven and Thomas Baum. Music: Brad Fiedel.

One can just see the NBC ad campaign on this one: "He's a rogue, a cop who's never read the rulebook. She's double trouble—a psychic cop with split personalities. They're HUNTER & SYBIL, fighting crime the hard way!" Actually they're surly, rumpled detective Tom Mackey and prescient Sally Peters, and in the pilot, they're after a serial killer who's stalking women.

Cast: Loryn Locklin (as Sally Peters), James Remar (Sgt. Tom Mackey), Penny Johnson (Luanne), Bruce MacVittie (Sgt. Stark), Francis X. McCarthy (Cmdr. Nathan Dowd), Mitch Pileggi (Capt. Stuart Keller), John Tenney (Martin), Mark Lindsay Chapman (Famous Actor), Angela Alvarado (Aura Lopez), Daniel Beer (Rocker), Kristen Corbett (Young Sally), Timothy Leary (New Age Minister), also Jessica Craven, Ron Howard George, John Benjamin Martin, Roxanna Michaels, Eric Rosse, Michele Roth, Dendrie Taylor, Bruce Wagner.

54. **905-WILD.** NBC 3/1/75. 60 minutes. Mark VII Productions and Universal Television. Executive Producer: Jack Webb. Producer: William Stark. Writers: Buddy Atkinson and Dick Connaway. Music: Gerald Fried.

This pilot for a proposed thirty-minute series aired as an episode of Webb's *Emergency!* The adventures of two officers (Mark Harmon and Albert Popwell) working for the Los Angeles Bureau of Animal Control who have to deal with mountain lions who wander into suburbia, seals who sneak into beach homes, skunks who stink up restaurants, and other bothersome beasts. David Huddleston is the staff veterinarian, Gary Crosby of *Adam-12* is their boss, and Roseanne Zecher is the unit secretary/clerk.

55. Northstar. ABC 8/10/86. 90 minutes. Phillips/Grodnick Productions and Warner Bros. Television. Director: Peter Levin. Executive Producers: Clyde Phillips and Dan Grodnick. Producer/Writer: Howard Lakin. Music: Brad Fiedel.

Originally titled *The Einstein Man*, this stars Greg Evigan as an astronaut who, while on a walk outside the spaceship, is zapped by a solar disturbance. When he gets back to earth, he has superhuman powers—and a superhuman mind—that's triggered by sunlight. But if he gets too much direct sunlight—without the protection of special sunglasses—he'll literally explode from overload. So, like his predecessor "The Six Million Dollar Man," he becomes a secret agent. Mitchell Ryan is his boss, Deborah Wakeman is the scientist who works with him.

Cast: Greg Evigan (as Major Jack North), Deborah Wakeman (Dr. Allison Taylor), Mitchell Ryan (Col. Evan Marshall), Mason Adams (Dr. Karl Janss), David Hay ward (Bill Harlow), Sonny Landham (Becker), Robin Curtiss (Jane Harlow), Richard Garrison (Agent), Steven Williams (Agent), Ken Foree (Astronaut).

56. Out of Time. NBC 7/17/88. 2 hours. TriStar Television. Director: Robert Butler. Executive Producer: Robert Butler. Producers: David Latt, Kerry Lenhart, and John J. Sakmer. Writers: Brian Alan Lane, Kerry Lenhart, and John J. Sakmer, from a story by Lane. Music: Andy Summers.

In this time-travel pilot, Bruce Abbott is a rogue future cop—living in the shadow of his long-dead, famous grandfather (Bill Maher)—who chases a notorious criminal (Adam Ant) one hundred years into the past, to Los Angeles circa 1988. The future cop ends up teaming with his forebear, now an underappreciated rookie officer, to find the bad guy and fight crime.

Cast: Bruce Abbott (as Channing Taylor), Bill Maher (Max Taylor), Adam Ant (Richard Markus), Rebecca Schaeffer (Pam Wallis), Kristian Alfonso (Cassandra Barber), Leo Rossi (Ed Hawkins), Ray Girardin (Capt. Stephen Krones), Barbara Tarbuck (Dr. Kerry Langdon), Arva Holt (Capt. Stuart), Tom LaGrua (Frank), Kimberley Sedgewick

(Salesgirl), also Chuck Lindsly, Arthur Mendoza, Rick Avery, Ashley Brittingham, Richard Lavin, Neal Penso, Jay Richardson, Shaun Toub, Martin Treat, Thomas Wagner, Patrick DeSantis.

57. The People. ABC 1/22/72. 90 minutes. Metromedia Producers Corp. and American Zoetrope. Director: John Korty. Executive Producer: Francis Ford Coppola. Producer: Gerald I. Isenberg. Writer: James M. Miller, from the novel *Pilgrimage* by Zenna Henderson. Music: Carmine Coppola.

A slow-moving, low-key pilot which casts Kim Darby as a schoolteacher who goes to an isolated California community and is puzzled by students who don't behave like kids at all—and have some unusual abilities. What she eventually discovers is that they, along with William Shatner and Diane Varsi, are the last descendants of a peaceful alien race that possesses awesome psychic powers.

Cast. Kim Darby (as Melodye Amerson), William Shatner (Dr. Curtis), Diane Varsi (Valency), Dan O'Herlihy (Sol Diemus), Laurie Walters (Karen Dingus), Chris Valentine (Francker), Johanna Baer (Bethie), Stephanie Valentine (Tabitha), Jack Dallgren (Kish), Andrew Chrichton (Thann), David Petch (Matt), Dorothy Drady (Dita), Mary Rose McMaster (Maras), Anne Walters (Obla), Tony Dario (Bram).

58. Planet Earth. ABC 4/23/74. 90 minutes. Warner Bros. Television. Director: Marc Daniels. Executive Producer/Creator: Gene Roddenberry. Producer: Robert H. Justman. Writers: Gene Roddenberry and Juanita Bartlett, from a story by Roddenberry. Music: Harry Sukman.

A reworking of the flop CBS pilot *Genesis II.* The title narration explained it like this: "This is the twenty-second century, the land renewed, the air and water pure again. The conflicts of the past are gone. It is a new Earth, with new peoples and new customs. In some places, bizarre savagery, in others, advanced cities. Everywhere, new challenge and new adventure. This is also the story of Dylan Hunt [this time played by John Saxon], lost in 1979 in a suspended animation accident. Over a century and a half later, in the year 2133, he was found and awakened by the people of this city called PAX, peace. The one place on Earth that escaped the final conflict of the twentieth century. The one place on earth where civilization did not perish. Dylan Hunt is one of them now, leader of a PAX science team exploring a much-changed world, part of the PAX dream of rebuilding a new and wiser civilization. Their mission is mankind, rebirth of Planet Earth." In the pilot, while his team is doing its thing, traveling in superspeed shuttles through underground tubes that honeycomb the earth, Dylan Hunt is captured by a society run by women and enslaved.

Cast: John Saxon (as Dylan Hunt), Janet Margolin (Harper-Smythe), Ted Cassidy (Isiah), Christopher Cary (Baylock), Diana Muldaur (Marg), Jo De Winter (Villar), Majel Barrett (Yuloff), Jim Antonio (Dr. Jonathon Connor), Sally Kemp (Treece), Claire Brennan (Delba), Corinne Comacho (Bronta), Sarah Chattin (Thetis), John Quade (Kreeg Commandant), Patricia Smith (Skylar), Raymond Sutton (Kreeg Captain), Rai Tasco (Paytre Kimbridge), Aron Kincaid (Gorda), James Bacon (Partha), Joan Crosby (Ayla), Lew Brown (Merlo), Craig Hundley (Harpsichordist).

59. The Possessed. NBC 5/1/77. 90 minutes. Warner Bros. Television. Director: Jerry Thorpe. Executive Producer: Jerry Thorpe. Producer: Philip Mandelker. Writer: John Sacret Young. Music: Leonard Rosenman.

James Farentino is a defrocked cleric (for adultery and alcoholism) who, after a serious car accident, is "saved" in order to battle supernatural evil wherever it lurks. In the pilot, it lurks at a girls' school, and Farentino is called upon to perform an exorcism. Future star Harrison Ford has a small role here.

Cast: James Farentino (as Kevin Leahy), Joan Hackett (Louise Gelson), Claudette Nevins (Ellen Sumner), Eugene Roche (Sgt. Taplinger), Ann Dusenberry (Weezie), Harrison Ford (Paul Winjam), Diana Scarwid (Lane), P.J. Soles (Marty), Susan Walden (Sandy), Dinah Manoff (Celia), Ethelinn Block (Barry).

60. The Power Within (aka The Man With the Power; aka The Power; aka The Power Man). ABC 5/11 /79. 90 minutes. Aaron Spelling Productions. Director: John Llewellyn Moxey. Executive Producers: Aaron

Spelling and Douglas S. Cramer. Producers: Alan Godfrey and E. Duke Vincent. Writer: William Clark. Creator: Ed Lasko. Music: John Addison.

This pilot went through many titles, but under any name, it would still be the same old story about a man who, thanks to a freak accident, acquires superpowers which he then uses to fight crime. Art Hindle is a decorated Vietnam hero who is struck by lightning, emerges with X-ray vision and the power to shoot electric bolts from his fingers, and takes on secret missions for this father, an Air Force general.

Cast: Art Hindle (as Chris Darrow), Edward Binns (General Tom Darrow), Joe Rassulo (Bill), Dick Sargent (Capt. Ed Holman), Susan Howard (Dr. Joanna Mills), Karen Lamm (Marvalee), Eric Braeden (Stephens), David Hedison (Danton), Isabell MacCloskey (Grandma), Chris Wallace (First Guard), John Dennis (Rancher).

61. Questor (aka The Questor Tapes). NBC 1 /23/74. 2 hours. Universal Television. Director: Richard A. Colla. Executive Producer/Creator: Gene Roddenberry. Producer: Howie Hurwitz. Writers: Gene L. Coon and Gene Roddenberry. Music: Gil Melle.

Gene Roddenberry's second post-*Star Trek* pilot. Robert Foxworth is an android called Questor searching the globe for the missing scientist—perhaps from another planet—who created him. Mike Farrell is the human scientist who accompanies him in his search, which brings them into contact with people in trouble. In the process, Questor's exposed to the constantly perplexing emotions of human beings. A humanoid robot would play a central role in Roddenberry's 1987 syndicated series, *Star Trek: The Next Generation*.

Cast: Robert Foxworth (as Questor), Mike Farrell (Jerry Robinson), John Vernon (Geoffrey Darro), Lew Ayres (Vaslovik), James Shigeta (Dr. Chen), Robert Douglas (Dr. Michaels), Ellen Weston (Allison Sample), Majel Barrett (Dr. Bradley), Reuben Singer (Dr. Gorlov), Walter Koenig (Administrative Assistant), Fred Sadoff (Dr. Audret), Gerald Sanderson (Randolph), Alan Caillou (Immigration Officer), Eydse Girard (Stewardess), Lai Baum (Col. Henderson), Patti Cibbison (Secretary).

62. **Return of the World's Greatest Detective (aka Alias Sherlock Holmes).** NBC 6/16/76. 90 minutes. Universal Television. Director: Dean Hargove. Producers/Writers: Dean Hargrove and Roland Kibbee. Music: Dick DeBenedictis.

An L.A.P.D. motorcycle cop with a love for Sherlock Holmes is knocked out in a traffic accident and, when he comes to, believes he actually is the famous detective. Now, with the help of a lady psychiatrist named Watson, he goes about solving cases and badgering his harried superior.

Cast: Larry Hagman (as Sherman Holmes), Jenny O'Hara (Dr. Watson), Nicholas Colasanto (Lt. Tinker), Woodrow Parfrey (Himmel), Helen Verbit (Landlady), Ivor Francis (Spiner), Charles Macauley (Judge Harley), Ron Silver (Dr. Collins), Sid Haig (Vince Cooley), Booth Colman (Psychiatrist), Lieux Dressier (Mrs. Slater), Benny Rubin (Klinger), Fuddle Bagley (Detective).

63. **Samurai.** NBC 4/30/79. 90 minutes. Danny Thomas Productions, Lamas Corporation, and Universal Television. Director: Lee H. Katzin. Executive Producers: Fernando Lamas and Danny Thomas. Producers; Allan Baiter and Ronald Jacobs. Writer: Jerry Ludwig. Music: Fred Karlin.

This ludicrous and unintentionally funny pilot starred Caucasian Joe Penny as half-American/half-Asian Lee Cantrall, a San Francisco district attorney by day and sword-wielding samurai warrior by night. In the pilot, the samurai D.A. tackles a dastardly villain who uses an "earthquake machine" to scare people into selling their property to him at a cut rate.

Cast: Joe Penny (as Lee Cantrall), Dana Elcar (Frank Boyd), James Shigeta (Takeo Chrisato), Beulah Quo (Hana Mitsubishi Cantrall), Norman Alden (Lt. Al DeNisco), Charles Cioffi (Amory Bryson), Geoffrey Lewis (Harold Tigner), Morgan Brittany (Cathy Berman), Ralph Manza (Irving Berman), Shane Sinutko (Tommy), Michael Pataki (Peter Lacey), James McEachin (Richardson), Philip Baker Hall (Professor Gordon Owens), Randolph Roberts (Phil Mercer), Diana Webster (Professor Helen Martell), Don Keefer (Norman Jonas), Michael Danahy (Harry Keller), Bob Minor (Zane), Fred Lerner (Powers), Tom Lupo (Frazier), Greg Barnett (Colfax), Jo McDonnell (Marianne).

64. Second Chance. ABC 2/8/72. 90 minutes. Metromedia Producers Corp. and Danny Thomas Productions. Director: Peter Tewksbury. Executive Producer: Danny Thomas. Producer: Harold Cohen. Writer: Michael Morris.

An overworked stockbroker (Brian Keith) buys a Nevada ghost town, renames it Second Chance, and makes it a haven for people who want a second chance at life. This semi-anthology would focus on the lives of the people who come to Second Chance. Shot on location in Arizona. Guest star Kenneth Mars would later play Brian Keith's brother in a 1986 episode of *Hardcastle and McCormick.*

Cast: Brian Keith (as Geoff Smith), Elizabeth Ashley (Ellie Smith), Brad Savage (Johnny Smith), Kenneth Mars (Dr. Julius Roth), William Windom (Stan Petryk), Pat Carroll (Gloria Petryk), Juliet Prowse (Martha Foster), Avery Schreiber (Robert Grazzari), Rosie Grier (Maxie Hill), Ann Morgan Guilbert (Charlene), Emily Yancy (Stella Hill), Vernon Weddle (Lester Fern), Bret Parker (Hardin), Bob Nichols (Dr. Strick), Oliver Dunbar (Dr. Willard).

65. Shadow Man. ABC 1969. Universal Television. Writers: Dean Riesner and Robert Soderberg.

A college professor, who is inadvertently responsible for the accidental death of his wife and child, agrees to have plastic surgery and assume the identity of a "Howard Hughes"-type billionaire. He uses the billionaire's vast wealth to assuage his guilt and do good deeds around the world.

66. Shangri-La Plaza. CBS 7/30/90. 30 minutes. Castle/Safan/ Mueller/ Schmaltzking Productions and CBS Entertainment. Director/ Writer: Nick Castle. Executive Producers: Nick Castle, Craig Safan, and Mark Mueller. Supervising Producer: Stephen Cragg. Producer: Mark Horowitz. Music: Craig Safan. Lyrics: Mark Mueller.

A surprisingly engaging, warmhearted musical sitcom set in a gaudy Los Angeles street-corner mini-mall. The pilot, told almost entirely in song, focuses on a widow (Melora Hardin) and her daughter (Allison Mack) who inherit a rundown donut shop and immediately win the attention of a couple of neighborhood mechanic brothers (Terrence Mann and

Jeff Yagher). A lively mixture of music, splashy production design, and energetic choreography made this pilot a successful half-hour of entertainment in its own right—even if it probably wouldn't have worked as a series.

Cast: Melora Hardin (as Amy), Allison Mack (Jenny), Jeff Yagher (George Bondo), Terrence Mann (Ira Bondo), Chris Sarandon (Victorio), Carmen Lundy (Geneva), Savion Glover (Chili), also Bernie Coulson, Hilary Shepard, Barry Bernal, Travis Payne, Lee Wilkof, Mark David, Victoria Stevens, Glen Chin, George Hamner.

67. **Shooting Stars (aka Hawke and O'Keefe).** ABC 7/28/83. 2 hours. Aaron Spelling Productions. Director: Richard Lang. Executive Producers: Aaron Spelling, Douglas S. Cramer, and E. Duke Vincent. Producers: Richard Lang and Michael Fisher. Writer: Michael Fisher, from a story by Fisher and Vernon Zimmerman. Music: Dominic Frontiere.

Billy Dee Williams and Parker Stevenson are a pair of TV detectives who, when fired by the show's jealous star (Efrem Zimbalist, Jr.), become real-life private detectives. They work out of a beachside cafe/ bar and utilize the skills of their various entertainment industry cronies (stunt men, makeup men, writers) to help solve crimes.

Cast: Billy Dee Williams (as Douglas Hawke), Parker Stevenson (Bill O'Keefe), John P. Ryan (Detective McGee), Edie Adams (Hazel), Fred Travalena (Teddy), Dick Bakalyan (Snuffy), Victoria Spelling (Danny), Frank McRae (Tubbs), Robert Webber (J. Woodrow Norton), Kathleen Lloyd (Laura O'Keefe), Denny Miller (Tanner), John Randolph (Stevenson), Efrem Zimbalist, Jr. (Jonathan Lieghton), Herb Edelman (Rex), Don Calfa (Driscoll), Kathryn Daley (Janie), D.D. Howard (Glenda), Lurene Tuttle (Mrs. Brand), Eric Server (Director), David Faustino (Patrick O'Keefe), Paul Tuerpe (Patrolman), Larry McCormick (Newscaster), Cis Rundle (Girl), Elisabeth Foxx (Tracy), Tim Haldeman (Propman), Stephen Miller (Newsman).

68. **Silent Whisper.** CBS 7/26/88. 60 minutes. Above the Line Productions, Maderlay Enterprises, and Lorimar-Telepictures. Director/Writer/ Creator: Jonathan Betuel. Executive Producers: Jonathan Betuel and Gary Adelson. Music: Bill Conti.

Aired as a segment of *CBS Summer Playhouse*. David Beecroft is a San Francisco police detective who discovers his family is about to be murdered by a serial killer, arrives too late, and is stabbed in the throat by the assailant. Now, his voice gone, he works as a special police operative and, in the pilot, stalks the killer who murdered his family. He's aided in his quest by a friend-on-the-force, his former partner (Richard Lawson).

Cast: David Beecroft (as Eric Bolan), Richard Lawson (as Nick Scott), Claudette Nevins (Capt. Bea Landry), Kate Vernon (Ellen Sanders), Rita Wilson (China Seasons), Joseph Kell (Colin Sanders), Steven Keats (Guido the Ghoul), James Greene (Nathan Sanders), Philip Levien (Dr. Mark Ryler), David Tress (Psychiatrist), Nancy Warren (Elvira Stout), John Brandon (Sergeant), Annie Gegen (Pat Bolari), Robert Factor (Serial Killer), Bridgett Helms (Bolan's Daughter), Brandon Stewart (Bolan's Son), Barney McGeary (Elderly Cop), Laurie Drake (Lady Cop), Al Pugliese (Mover), Robert Lee (Mayor), Gloria Delaney (Nurse), Marie Halton (Mourner), Justin Whelan (Soccer Player), Gregory Deason (David Sanders).

69. Stranded. NBC 1966. 60 minutes. Universal Television. Director: Leon Benson. Executive Producer: Frank Price. Producer: Frank P. Rosenberg. Writer: Dick Nelson, from a story by Nelson and Larry Marcus. Music: Jack Elliott.

Richard Egan leads a group of plane-crash survivors, lost in the Andes amid ancient Inca ruins, who must form their own civilization until rescued. Among the survivors are Fernando Lamas as a murderer being escorted back to Bolivia by a cop; Peter Graves as a writer and big-game hunter; Karen Sharpe as a stewardess; Joby Baker as a famous singer and actor; Harry Guardino as an ex-alcoholic comic on the way to his big comeback gig; Julie Adams as a shy schoolteacher; Leonard Nimoy as a Miami lawyer, and Otis Young as a black doctor.

Producer Price apparently loved this concept and would revive it in several dramatic and comedic incarnations in following years, including *Lost Flight* (1969) with Lloyd Bridges and *Stranded* (1976) with Kevin Dobson. The pilot was released theatrically as *Valley of Mystery* with forty minutes of extra footage that includes entirely new scenes with Lois

Nettleton and ends with the castaways getting rescued. The film credits Joseph Leytes as director, Harry Tattelman as producer, and the screenplay to Richard Neal and Lowell Barrington, from a story by Neal and Larry Marcus.

Cast: Richard Egan (as Wade Cochran), Peter Graves (Ben Barstow), Karen Sharpe (Connie Lane), Joby Baker (Pete Patton), Harry Guardino (Joey O'Neill), Julie Adams (Joan Simon), Fernando Lamas (Francisco Rivera), Lee Patterson (Dino Doretti), Leonard Nimoy (Spence Atherton), Otis Young (Dr. John Quincy), Lisa Gaye (Margo Yorke).

70. Stranded. CBS 5/26/76. 60 minutes. Universal Television. Director: Earl Bellamy. Executive Producer: David Victor. Producer: Howie Horowitz. Writer: Anthony Lawrence. Music: Gordon Jenkins.

A straight "Gilligan's Island" that was tried once before as *Lost Flight*. An Australia-bound airliner crash-lands on an uncharted South Pacific island, and the survivors, led by a New York cop (Kevin Dobson), create their own civilization. Characters include a streetwise ghetto kid who was a stowaway, the criminal the cop was taking back to Australia, a retired construction worker who is revitalized by building the island community, a woman who was on her way to get married in Australia, and a teenage brother and sister whose parents are killed in the crash.

Cast: Kevin Dobson (as Sgt. Rafe Harder), Lara Parker (Crystal Norton), Marie Windsor (Rose Orselli), Devon Ericson (Julie Blake), Jimmy McNichol (Tim Blake), Rex Everhart (John Rados), Erin Blunt (Ali Baba), Lai Baum (Burt Hansen), James Cromwell (Jerry Holmes), John Fujioka (Charley Lee).

71. Strange New World. ABC 7/13/75. 2 hours. Warner Bros. Television. Director: Robert Butler. Executive Producers: Ronald F. Graham and Walon Green. Producer: Robert E. Larson. Writers: Al Ramrus, Ronald F. Graham, and Walon Green. Music: Elliot Kaplan and Richard Clements.

A reworking of the flop pilot *Planet Earth* (a sequel to the failed pilot *Genesis II*) which starred John Saxon as a scientist who wakes up several hundred years after being placed in suspended animation. This time, producer Gene Roddenberry is not involved and the concept has been altered. Now Saxon, Kathleen Miller, and Keene Curtis are three astronauts who return to post-apocalypse earth after floating in space in suspended animation for two hundred years. Director Robert Butler made the original *Star Trek* pilot ten years earlier.

Cast: John Saxon (as Capt. Anthony Vico), Kathleen Miller (Dr. Allison Crowley), Keene Curtis (Dr. William Scott), James Olson (The Surgeon), Martine Beswick (Tana), Reb Brown (Sprang), Ford Rainey (Sirus), Bill McKinney (Badger), Gerritt Graham (Daniel), Cynthia Wood (Araba), Catherine Bach (Lara), Norland Benson (Hide), Richard Farnsworth (Elder).

72. **The Stranger.** ABC 2/26/73. 2 hours. Bing Crosby Productions. Director: Lee H. Katzin. Executive Producer: Andrew J. Fenady. Producer: Alan A. Armer and Gerald Sanford. Writer/Creator: Gerald Sanford. Music: Richard Markowitz.

Glenn Corbett is Stryker, an astronaut on a deep-space probe, who crash-lands on Earth—only to find out it isn't Earth but rather a "parallel world" called Terra, hidden behind the sun. They have everything we have (including Chryslers), except freedom. This alternate Earth is run by an evil dictatorship that wants Stryker dead because he preaches free speech and other rights that he had on Earth. The series would depict Stryker's efforts to elude death (wielded by Cameron Mitchell), escape Terra, and return home.

Cast: Glenn Corbett (as Neil Stryker), Cameron Mitchell (George Benedict), Sharon Acker (Dr. Bettina Cooke), Lew Ayres (Prof. Dylan MacAuley), George Coulouris (Max Greene), Steve Franken (Henry Maitland), Dean Jagger (Carl Webster), Tim O'Connor (Dr. Revere), Jerry Douglas (Steve Perry), Arch Whiting (Mike Frame), H.M. Wynant (Eric Sconer), Virginia Gregg (Secretary), Buck Young (Tom Nelson), William Bryant (Trucker).

73. **Stunt Seven.** CBS 5/30/79. 2 hours. Martin Poll Productions. Director: John Peyser. Producers: Martin Poll and William Craver. Writer: David Shaw. Music: Bill Conti.

Christopher Connelly heads a versatile, seven-member Hollywood stunt team who, in the lighthearted pilot, save a movie star (Elke Sommer) held prisoner by a pirate (Patrick Macnee) in an island fortress.

Cast: Christopher Connelly (as Hill Singleton), Christopher Lloyd (Skip Hartman), Morgan Brittany (Elena Sweet), Bob Seagren (Wally Ditweiler), Soon-Teck Oh (Kenny Uto), Brian Brodsky (Horatio Jennings), Juanin Clay (Dinah Lattimore), Bill Macy (Frank Wallach), Peter Haskell (Phil Samson), Patrick Macnee (Maximilian Boudeau), Elke Sommer (Rebecca Wayne), Morgan Paull (John Heinlein), Robert Ritchie (Harrison), Lynda Beattie (Monica).

74. **Stunts Unlimited.** ABC 1 /4/80. 90 minutes. Paramount Television and Lawrence Gordon Productions. Director: Hal Needham. Executive Producer: Lawrence Gordon. Producer: Lionel E. Siegel. Writer: Laurence Heath. Music: Barry DeVorzon.

Glenn Corbett is an ex-C.I.A. agent who recruits three stunt experts (Sam Jones, Chip Mayer, Susanna Dalton) to form an elite counterespionage team which, in the pilot, retrieves a stolen laser. *People* magazine thought "the idea is ingenious; it ought to be a series." Apparently, nobody else did.

Cast: Chip Mayer (as Matt Lewis), Susanna Dalton (C.C. Brandt), Sam Jones (Bo Carlson), Glenn Corbett (Dirk Macauley), Linda Grovernor (Jody Webber), Alejandro Rey (Fernando Castilla), Vic Mohica (Tallis), Mickey Gilbert (Horse Gilbert), Charles Picerni (Stuntman).

75. **Tag Team.** ABC 1/26/91. 60 minutes. IndeProd Productions and Walt Disney Television. Director: Paul Krasny. Executive Producer: Bruce Sallan. Producer: Ric Rondell. Writer: Robert L. McCullough. Music: Jay Ferguson.

The adventures of "The Lizard Brothers," tag-team wrestlers-turned-undercover-cops who use their big ring skills to nab bad guys. This concept was designed, according to ABC development reports, to capitalize on the "enormous popularity of wrestling within a traditional television franchise."

Cast: Jesse "The Body" Ventura (as Billy "The Body" Youngblood), "Rowdy" Roddy Piper ("Tricky" Rick MacDonald), Robin Curtis

(Capt. Steckler), Phill Lewis (Officer Tyler), Michael Genovese (Hatch), Raymond O'Connor (Sgt. Harrigan), Jennifer Runyon (Rita Valentine), Shannon Tweed (Lena Lewis), also Sean Baca, Mark Gintner, Robert Hanley, Mark Lenow, Michael M. Vendrell.

76. **Time Travelers.** ABC 3/19/76. 90 minutes. Irwin Allen Productions and Twentieth Century Fox Television. Director: Alexander Singer. Producer: Irwin Allen. Writer: Jackson Gillis, from a story by Rod Serling and Irwin Allen. Music: Morton Stevens.

Rod Serling lent his creativity to this reworking of Irwin Allen's old *Time Tunnel* series. This time, the stories would revolve around a doctor and a research scientist who go back in time for the good of mankind. In the pilot, a dangerous epidemic is spreading across the country. Scientists believe a cure was once found for the disease, but the antidote and the man who developed it perished in the great Chicago fire over one hundred years ago. Heroes Sam Groom and Tom Hallick go back to the days just before the fire in hopes of finding the antidote before everything goes up in flames. The pilot utilized the Twentieth Century-Fox backlot sets remaining from *Hello, Dolly!* and footage from the 1938 film *In Old Chicago*.

Cast: Sam Groom (as Dr. Clint Earnshaw), Tom Hallick (Jeff Adams), Richard Basehart (Dr. Joshua Henderson), Trish Stewart (Jane Henderson), Booth Colman (Dr. Cummings), Francine York (Dr. Helen Sanders), Walter Burke (Dr. Stafford), Baynes Barron (Chief Williams), Dort Clark (Sharkey).

77. **Toni's Boys (aka Toni's Devils).** ABC 4/2/80. 60 minutes. Spelling / Goldberg Productions. Director: Ron Satlof. Executive Producers: Aaron Spelling and Leonard Goldberg. Producer: Robert James. Writer: Kathryn Michaelian Powers. Music: Jack Elliott and Allyn Ferguson.

An obvious reworking of *Charlie's Angels*, the hit show which hosted the pilot episode. Barbara Stanwyck is the matriarchal private eye who solves cases with the help of three hunks (Bob Seagren, Stephen Shortridge, and Bruce Bauer) and her butler (James E. Broadhead). Stanwyck would later star in *The Colbys*, a spin-off of *Dynasty*, which starred *Charlie's Angels* title character played by John Forsythe.

Cast: Barbara Stanwyck (as Antonia Blake), Bob Seagren (Bob Sorenson), Stephen Shortridge (Cotton Harper), Bruce Bauer (Matt Parrish), James E. Broadhead (Rolph), Robert Loggia (Michael Durrano), Cheryl Ladd (Kris Munroe), Jaclyn Smith (Kelly Garrett), Shelley Hack (Tiffany Wells), David Doyle (John Bosley), John Forsythe (Charlie).

78. **Tut and Tuttle (aka Through the Magic Pyramid).** NBC 12/6/81 and 12/13/81. 2 hours (2 x 60 minutes). Major H Productions. Director: Ron Howard. Executive Producer: Ron Howard. Producers: Ron Howard and Herbert J. Wright. Writers/Creators: Rance Howard and Herbert J. Wright. Music: Joe Renzetti.

    The misadventures of a boy (Christopher Barnes) who gets a toy pyramid for his birthday—a pyramid that is actually a magic device that can transport him back to ancient Egypt, where he befriends young King Tut and helps him deal with his problems. This two-hour pilot (directed and coproduced by Ron Howard for his own company and co-created and cowritten by his dad, Rance) was sliced in half and broadcast as two hour-long specials, which were nominated for an Emmy as Outstanding Children's Special.

    Cast: Christopher Barnes (as Bobby Tuttle), James Hampton (Sam Tuttle), Betty Beaird (as Eleanor Tuttle), Robbie Rist (Bonkers), Olivia Barash (Princess Baket), Hans Conried (Ay), Vic Tayback (Horembeb), Kario Salem (Akenaten), Eric Greene (Tutankamen), Jo Anne Worley (Mutjnedjmet), Mel Berger (Yuzannout), Mary Carver (Tiye), Daniel Leon (Guard), Gino Conforti (Hotep), Elaine Giftos (Neferiti), David Darlow (Taduhk), Sydney Penny (Princess).

79. **Twin Detectives (aka Gemini).** ABC 5/1/76. 90 minutes. Charles Fries Productions. Director: Robert Day. Executive Producer: Charles Fries. Producer: Everett Chambers. Creator: Don Sharpe. Writer: Robert Specht, from a story by Everett Chambers, Robert Carrington, and Specht. Music: Tom Scott. Songs: "Spinning the Wheel" and "Hard on Me" by the Hudson Brothers.

Country singers Jim and Jon Hager, who became famous on *Hee Haw*, starred in this pilot for a series about identical twins who pretend to be a single private eye, thereby using their ability to be in two places at once as an edge in crime-fighting. In the pilot, through their twin ruse they unmask a phony psychic, solve a murder, and recover stolen money belonging to Lillian Gish (in her TV movie debut).

Cast: Jim Hager (as Tony Thomas), Jon Hager (Shep Thomas), Lillian Gish (Billy Jo Haskins), Patrick O'Neal (Leonard Rainer), Michael Constantine (Ben Sampson), Otis Young (Cartwright), Barbara Rhoades (Sheila Rainer), David White (Marvin Telford), Fred Beir (Dr. Hudson), Lynda Day George (Nancy Pendleton), Randy Oakes (Jennie), James Victor (Lt. Martinez), Frank London (Hutchins), Billy Barty (Bartender).

80. The Ultimate Impostor. NBC 5/12/79. 2 hours. Universal Television. Director: Paul Stanley. Producer/Writer: Lionel E. Siegel, from the novel *Capricorn Man* by William Zacha, Sr. Music: Dana Kaproff.

A secret agent (Joseph Hacker) whose brain is "erased" by bad guys has a computer surgically implanted in his skull, allowing him to be programmed with an all-new personality and set of skills. The catch is the programming fades after seventy-two hours. You can just imagine how each episode in the proposed series would have ended. Keith Andes is the scientist who programs him, Macon McCalman gives him his assignments, and Erin Gray is a fellow agent.

Cast: Joseph Hacker (as Frank Monihan), Keith Andes (Eugene Danziger), Macon McCalman (Jake McKeever), Erin Gray (Beatrice Tate), Tracy Brooks Swope (Danielle Parets), John Van Dreelen (Reuben Parets), Rosalind Chao (Lai-Ping), Bobby Riggs (Tennis Pro), Norman Burton (Papich), Robert Phillips (Red Cottle), Greg Barnett (Sgt. Williger), Thomas Bellin (Joe Mason), Loren Berman (Dominic), Bill Capizzi (Tony), Cindy Castillo (Esteban), Joseph Hardin (Eddie), Mark Garcia (Felippe), Gray don Gould (Carl Lathrop), Chip Johnson (Martin), Mike Kulcsar (Vaya Makov), Betty Kwan (Ms. Wang), Bob Thomas (Tomas), W.T. Zacha (Weeks).

81. Vampire. ABC 10/7/79. 2 hours. MTM Enterprises and Company Four. Director: E.W. Swackhamer. Executive Producer: Steven Bochco. Producer: Gregory Hoblit. Writers/Creators: Steven Bochco and Michael Kozoll. Music: Fred Karlin.

This offbeat black comedy pilot comes from the same production team that later would be responsible for *Hill Street Blues*. Architect John Rawlins (Jason Miller) builds a San Francisco church and unknowingly offends a vampire (Richard Lynch). When the enraged, centuries-old vampire kills Rawlins' girlfriend for vengeance, the architect teams up with a retired cop (E.G. Marshall) to pursue and destroy the bloodsucking beast. "The pilot was a longshot," says Bochco. "In a sense, it was a cop show with a little bit of the *Night Stalker*. It was fun. But making pilots *is* fun. It's what happens after they sell where it gets ugly."

Cast: Jason Miller (as John Rawlins), Richard Lynch (Anton Voytek), E.G. Marshall (Harry Kilcoyne), Kathryn Harrold (Leslie Rawlins), Barrie Youngfellow (Andrea Parker), Michael Tucker (Christopher Bell), Jonelle Allen (Brandy), Jessica Walter (Nicole DeCamp), Adam Starr (Tommy Parker), Wendy Cutler (Iris), Scott Paulin (Father Hanley), David Hooks (Casket Salesman), Brendon Dillon (Father Devlin), Joe Spinell (Captain Desher), Byron Webster (Selby), Ray K. Gorman (Detective), Nicholas Gunn (Dance Instructor), Herb Braha (Felon), Tony Perez (Cop).

82. Velvet. ABC 8/27/84. 2 hours. Aaron Spelling Productions. Director: Richard Lang. Executive Producers: Aaron Spelling and Douglas S. Cramer. Producers: E. Duke Vincent and Richard Lang. Writers: Ernest Tidyman and Ned Wynn. Music: Dominic Frontiere.

Yet another attempt to clone Aaron Spelling's hit *Charlie's Angels*, this time by Spelling himself. Four attractive aerobic dancers (Leah Ayres, Shari Belafonte-Harper, Mary-Margaret Humes, and Sheree Wilson) are actually secret agents using Polly Bergen's Velvet International health spas as a front for their espionage activities.

Cast: Leah Ayres (as Cass Dayton), Shari Belafonte-Harper (Julie Rhodes), Mary-Margaret Humes (Lauren Dawes), Sheree Wilson (Ellen Stockwell), Polly Bergen (Mrs. Vance), Michael Ensign (Stefan), Leigh

McCloskey (James Barstow), Bruce Abbott (Breed), Judson Scott (Mats Edholm), Bo Brundin (Prof. Charles Vandemeer), Clyde Kusatsu (Dr. Edward Yashima), William Windom (Government Official), Ellen Greer (Nora Vandemeer), David Faustino (Billy Vandermeer), Bill Quinn (Dr. Harmon), Stanley Bower (Cullom), Stephen Davies (Farrow), Holly Butler (Receptionist), Carrie Rhodes (Instructor), Paul Tuerpe (Contact), Danny Wells (Producer), Anthony DeLongis (Rawls), Tim Haldeman (Sammy), Cis Rundle (Flight Attendant), Alya Swan (Dowager).

83. Weekend Nun. ABC 12/20/72. 90 minutes. Paramount Television. Director: Jeannot Szwarc. Producers: Tom Miller and Edward Milkis. Writer: Ken Trevey. Music: Charles Fox.

Joanna Pettet is a nun who doubles as a probation officer in this pilot based on the real-life exploits of Joyce Duco.

Cast: Joanna Pettet (as Sister Mary Damian/Marjorie Walker), Vic Morrow (Chuck Jardine), Ann Sothern (Mother Bonaventure), James Gregory (Sid Richardson), Beverly Garland (Bobby Sue Prewitt), Kay Lenz (Audree Prewitt), Michael Clark (Rick Seiden), Tina Andrews (Bernetta), Judson Pratt (Priest), Barbara Werle (Sister Gratia), Lynn Borden (Connie), Marion Ross (Mrs. Crowe), Stephen Rogers (Arlen Crowe), Ann Summers (Administrator).

84. Wishman. CBS 6/23/83. 60 minutes. Viacom Enterprises. Director: James Frawley. Executive Producers: Terry Morse, Jr., Rick Rosenberg, and Robert Christiansen. Producer: Chris Seitz. Writer: John Stern. Music: Fred Karlin.

This flop features a creature modeled after *ET* and a timeworn concept that simply refuses to die—the [FILL IN THE BLANK] and his/ her friend [FILL IN THE BLANK] pursued by an obsessed [FILL IN THE BLANK] intent on: a) dissecting him/her/it, or: b) prosecuting him/her/it for a crime he/she/it didn't commit, or: c) [FILL IN THE BLANK]. This time, bioengineer Joseph Bottoms creates a lovable creature in his lab and is forced to flee, along with fashion photographer/ wife Linda Hamilton, when the evil corporation wants to exploit the cute beastie for profit. James Keach is their obsessed pursuer.

Cast: Joseph Bottoms (as Dr. Alex MacGregor), Linda Hamilton (Mattie MacGregor), James Keach (Galen Reed), Margarita Fernandez (Wishman), John Reilly (Sam), Jean Bruce Scott (Karen Kaleb), Sam Weisman (Nat Kaleb), Robin Gammell (Dr. Harold Wish), Jason Presson (Bruce Kaleb), Seamon Glass (Gate Guard), Burt Edwards (Ed).

85. **The World of Darkness.** [Pilot #1]. CBS 4/17/77. 60 minutes. Talent Associates. Director: Jerry London. Executive Producer: David Susskind. Producer: Diana Karew. Writer/Creator: Art Wallace. Music: Fred Karlin.

The first of two pilots about a sportswriter (Granville Van Dusen) who, after a serious accident, "dies" for two minutes on the operating table and awakens with a supernatural, psychic tie to "the world beyond" (which, incidentally, is the title of the second pilot). Voices from beyond the grave send him on missions to help people facing supernatural dangers.

Cast: Granville Van Dusen (as Paul Taylor), Tovah Feldshuh (Clara Sanford), Beatrice Straight (Joanna Sanford), Gary Merrill (Dr. Thomas Madsen), James Austin (John Sanford), Shawn McCann (Matty Barker), Jane Eastwood (Helen), Al Bernardo (Max).

85a. **The World Beyond.** [Pilot #2]. CBS 1/27178. 60 minutes. Talent Associates. Director: Noel Black. Executive Producer: David Susskind. Producer: Frederick Brogger. Writer/Creator: Art Wallace. Music: Fred Karlin.

A second attempt to sell the concept of a sportswriter (again played by Granville Van Dusen) who nearly expires on the operating table following an accident and now gets messages from "beyond" to help people in supernatural danger.

Cast: Granville Van Dusen (as Paul Taylor), JoBeth Williams (Marian Faber), Barnard Hughes (Andy Borchard), Richard Fitzpatrick (Frank Faber), Jan Van Evers (Sam Barker).

86. **Wurlitzer.** Fox 1989. 60 minutes. Patrick Hasburgh Productions. Executive Producer/Writer: Patrick Hasburgh.

Scott Maldovan inherits a run-down diner, and in it, an antique, mahogany Wurlitzer jukebox which not only plays timeless hits, but hurls our hapless hero into the past, to the time when each particular song was popular. In the unproduced pilot, Scott is sent to 1968 San Francisco to help a woman in her battle against drug addiction. Hasburgh, with Stephen J. Cannell, created *21 Jump Street*, which was the cornerstone of the fledgling Fox network.

SITCOMS

87. **America 2100.** ABC 7/24/79. 30 minutes. Rothman/Ganz Productions and Paramount Television. Director: Joel Zwick. Executive Producers/Writers: Austin Kalish and Irma Kalish. Producer: Gary Menteer. Creators: Mark Rothman and Lowell Ganz. Music: Jonathan Tunick.

Two nightclub comics (Jon Cutler and Mark King) are accidentally put into suspended animation, wake up in the year 2100, in a world now run by a friendly computer named Max (Sid Caesar), and are befriended by a female scientist (Karen Valentine).

Cast: Karen Valentine (as Dr. Karen Harland), Jon Cutler (Chester Barnes), Mark King (Phil Keese), Sid Caesar (Voice of Max).

88. **The Astronauts.** CBS 8/11/82. 30 minutes. Elmar Productions. Director: Hal Cooper. Executive Producers: Rod Parker and Hal Cooper. Producer: Rita Dillon. Writer: Rod Parker. Creators: Hal Cooper and Rod Parker. Music: Billy Byers.

Based on the BBC sitcom, a *Three's Company* in outer space with two men and a beautiful woman stuck in an orbiting space station, dubbed Scilab. McLean Stevenson is their earthbound commanding officer.

Cast: Granville Van Dusen (as Capt. Roger Canfield), Brianne Leary (Astronaut Jennifer Tate), Bruce Davison (Astronaut David Ackroyd), McLean Stevenson (Col. Michael C. Booker), Nathan Cook (Scotty).

89. **Ben Blue's Brothers.** CBS 6/28/65. 30 minutes. Hal Roach Productions. Director: Norman Z. McLeod. Producer: Jerry Stagg. Writers: Marion Hargrove and Russel Beggs.

Veteran stage and screen comic Ben Blue would portray four different brothers: an aristocrat, a bum, a vaudeville performer, and an average joe.

The only other recurring character not portrayed by Blue was his mother, played by Ruth McDevitt. The pilot was shot in 1958 but remained unaired until 1965. Costarred Barbara Heller, Robin Raymond, Lillian Culver, Yvette Vickers, Jane McGowan, Fred Easier.

90. **Bungle Abbey.** NBC 5/31/81. 30 minutes. Lucille Ball Productions. Director: Lucille Ball. Executive Producers: Gary Morton and Lucille Ball. Writers/Creators: Seamon Jacobs and Fred Fox.

Charlie Callas, Graham Jarvis, Antony Alda, Peter Palmer, Guy Marks, and Gino Conforti are among the wacky monks in this zany monastery. Gale Gordon stars as the Abbott. William Lanteau guest starred in the pilot, which had the monks scheming to sell the portrait of monastery founder Brother Bungle to raise money for an orphanage.

91. **Captain Ahab.** CBS 9/3/65. 30 minutes. Director: Richard Crenna. Producer: Hal Kanter. Writers: Hal Kanter and Michael Fessier.

Two distant cousins—a naïve southern girl (Judy Canova) and a streetwise Las Vegas showgirl (Jaye P. Morgan)—inherit their uncle's New York town house, a lot of money, and Captain Ahab, a ninety-year-old talking parrot. To keep the money, the two cousins have to live together and care for the smart-mouth parrot.

Cast: Judy Canova (as Tillie Meeks), Jaye P. Morgan (Maggie Feeney), Don Porter (Battersea), Sid Gould (Angelo), Francine York (Miss Langdon), Eddie Quillan (Emcee), Larry Blake (Hardhat), Tom Lound (Chauffeur), Maury Hill (Cop), Tommy Alende (Delivery Boy).

92. **Danny and the Mermaid.** CBS 5/17/78. 30 minutes. Ivan Tors Productions. Director: Norman Abbott. Executive Producer/Creator: Ivan Tors. Producer/Writer: Budd Grossman.

Danny Stevens is an oceanography student having troubles with his studies, who secretly befriends a mermaid named Aqua, her dolphin, and her sea lion, all of whom help him explore the ocean.

Cast: Harlee McBride (as Aqua), Patrick Collins (Danny Stevens), Ray Walston (Prof. Stoneman), Rick Fazel (Turtle), Conrad Janis (Psychiatrist), Ancel Cook (Pilot).

93. The Darwin Family. NBC 1956. Production Company: William Morris.

A spin-off from the *NBC Comedy Hour*. While monkeys frolic on the set, offscreen actors provide "their voices." Twenty years later, ABC would do a Saturday morning children's series, entitled *Lancelot Link*, based on the same notion.

94. Ethel Is an Elephant. CBS 6/18/80. 30 minutes. Columbia Pictures Television. Director: John Astin. Executive Producers: Bob Sweeney, Larry Rosen, and Edward H. Feldman. Producer: Larry Rosen. Writer: Larry Tucker. Music: Ken Harrison.

Todd Susman is a New York photographer who shares his apartment with a baby elephant abandoned by a circus. The proposed series would chronicle this awkward living arrangement and his constant battles with the city and his landlord to keep the animal. *People* called it a "smartly written bit of Aesopian whimsy."

Cast: Todd Susman (as Eugene Henderson), Steven Peterman (Howard Dimitri), Liberty Godshall (Dr. Diane Taylor), Ed Barth (Harold Brainer), Stephen Pearlman (Prosecutor), John C. Becher (Judge), Bernie McInerney (Cop).

95. Good Old Days. NBC 7/11/66. 30 minutes. Desilu. Director: Howard Morris. Producers/Writers: Hal Goodman and Larry Klein.

A comedy about the problems of a prehistoric family a la *The Flintstones*. In the pilot, teenage caveman Rok meets beautiful cavegirl Pantha.

Cast: Darryl Hickman (as Rok), Kathleen Freeman (Mom), Ned Glass (Dad), Chris Noel (Pantha), Dodo Denny (Ugh), Beverly Adams (Cavegirl), Dean Moray (Kid), Jacques Aubuchon (Soc), Joe Bova (Kook), Bruce Yarnall (Slag), Charles Horvath (Brute).

96. Great Day. ABC 5/23/77. 30 minutes. Aaron Ruben Productions. Director: Peter Baldwin. Executive Producer/Writer/Creator: Aaron Ruben. Producer: Gene Marcione. Music: Peter Matz.

This pilot was supposed to illustrate how fun life is as a skid row bum in New York's bowery. It failed.

Cast: Al Molinaro (as Peavey), Dub Taylor (Doc), Guy Marks (Boomer), Spo-De-Odee (Jabbo), Joseph Elic (Moose), Billy Barty (Billy), Pat Crenshaw (Pop), Alice Nunn (Molly), Audrey Christie (Mrs. Graham), Dorothy Konrad (Woman).

97. **Katmandu.** ABC 1980. 30 minutes. Paramount Television. Producer: Garry Marshall. Writer: Jeff Ganz.

A teenage prince and princess of an exotic foreign land and their beautiful female bodyguard Kat are on-the-run from the country's evil king and take refuge with a typical American family. Stars include Vicki Lawrence, Victor Buono, Alice Ghostley, and Deborah Pratt. Although the *Katmandu* pilot never aired, the character appeared on the *Happy Days* episode "Fonzie Meets Kat" on 9/25/79. Deborah Pratt, later producer of *Quantum Leap*, starred as Kat.

98. **A Little Bit Strange.** NBC 4/23/89. 30 minutes. NBC Productions. Director: Jack Shea. Executive Producers/Writers: Topper Caren and David Duclon. Producer: Michael Holt. Music: Greg Poree. Theme: Ron Bussard.

An attempt at melding *The Addams Family* and *The Brady Bunch* brands of 1960s comedy, with a touch of *Cosby* for contemporary audiences. Michael Warren is a widower raising a most unusual family—he and his son are warlocks, his daughter is a witch, his mother is psychic, his brother a soul-singing bat, and his nephew is made of mud. Enter single mother Marilyn McClane, a "normal" woman who marries into a family that is—cue the theme song—"A Little Bit Strange."

Cast: Michael Warren (as Ben Masterson), Vanessa Bell Calloway (Marilyn McClane), Shawn Skie (TJ), Cherie Johnson (Tasha), Martin Lawrence (Sydney), Myra J (Maggie), Finis Henderson (Uncle Frank), Thomas Ryan (Customer), Raymond Davis (George Washington).

99. **Love at First Sight.** [Pilot #1]. CBS 10/13/80. 30 minutes. Filmways. Director: Bill Persky. Executive Producer/Writer/Creator: Nick Arnold. Producer: Peter Locke. Music: Jose Feliciano.

The first of two pilots about a woman (Susan Bigelow) with conservative parents (Robert Rockwell and Peggy McCay) who marries a blind musician (Philip Levien) who writes jingles for an ad agency.

Cast: Philip Levien (as Jonathan Alexander), Susan Bigelow (Karen Alexander), Pat Cooper (Francis Fame), Deborah Baltzell (Genevieve Lamont), Angela Aames (Denise), Robert Rockwell (Mr. Bellamy), Peggy McCay (Mrs. Bellamy).

99a. Love at First Sight. [Pilot #2]. CBS 3/29/82. 30 minutes. Filmways. Director: Nick Havinga. Executive Producer/Writer/Creator: Nick Arnold. Producer: Peter Locke. Music: Jose Feliciano.

The Alexanders think about buying a gun after they are robbed.

Cast: Philip Levien (as Jonathan Alexander), Susan Bigelow (Karen Alexander), Macon McCalman (Mr. Sawyer), Reni Santoni (Stan).

100. The Many Wives of Patrick. CBS 1980. 30 minutes. NRW Productions. Producers: Don Nicholl, Mickey Ross, and Bernie West. Writer: Budd Grossman.

From the folks behind Three's Company comes this adaptation of a BBC sitcom about an insurance agent who has been married and divorced six times. The comedy would arise from myriad complications of life with his six former spouses and his various children.

101. Mars: Base One. CBS 1988. 30 minutes. Mebzor Productions. Executive Producers: Edward K. Milkis and Dan Aykroyd. Writer/Creator: Dan Aykroyd.

The misadventures, a la *The Jetsons*, of a family adjusting to life on Mars, where they live next door to a Soviet technician and his American-stripper wife. The 1988 Writers Guild strike forced production of the pilot—and any serious consideration of it for the network schedule—to be put on the back burner.

102. Merlin the Magician. George Huskin and Associates, 1959. Writer: Phil Rapp.

British vaudeville comic Richard Hearn stars in this "zany comedy" about the famed magician in King Arthur's court. The twist is he always conjures up such modern objects as gas ranges, cars and the like to solve his problems. The series would try to capture the tone of Mark Twain's *A Connecticut Yankee in King Arthur's Court.*

103. **Mickey and the Contessa.** CBS 8/12/63. 30 minutes. Desilu. Director: William Asher. Producer: Cy Howard. Writers: William Davenport and Cy Howard.

Eva Gabor stars as a dispossessed woman of nobility who comes to America and is hired as a housekeeper by Mickey Shaughnessy, a basketball coach with two kids who knows nothing about culture or high society.

Cast: Mickey Shaughnessy (as Mickey Brennan), Eva Gabor (Contessa Czigoina), Ann Marshall (Sissy Brennan), Bill St. John (Mike Brennan), John Fiedler (Arney Tanner), Michael Green (Butch Gorkey).

104. **Mixed Nuts.** ABC 5/12/77. 30 minutes. Mark Carliner Productions and Viacom Enterprises. Directors: Peter H. Hunt and Jerry Belson. Executive Producer: Mark Carliner. Producer: Michael Leeson. Writers: Jerry Belson and Michael Leeson. Creator: Jerry Belson.

The lives and misadventures of the doctors and psychiatric patients at the Willow Center Hospital. In the pilot, the staff lets the patients choose where to go on a field trip—and they pick a singles bar.

Cast: Zohra Lampert (as Dr. Sarah Allgood), Emory Bass (Dr. Folder), Dan Barrows (Bugs), Richard Karron (Logan), Morey Amsterdam (Moe), James Victor (Gato), Ed Begley, Jr. (Jamie), Conchata Ferrell (Nurse Cassidy).

105. **Mr. and Mrs. Dracula.** [Pilot #1]. ABC 9/5/80. 30 minutes. ABC Circle Films. Director: Doug Rogers. Executive Producer/Writer/ Creator: Robert Klane. Producer: Stanley Korey. Music: Ken Lauber.

The Dracula family is forced by a villagers' uprising to move from their Transylvania castle to a New York apartment. The proposed series would have focused on their troubles adjusting to a new way of life.

Cast: Dick Shawn (as Dracula), Carol Lawrence (Sonia Dracula), Gail Mayron (Minna Dracula), Anthony Battaglia (Sonny Dracula), Johnny Haymer (Gregor the Bat), Barry Gordon (Cousin Anton), Rick Aviles (Mario).

105a. Mr. and Mrs. Dracula. [Pilot #2]. ABC 1981. 30 minutes. Marble Arch Productions and ABC Circle Films. Director: Doug Rogers. Executive Producer: Robert Klane. Producer: Stanton Corey. Creators: Dick Clement and Ian LaFranais.

A reworking of the previous season's pilot. Dick Shawn is back as Dracula, who moves with his family from Transylvania to the South Bronx. Paula Prentiss replaces Carol Lawrence as Mrs. Dracula.

106. My Wife Next Door. NBC 1974. 30 minutes. Concept II Productions. Producers: Bill Persky and Sam Denoff. Writer: Jerry Davis.

A divorced couple (James Farentino and Julie Sommers) coincidentally move into adjoining apartments on the beach.

107. My Wife Next Door. CBS 9/11/80. 30 minutes. Marble Arch Productions and Witzend Productions. Director: Bill Persky. Executive Producer: Martin Starger. Producers: Ian LeFrenais and Allan McKeown. Writers: Dick Clement and Ian LaFrenais.

Based on BBC sitcom. TV producer Lee Purcell and baseball player Granville Van Dusen just got a divorce—and now they discover they've inadvertently bought condominiums next door to each other. Bill Persky directed a flop pilot, also called *My Wife Next Door*, for NBC in 1974.

Cast: Lee Purcell (as Lisa Pallick), Granville Van Dusen (Paul Gilmore), Desiree Brochetti (Jan Pallick), Michael Delano (Vinnie Messina), Frank Dent (Lionel), Phil Rubenstein (Artie).

108. Off the Boat (aka Big Shots in America). NBC 6/20/85. 30 minutes. The Brillstein Company. Director: James Burrows. Executive Producers: Bernie Brillstein and Lome Michaels. Writer: Alan Zweibel.

From the creators and writers of *Saturday Night Live* comes this sitcom pilot that, not coincidentally, has characters reminiscent of the "two wild and crazy guys" created by Dan Aykroyd and Steve Martin on the show. The proposed series would follow the comic misadventures of two immigrants—Jovan and Enci Shegula—from an unnamed Eastern European country who come to America and end up managing a Brooklyn apartment house.

Cast: Joe Mantegna (as Jovan Shegula), Keith Szarabajka (Enci Shegula), Dan Vitale (Dae), Christine Baranksi (Cara).

109. Out of the Blue. CBS 8/12/68. 30 minutes. CBS Entertainment. Director: Sherman Marks. Producer/Writer: Sol Saks.

Shirley Jones, Barry Dennen, Carl Ballantine, and Marvin Kaplan are aliens from an overpopulated planet who come to Earth to see whether or not they should move some of their people here. They befriend a physics professor (John McMartin) living in Hollywood, who helps them understand our often confusing world.

Cast: Shirley Jones (as Dr. Aphrodite), John McMartin (Professor Josh Enders), Carl Ballantine (Claude), Marvin Kaplan (Ethel), Barry Dennen (Solly), Richard Erdman (Murphy), Nydia Westman (Woman), Richard Jury (Man), John Hubbard (Captain), Rick Richards (Private).

110. Poor Richard (aka The George Hamilton Show). CBS 1/21/84. 30 minutes. MGM/UA Television. Director: Rod Daniel. Executive Producer: Jerry Weintraub. Producers: Tim Berry and Hal Dresner. Writer: Hal Dresner. Music: Harry Lojewski.

George Hamilton is a millionaire who squanders his fortune and is forced to fire his servants and sell his mansion. He's standing alone in his mansion when the new owners—a *Beverly Hillbillies*-type family that made a fortune on a new pig feed—arrive and mistake him for the butler. He plays along, hiding his true identity from his employers and his new identity from his friends—who think he's still the wealthy master of the house.

Cast: George Hamilton (as Rich Manning), Geoffrey Lewis (Rudy Hopper), Alley Mills (Terry), Cynthia Sikes (Vicki), Nancy Stafford (Randi), John Hunsaker (Jimmy), Glynn Turman (Jonathan).

111. S.A.M. ABC 1971. MGM Television. Producer/Writer: James Komack.

The title means "Stories About Men." It's also the first name of the hero, a guy (played by Paul Sand) in the Public Works Department at City Hall who arbitrates the opinionated battles between his coworkers, neighbors, and people on the street.

112. The Secret Life of James Thurber (aka The Secret Life of John Monroe). [Pilot #1]. NBC 6/8/59. 30 minutes. Screen Gems. Director: James Sheldon. Producer: Jules Goldstone. Writer: Mel Shavelson, from the stories by James Thurber.

Aired as the "Christabel" episode of *Alcoa/Goodyear Theatre*. Arthur O'Connell is magazine writer and cartoonist John Monroe who often escapes into the fantasy world of his drawings—which came alive through animation by UPA Pictures. In the pilot, Monroe's daughter's dog Christabel dies. Although this didn't sell, another pilot was made in 1961 called *The Secret Life of James Thurber*, this time starring Orson Bean. It, too, failed to spawn a series. A decade later, however, Thurber's life and tales became the basis for *My World and Welcome to It*, starring William Windom as John Monroe, Joan Hotchkis as his wife Ellen, Lisa Gerristen as daughter Lydia. The highly acclaimed last-named series, produced by Sheldon Leonard and Danny Arnold, mixed animation and live action and survived for a single season.

Cast: Arthur O'Connell (as John Monroe), Georgann Johnson (Ellen Monroe), Susan Gordon (Lydia Monroe), Charles Herbert (Charlie), Dabbs Greer (Policeman).

112a. The Secret Life of James Thurber. [Pilot #2]. CBS 3/20/61. 60 minutes. Four Star.

Aired as an episode of *The June Allyson Show*. Orson Bean played James Thurber, here a magazine writer and cartoonist who often slips into a fantasy world populated by his drawings, which come to life. Adolphe Menjou costarred. This was another attempt at adapting the Thurber stories and artwork to a television series. The first, the 1959 pilot *The Secret Life of John Monroe* starred Arthur O'Connell.

113. **Sgt. T.K. Yu.** NBC 4/10/79. 30 minutes. Hanna-Barbera Productions. Director: Paul Stanley. Executive Producer: Joseph Barbera. Producer: Terry Morse, Jr. Writer: Gordon Dawson. Music: Al Kasha.

Real-life Korean-born standup comic Johnny Yune is a Korean L.A.P.D. detective who works part-time as a standup comic. Writer Dawson later would create and produce *Bret Maverick*.

Cast: Johnny Yune (as Sgt. T.K. Yu), Marty Brill (Sam Palfy), John Lehne (Lt. Robert Ridge).

114. **Silver Springs (aka Mike and the Mermaid).** ABC 1/5/68. 30 minutes. Robert Maxwell Productions. Producer: Rudy Abel.

Aired as an episode of *Off to See the Wizard*. A boy, living with his parents and his grandfather, meets a mermaid who followed a school of fish into Florida waters and now can't find her way home.

Cast: Kevin Brodie (as Mike Malone), Jerri Lynn Fraser (Mermaid), Med Flory (Jim Malone), Rachel Ames (Nellie Malone), also, Dan Tompkins.

115. **Starstruck.** CBS 6/9/79. 30 minutes. Herbert B. Leonard Productions. Director: Al Viola. Executive Producer: Herbert B. Leonard. Producer: Bob Kiger. Writer/Creator: Arthur Kopit. Music: Alan Alper.

The misadventures of a family operating an orbiting space station restaurant—the only place in the galaxy that still makes apple pie. The family includes widower Ebeneezer McCallister, whose ancestors helped settle California; his stoic mother Abigail; his 172-year-old great-great-great-great grandfather Ezra; and his three children. There are also two robots, Hudson and Bridges, who are in love with each other. The envisioned series would focus on the family and the bizarre assortment of aliens who visit their galactic diner.

Cast. Beeson Carroll (as Ebeneezer McCallister), Tania Myren (Kate McCallister), Meegan King (Mark McCallister), Kevin Brando (Rupert McCallister), Guy Raymond (Ezra McCallister), Elvia Allman (Abigail McCallister), Lynne Lipton (Amber LaRue), Sarah Kennedy (Delight), Robin Strand (Chance), Joe Silver (Max), Roy Brocksmith (Orthwaite Frodo), Herb Kaplowitz (Dark), Robert Short (Hudson), Buddy

THE BEST TV SHOWS THAT NEVER WERE

Douglas (Mrs. Bridges), J.C. Wells (Tashko), Chris Wales (Mary-John), Cynthia Latham (Madame Dumont).

116. Stick Around. ABC 5/30/77. 30 minutes. Humble Productions and T.A.T. Communications. Director: Bill Hobin. Producers/Writers: Fred Freeman and Lawrence J. Cohen.

An attempt at a live-action *Jetsons* with Fred McCarren and Nancy New as a typical married couple in the year 2055. In the pilot, they fight over whether to trade in their out-dated robot Andy (Andy Kaufman) for a new one.

Cast. Nancy New (as Elaine Keefer), Fred McCarren (Vance Keefer), Andy Kaufman (Andy), Cliff Norton (Joe Burkus), Craig Richard Nelson (Earl), Jeffrey Kramer (Ed), Liberty Williams (Lisa), Priscilla Morrill (Customer).

117. Take Me to Your Leader. ABC 1964. 30 minutes. MGM Television.

The story of two aliens from Venus who come to earth, meet an inventor, and go into business with him selling to unknowing earthlings products created for another planet.

118. There Goes the Neighborhood. NBC 6/4/83. 30 minutes. Saul Ilson Productions and Columbia Pictures Television. Director: Dick Martin. Executive Producer: Saul Ilson. Writer: David Duclon.

Buddy Hackett, G.W. Bailey, and Patrick Collins are three hobos who inherit the estate of a Bel Air millionaire, and proceed to shock and embarrass the dead man's servants, family, and neighbors. The hobos hire a business manager (Graham Jarvis) who watches out for them, to the dismay of his snobbish wife (Sue Ann Gilfillan). In the book *The Sweeps*, authors Mark Christianson and Cameron Stauth say the pilot was killed by Hackett, who was funny during rehearsals but "froze up" when the cameras started rolling, so that his "screwball attitude congealed into a stilted, painful tightness that brought the entire production down around him." The show was "written off as a $500,000 bath."

Cast: Buddy Hackett (as Boxcar), Patrick Collins (The Kid), G.W. Bailey (Barney), Graham Jarvis (Milton Crocker), William Glover (Filkins), Sue Ann Gilfillan (Hortense Crocker), Keene Curtis (Charles Hawthorne).

119. **13 Thirteenth Avenue.** CBS 8/15/83. 30 minutes. Paramount
Television. Director: John Bowab. Executive Producer: Chris
Thompson. Producers: Lenny Ripps and Don Van Atta. Writer: Lenny
Ripps. Music: Michel Rubini.

The misadventures of a widower (A.C. Weary) and his son (Wil
Wheaton), who move into a Greenwich Village apartment building
inhabited by a model who's a witch (Ilene Graff), a C.P.A. who's a were-
wolf (Robert Harper), a lawyer who's a vampire (Paul Kreppel), a superintendent who's a troll (Ernie Sabella), and their psychiatrist (Clive Revill).

Cast: Clive Revill (as Dr. Carey), A.C. Weary (Jack Gordon), Ilene
Graff (Melinda York), Paul Kreppel (Roland Keats), Robert Harper (Marv
Hoberman), Ernie Sabella (Vlastock Spoltechzep), Wil Wheaton (Willie
Gordon), Elizabeth Savage (Joan Arthur), Stanley Brock (Mr. Epstein).

120. **Tickets, Please.** CBS 9/6/88. 30 minutes. Walt Disney Television and
Charlie Peters Films. Director: Art Dielhenn. Executive Producers:
Charlie Peters and Bill Dial. Producer: George Sunga. Writer/Creator:
Charlie Peters. Music: David Benoit.

Aired as a segment of *CBS Summer Playhouse.* An ensemble comedy
revolving around the regular riders of a New York commuter train "club
car." Cleavon Little is the bartender who runs the car, Yeardley Smith is
a law student working as a ticket-taker, David Marciano the conductor,
Marcia Strassman a divorced lawyer with a teenager daughter, Barbara
Howard an actress, and Bill Macy a pesticide executive.

Cast: Cleavon Little (as "Bake" Baker), David Marciano (Sal
Bernardini), Yeardley Smith (Paula Bennett), Marcia Strassman (Elaine),
Bill Macy (Sam), Harold Gould (Jack), Joe Guzaldo (Ted), Barbara
Howard (Ginger).

121. **Where's Everett?** CBS 4/18/66. 30 minutes. Screen Gems and Proctor
& Gamble Productions. Director: Gene Nelson. Producer/Writer: Ed
Simmons. Music: Frank DeVol.

Alan Alda is a young father who goes to get the morning paper and
finds that aliens have left an invisible baby on his doorstep—a baby which
his wife and kids gladly adopt and name Everett.

Cast: Alan Alda (as Arnold Barker), Patricia Smith (Sylvia Barker), Doreen Miller (Lizzie Barker), Nicolas Coster (Dr. Paul Jellico), Frank DeVol (Murdock), Robert Cleaves (Milkman).

122. Which Way to the Mecca, Jack? Independent 1965. 30 minutes. Producer: Harry Ackerman. Writer: William Peter Blatty.

Based on Blatty's book about a Middle East king who is a swinger and uses American aid to build his harem, to the consternation of the U.S. emissary who is supposed to control the money. This is a variation on Blatty's 1964 movie, *John Goldfarb, Please Come Home*, starring Shirley MacLaine, Richard Crenna and Peter Ustinov.

123. Yazoo (aka Wizzle Falls). NBC 1984. 30 minutes. Carson Productions. Director: Perry Rosemond. Executive Producer: April Kelly. Producers: Jim Gentry and Dave Pavelonis. Writers: Jeff Franklin and April Kelly.

William Conrad is a widowed journalist who goes fishing one day, falls asleep in the boat, and wakes up in a magical world called Yazoo, populated by the Peppercorn Puppets. Although he can leave, he finds a contentment there. The proposed series would follow him as he learns about their world, and they learn about his. The original concept had him crashing his single-engine plane in the mystery land, then dubbed Wizzle Falls.

GHOSTS, ANGELS AND DEVILS

Some high concepts keep repeating themselves—particularly those involving robots, extraterrestrials, ghosts, and wacky animals.

The annals of television are bursting with concepts about ghosts returning to haunt their newly wedded spouses, about robots that develop minds of their own, about kindly extraterrestrials pursued by evil humans, about angels coming to help their errant mortal charges, and about lovable pets who are more human than their owners.

What they all have in common is that as often as they fail, they also succeed. So take a good look at these flops—because no matter how familiar they are, how disastrously they failed, or how ridiculous they seem, the concept is bound to return…and return.

124. After George. CBS 6/6/83. 30 minutes. Humble Productions and MGM Television. Director: Linda Day. Producers: Fred Freeman and Lawrence J. Cohen. Writers: Dennis Danziger and Ellen Sandler. Music: James DiPasquale.

Susan Saint James stars as a widow who discovers that her late husband, who died in a car accident, programmed his personality into the computer that operates their house.

Cast: Susan Saint James (as Susan Roberts), Joel Brooks (Cal Sloan), Susan Ruttan (Marge), Allyn Ann McLerie (Rose), Richard Schaal (Voice of George), John Reilly (Walt), George Pentecost (Frank), Steve Anderson (Charles).

125. Back Together. CBS 1/25/84. 30 minutes. Chagrin Productions and Lorimar Productions. Director: Peter Bonerz. Executive Producer/ Writer: Charlie Hauck. Music: David Franco and Willie Wilkerson.

Herkie Burke is dead, but an administrative foul-up in heaven prevents him from passing through the Pearly Gates. He chooses to wait things out with his old college friends, the Harringtons, who aren't wild about having a ghost in the house—especially one who doesn't care how he behaves since there's nothing to lose, he's dead anyway.

Cast: Paul Provenza (as Herkie Burke), Jamie Widdoes (Elliot Harrington), Grace Harrison (Anne Harrington), Lisa Jane Persky (Dora Holloway), Richard Hamilton (Mr. Christopher), Mina Kolb (Mrs. Burke).

126. Barnaby (aka Mr. O'Malley). CBS 12/20/59. 30 minutes. Director: Sherman Marks. Producer: Stanley Rubin. Writer: Louis Pelletier.

Aired as an episode of *G.E. Theatre,* this was based on Crockett Johnson's comic strip "Barnaby and Mr. O'Malley." A young boy (Ron Howard) wishes for a fairy godmother and gets a cigar-smoking fairy godfather (Bert Lahr).

Cast: Bert Lahr (as Mr. O'Malley), Ron Howard (Barnaby Baxter), June Dayton (Alice Baxter), William Redfield (George Baxter), Mel Blanc (The Leprechaun Voice), Don Beddoe (Dr. Harvey), Debbie Megowan (Janie).

127. Charlie Angelo. CBS 8/26/62. 30 minutes. Director/Writer: Don McGuire. Producer: Jackie Cooper. Music: Sonny Burke.

James Komack, who would become a top TV producer and director, stars as an angel who tries to convince people not to do evil things—bad deeds encouraged by Dan Devlin aka The Devil (Larry Storch). In the pilot, Charlie tries to convince a debt-ridden nightclub owner (Bernard Kates) not to set his building aflame to collect the insurance money.

Cast: James Komack (as Charlie Angelo), Larry Storch (Dan Devlin), Bernard Kates (Chico Hernandez), Robert Carricart (Tony), Len Lesser (Holdup Man), Ben Wright (George).

128. Finch Finds a Way (aka Slightly Fallen Angel). NBC 5/4/59. 30 minutes. Screen Gems. Director: Robert Ellis Miller. Producer: William Sackheim. Writers: Sol Saks, William Cowley, and Peggy Chantler.

Aired as an episode of *Alcoa/Goodyear Theatre.* Mr. Finch (Walter Slezak) is an angel who comes to earth to fix our human problems—but usually just makes the problems worse. This is a popular concept in television, a concept that would be pitched many times and become such series as *Good Heavens* and *Highway to Heaven.* Costarred are Lee Bergere, David White, Elizabeth Watts, Jeffrey Roland, Paul Reed and Sid Raymond.

129. Free Spirit. ABC 1987. 60 minutes. Aaron Spelling Productions. Director: Paul Aaron. Executive Producer: Aaron Spelling. Writer: Richard Shapiro.

Yet another failed attempt to sell a series about a widow (Lisa Eilbacher) who remarries (Robin Thomas), only to be haunted by the ghost of her dead first husband (Michael Des Barres)—and yet another in a long line of ripoffs of *Dona Flor and Her Two Husbands* and its Americanized remake, *Kiss Me Goodbye.*

130. Freeman. ABC 6/19/76. 30 minutes. Harry Stoones, Inc. Director: Hal Cooper. Executive Producers: Bernie Kukoff, Jeff Harris, and Paul Mooney. Writer: Paul Mooney.

Freeman is a black ghost inhabiting a colonial mansion occupied by a wealthy white family. Neither is willing to leave, and it's from this conflict that the laughs were supposed to come. They didn't.

Cast: Stu Gilliam (as Freeman), Linden Chiles (Dwight Wainright), Beverly Sanders (Helen Wainright), Jimmy Baio (Timmy Wainright), Melinda Dillon (Madam Arkadina).

131. Ghost of a Chance. ABC 7/7/81. 30 minutes. Arim Productions and Paramount Television. Director: Nick Havinga. Executive Producers/ Writers: Austin and Irma Kalish. Producer: Gene Marcione. Music: Earle Hagen.

A pale imitation of the then-popular feature *Dona Flor and Her Two Husbands.* When Shelley Long marries Barry Van Dyke, the ghost of her dead first husband (Steven Keats) comes back to haunt her. Gretchen Wyler played Long's mother. Ironically, Dick Van Dyke, Barry's dad, also did a pilot called *Ghost of a Chance* six years later—playing a narco cop who accidentally gets himself killed and returns to help wrap up the case he was working on.

Cast: Shelley Long (as Jenny Clifford), Barry Van Dyke (Wayne Clifford), Steven Keats (Tom Chance), Gretchen Wyler (Frances), Archie Hahn (Michael), Rosalind Kind (Leslie), John O'Leary (Minister).

132. Heaven Help Us. CBS 8/14/67. 30 minutes. Twentieth Century Fox Television. Director: Richard Whorf. Executive Producer: William Dozier. Producer: Stan Shpetner. Writer: Sol Sachs.

Barry Nelson is a widower whose romantic life is frustrated by the ghost of his dead wife (Joanna Moore), who has a mean jealous streak and relishes interfering with his love life.

Cast: Barry Nelson (as Dick Cameron), Joanna Moore (Marge Cameron), Mary Grace Canfield (Mildred), Bert Freed (Mr. Walker), Skip Ward (Collins), Sue Randall (Ruth), Sandra Warner (Linda).

133. **Jeremiah of Jacob's Neck.** CBS 8/13/76. 30 minutes. Palomar Productions and Twentieth Century Fox Television. Director: Ralph Senesky. Producers: Art Stolnitz and Ed Scherick. Creator/Writer: Peter Benchley. Music: Harry Sukman.

The author of the novel *Jaws* created this thirty-minute pilot for an envisioned sixty-minute comedy/drama about a police chief and his family who move into a New England mansion inhabited by the cantankerous ghost of a smuggler.

Cast: Keenan Wynn (as Jeremiah the Ghost), Ron Masak (Chief Tom Rankin), Arlene Golonka (Anne Rankin), Brandon Cruz (Clay Rankin), Quinn Cummings (Tracy Rankin), Elliot Street (Deputy Wilbur Swift), Pitt Herbert (Mayor Dick Barker), Amzie Strickland (Abby Penrose), Alex Hentelhoff (Leonard), Les Lannom (Max), Tom Palmer (Crabtree), Don Burleson (Bob Peabody).

134. **Judgment Day.** NBC 12/6/81. 60 minutes. Ed Friendly Productions and NBC Productions. Director: Alan J. Levi. Executive Producer: Ed Friendly. Writer: William Froug. Music: Morton Stevens.

An anthology that features different people each week who turn up at the Pearly Gates to face sentencing to heaven or hell by the judge (Barry Sullivan) of the celestial court. Heaven is represented by Victor Buono, who tells us in flashbacks about the person's good deeds, while the Devil, represented by Roddy McDowall, shows us what this person did to deserve hell. This pilot reportedly cost $1.3 million to produce.

Cast: Barry Sullivan (as the Judge), Victor Buono (Mr. Heavener), Roddy McDowall (Mr. Heller), Carol Lynley (Harriet Egan), Beverly Garland (Vicki Connors), Robert Webber (Charles Egan), John Larch (Burton Randolph), Hari Rhodes (Joseph Pierson), Joseph Chapman (Bob Simmons), Priscilla Pointer (Mrs. Miller).

135. **Justin Case.** ABC 5/15/88. 90 minutes. Walt Disney Television and Blake Edwards Company. Director: Blake Edwards. Executive Producer: Blake Edwards. Producer: Tony Adams. Writer: Blake Edwards, from a story by Jennifer Edwards and Blake Edwards. Music: Henry Mancini.

Aired as an episode of *The Disney Sunday Movie*. A ditzy unemployed actress (Molly Hagan) applies for a secretarial job at a detective agency, only to find the private eye (George Carlin) has been murdered. So she helps his ghost search for the killer. (This was made as a two-hour movie but was chopped to 90 minutes on the eve of its premiere.)

Cast: George Carlin (as Justin Case), Molly Hagan (Jenny Spaulding), Timothy Stack (Detective), Kevin McClarnon (Detective), Gordon Jump (Psychic), Douglas Sills (Paramedic), Paul Sand (Cab Driver), Valerie Wildman (Woman in Black), Todd Susman (Aaron Slinker), Rod McCary (Simon Fresca), Philippe Denham (Paul Arkin), Richard McGonagle (Dr. Weintraub), also Jay Thomas, Kenneth Tigar, Kay Perry, John Lavachielli, Dotty Colorso, Reed McCants, Joe Mays, Lily Mariye, Andrew Nadell, Nina Mann, Jerry Martin, Stuart Tanney.

136. **Lady Luck.** NBC 9/12/73. 30 minutes. Universal Television. Producer/Director: James Komack. Writers: Dean Hargrove, Charles Shyer, and Alex Mandel. Creator: Hunt Stromberg, Jr. Music: Hal Mooney.

Valerie Perrine is a beautiful—perhaps supernatural—woman who helps people in trouble.

Cast: Valerie Perrine (as Lady Luck), Paul Sand (Roger), Bert Convy (Clay), Sallie Shockley (Penny), J.D. Cannon (Walter), Carole Cook (Fran).

137. **Landon, Landon and Landon (aka Gumshoes).** CBS 6/14/80. 60 minutes. Quinn Martin Productions. Director: Charles Dubin. Executive Producer: Don Reo. Producers/Writers: Bruce Kalish and Philip John Taylor. Music: Perry Botkin, Jr.

A brother (Daren Kelly) and sister (Nancy Dolman) share a detective agency with the ghost of their dead P.I. father (William Windom). *People* said: "William Windom is a private eye who returns from the grave to solve his own murder, but the real zombie is this sitcom pilot." This concept was reworked in 1981 as *Quick and Quiet*, and only Windom as the ghost and Millie Slavin as the agency secretary survived.

Cast: William Windom (as Ben Landon), Nancy Dolman (Holly Landon), Daren Kelly (Nick Landon), Millie Slavin (Judith Saperstein),

Richard O'Brien (Inspector Ulysses Barnes), Norman Bartold (George Rumford), Sudie Bond (Billie), Jason Wingreen (Daryl Goren), Wil Albert (Reggie Ozer), Pat Studstill (Capt. Nestor), Maurice Hill (Cy Vorpal).

138. Mr. Bevis. CBS 6/3/60. 30 minutes. Cayuga Productions. Director: William Asher. Producer: Buck Houghton. Writer/Creator: Rod Serling.

A spin-off from *The Twilight Zone*. A fantasy/comedy about the problems of Mr. Bevis, who discovers that his guardian angel, J. Hardy Hempstead, has come down to live with him. Burgess Meredith was originally envisioned as the angel but turned the role down. Serling would try this concept again as the "Cavender Is Coming" episode of *The Twilight Zone*, with Jesse White as the angel.

Cast: Orson Bean (as Mr. Bevis), Henry Jones (J. Hardy Hempstead), Charles Lane (Mr. Peckinpaugh), William Schallert (Policeman), House Peters, Jr. (Policeman), Colleen O'Sullivan (Lady), Horace McMahon (Bartender), Florence MacMichael (Margaret), Dorothy Neuman (Landlady), Vito Scotti (Peddler), Timmy Cletro (Little Boy).

139. Mr. and Mrs. and Mr. CBS 9/1/80. 30 minutes. Director: Hal Cooper. Executive Producers: Hal Cooper and Rod Parker. Producers: Rod Dames, Bob Fraser, and Rita Dillon. Writer: Rod Parker. Music: Billy Byers.

Widow Jenny Collins (Rebecca Balding) marries Jeff (Patrick Collins) only to discover afterwards that her first husband (Kale Browne)—believed dead in a plane crash—is still alive. In this *Enoch Arden*-themed plot, she has to pick which husband to keep, and while she thinks about it, they stay in the guest room.

Cast: Rebecca Balding (as Jenny Collins), Kale Browne (Jimmy York), Patrick Collins (Jeff Zelinka), Eda Zahl (Susan Masters).

140. Poor Devil. NBC 2/14/73. 90 minutes. Paramount Television.

Director: Robert Scheerer. Executive Producers/Creators: Arne Sultan and Earl Barret. Producer: Robert Stambler. Writers: Arne Sultan, Earl Barret, and Richard Bare. Music: Morton Stevens.

Sammy Davis, Jr., stars as the earnest but inept disciple of the devil (Christopher Lee) who constantly fails to win over souls in this long-form pilot for a half-hour sitcom.

Cast: Sammy Davis, Jr. (as Sammy), Christopher Lee (Lucifer), Jack Klugman (Burnett Emerson), Adam West (Crawford), Gino Conforti (Bligh), Emily Yancy (Chelsea), Madlyn Rhue (Frances Emerson), Alan Manson (Mr. Moriarty), Ken Lynch (Desk Sergeant), Byron Webster (Blackbeard), Buddy Lester (Al Capone), Owen Bush (Tom), Nick Georgiade (Bob Younger), Don Ross (Eddie), Lila Teigh (Woman), Stephen Coit (Father-in-law), Jo DeWinter (Secretary), George Kramer (Cole Younger), Clyde Ventura (Clyde Barrow), Nancy Reichert (Bonnie), Tom Wize (John Younger), David Young (James Younger).

141. **Quick and Quiet.** CBS 8/18/81. 30 minutes. Quinn Martin Productions and Brademan/Self Productions. Director: Don Weis. Executive Producers: Ed Self and Bill Brademan. Producer: Michael Rhodes. Writers: Sam Bobrick, Bruce Kalish, and Philip John Taylor. Music: Jack Elliott.

A reworking of the 1980 pilot *Landon, Landon and Landon.* William Windom returns as the ghost of a dead private eye who, this time, haunts his fun-loving, irresponsible, irreverent son (Rick Lohman) and reluctantly helps him solve crimes. Millie Slavin once again plays the agency secretary.

Cast: William Windom (as Thaddeus Clark "T.C." Cooper), Rick Lohman (Elliot Cooper), Millie Slavin (Camille), Lynda Day George (Margo Hilliard), Henry Jones (Walter Hilliard), Warren Berlinger (Leonard Plumb), Lois Areno (Bambi Wilson), Joan Roberts (Trixie Hilliard), Dallas Alinder (Minister), Jerry Marren (Harry Romero), David Pritchard (David), Lee Crawford (Woman).

142. **Satan's Waitin'.** CBS 9/12/64. 30 minutes. Director: Charles Haas. Producer: Joel Malone. Writers: Joel Malone and Tom Tomlinson.

Ray Walston is The Stranger, actually Satan, who each week would try to ruin someone's life by tempting him to indulge in avarice, jealousy, greed, and vice. Walston also played the Devil in *Damn Yankees.*

Cast: Ray Walston (as The Stranger), Jo Van Fleet (Velma Clarke), Lee Phillips (Walter Leighton), Sue Randall (Linda), Tom Greenway (Police Lieutenant), Simon Twigg (Minister).

143. Shivers. CBS 7/4/89. 30 minutes. Columbia Pictures Television.

Director: Peter Baldwin. Executive Producers: Jack Schwartzman and Larry Molin. Producer/Writer: Pamela Pettier. Music: Fred Mollin.

James Eckhouse is a divorced father who moves with his two kids into a house haunted by a Revolutionary War rogue (Mark Lindsay Chapman), his sexy girlfriend (Lesley-Anne Down), and a nasty pig-slopper (Courtney Gains)—all of whom make themselves visible to the new family but, of course, to nobody else.

Cast: Mark Lindsay Chapman (as Jack Marlowe), Lesley-Anne Down (Cassandra), James Eckhouse (David), Courtney Gains (Silas), Amber Susa (Amanda), Tim Eyster (Matthew), Priscilla Morrill (Miss Gordon), Tim Winters (Professor Frolich).

144. The Side of the Angels (aka Cavender Is Coming). CBS 5/25/62. 30 minutes. Cayuga Productions. Director: Christian Nyby. Producer: Buck Houghton. Writer: Rod Serling.

"Submitted for your approval: the case of one Agnes Grep, put on earth with two left feet, an overabundance of thumbs and a propensity for falling down manholes. In a moment, she will be up to her jaw in miracles, wrought by apprentice angel Harmon Cavender, intent on winning his wings. And, though it's a fact both of them should have stayed in bed, they will tempt all the fates by moving into the cold, gray dawn of *The Twilight Zone.*" Sound familiar? It should. *Cavender Is Coming* is Serling's second attempt to sell the concept he showcased in *Mr. Bevis*, which was also aired as a *Twilight Zone* episode. Though it didn't come across like a comedy, this had a laugh track.

Cavender is a hapless angel who must earn his wings by helping chronically unemployed and clumsy Agnes Grep (Carol Burnett) support herself. He botches the assignment, but the end result is a happy one and his boss, Mr. Polk, decides perhaps Cavender can help other mortals in distress. (In the first pilot, Mr. Bevis was the angel's permanent assignment.) Although it didn't sell, ten years later others with the similar notion were a little more successful—*Out of the Blue*, about an angel who helps a family, and *Good Heavens*, about an angel who helps people in need. Both became series…and lasted less than a month. "A word to the wise now to any and all who might suddenly feel the presence of a cigar-smoking helpmate who takes bankbooks out of thin air. If you're suddenly aware of such celestial aids, it means that you're under the beneficent care of one Harmon Cavender, guardian angel. And this message from the Twilight Zone: lotsa luck!"

Cast. Carol Burnett (as Agnes Grep), Jesse White (Harmon Cavender), Howard Smith (Mr. Polk), William O'Connell (Field Rep), Pitt Herbert (Field Rep), John Fiedler (Field Rep), G. Stanley Jones (Field Rep), Frank Behrens (Stout), Albert Carrier (French Man), Roy Sickner (Bus Driver), Norma Shattuc (Little Girl), Rory O'Brien (Little Boy), Sandra Gould (Woman), Adrienne Marden (Woman), Jack Younger (Truck Driver), Danny Kulick (Child), Donna Douglas (Woman), Maurice Dallimore (Man), Barbara Morrison (Woman).

145. Three Wishes. NBC 7/29/63. 30 minutes. Don Sharpe Productions. Director: Andrew McCullough. Executive Producer: Don Sharpe. Producer: Robert Welch. Writer: Robert Riley Crutcher.

Although originally made for NBC in 1960, this pilot appeared on CBS three years later. Diane Jergens stars as a woman who finds an antique lamp, rubs it, and a genie, that only she can see, appears to grant wishes to her and her friends to help them out of trouble.

Cast: Diane Jergens (as Annie Brenner), Gustavo Rojo (The Genie), George Grizzard (Henry), Wallace Ford (Uncle Jonas), Gage Clark (Miles Bunker), Dan Tobin (John Bunker).

146. Where's Momma? NBC 1973. 30 minutes. Lorimar Productions. Producer/Director: Carl Reiner. Executive Producer: Lee Rich. Writer/Creator: Muriel Resnick.

Yet another rehash of the dead-spouse-from-beyond-returns premise. This time, it's Richard Mulligan as a widowed real estate agent having a hard time juggling work and the responsibility of raising his two five-year-old twin boys—so his wife (Michele Carey) returns from the grave to help him out. Only he, of course, can see her. (Not to be confused, of course, with Reiner's cult movie, *Where's Poppa?*)

147. Who Goes There? CBS 1965. 30 minutes. CBS Productions. Producer: Stanley Kallis. Director: Jack Arnold.

Two troublesome ghosts haunting a southern California tract home materialize as General Custer (Pat Hingle) and Indian Chief Running Dog (Ben Blue), because pictures of those historical figures are on the wall, and roam the neighborhood.

REAL DOGS

148. Bear Heart. Rand-Brooks Productions, 1963. 30 minutes. Director: Randy Brooks. Producer: Robert Huddleston.

Two half-hour pilots were shot in Big Bear, California, starring Marshall Reed as a widower who brings his two teenage children to a trading post he recently bought in the High Sierras, where they befriend a wild German shepherd named Bear Heart. The first story shows how Bear Heart was mistreated by his owner, the former manager of the trading post, and became wild. The second story shows how the animal became a part of this new family.

149. McGurk (aka A Dog's Life). NBC 6/15/79. 30 minutes. TAT Communications. Director: Peter Bonerz. Producer: Charlie Hauck. Writers/Creators: Arthur Julian and Charlie Hauck.

A classic unsold pilot, an embarrassing disaster from the company responsible for such landmark shows as *All in the Family* and *Maude*. Barney Martin headed a cast of actors who dressed in dog suits and barked one-liners at each other. The idea, supposedly, was to offer wry observations about man through the eyes of his best friend.

Cast: Barney Martin (as McGurk), Beej Johnson (Iris), Sherry Lynn (Camille), Charles Martin Smith (Tucker), Hamilton Camp (Spike), Michael Huddleston (Turk).

150. Duffy. CBS 5/6/77. 30 minutes. Universal Television. Director: Bruce Bilson. Producer: George Eckstein. Writer: Richard DeRoy.

Duffy is the canine mascot of an elementary school. Everyone likes good old Duffy except the principal (Roger Bowen), the typical, red-cheeked, stuffy TV stereotype.

Cast: Duffy (as Himself), Fred Grandy (Cliff Sellers), Lane Binkley (Marty Carter), Roger Bowen (Thomas N. Tibbies), George Wyner (Happy Jack), Jane Lambert (Mrs. Dreifuss), Dick Yarmy (Postman), John Sheldon (Nick), Jarrod Johnson (Danny), John Herbsleb (Craig), Stephen Manley (Josh), Robert E. Ball (Hobo), Jane Dulo (Neighbor).

151. I Married a Dog. NBC 8/4/61. 30 minutes.

Hal March stars as a man who's constantly hampered by Noah, his wife's (Marcia Henderson) bothersome dog.

Cast: Hal March (as Peter Chance), Marcia Henderson (Joyce Nicoll-Chance), Mary Carver (Madge Kellogg).

152. K-Nine Patrol. Don Sharpe Productions, 1961.

John Lupton and Jesse White as police officers in a series pilot based on the case histories of the canine squad of the Baltimore Police Department.

153. K-9000. Fox 6/1/91. 2 hours. Fries Entertainment. Director: Kim Manners. Executive Producer: Steven E. DeSouza. Producer: Rick Dumm. Writers: Michael Part and Steven E. DeSouza.

Chris Mulkey is Eddie Monroe, a loose cannon on the L.A.P.D. who has a microchip implanted in his brain by scientist Catherine Oxenberg. This enables him to talk telepathically with his new partner, Niner, a genetically-enhanced German shepherd, who was also a cell phone. No kidding. A cell phone. Imagine the conversation Eddie and Niner might have had as they fought crime each week (Niner: "I really want to sniff some butt." Eddie: "Later. We got a murder to solve."). Fox Television Network, trying to build a name for itself as a network of innovation, ordered several scripts based on the concept.

Cast: Chris Mulkey (as Eddie Monroe) Catherine Oxenberg (Aja Turner), Dennis Haysbert (Nick Sanrio), Dana Gladstone (Capt. DeLillo)

Jerry Houser (Niner's voice) Judson Earney Scott (Anton Zeiss) Anne Haney (Mrs. Wiffington), Tom McFadden (Banks) David Renan (Zeiss Man).

154. Mutts. ABC 1988. 30 minutes. Ron Howard/Brian Grazer Productions and Imagine Entertainment. Director: Linda Day. Executive Producer: Brian Grazer. Producers/Writers: Howard Bendetson and Bob Bendetson. Music: Alf Clausen. Theme: Harry Nilsson, sung by Rick Riccio.

The adventures of a boy (Stephen Dorff) and his telepathic dog. In the pilot, they try to win the affections of the girl next door (Amy Hathaway).

Cast: Stephen Dorff (as Eric Gillman), Wendy Schaal (Janice Gillman), Geoff Pierson (Stuart Gillman), Amy Hathaway (Chris Hayden), Mike the Dog (Jeepers), Ray Buktenica (Glen), Jennifer Darling (Michelle), Sam Ballantine (Attendant), Catherine Ann Christianson (Customer).

155. Poochinski. NBC 7/9/90. 30 minutes. Adam Productions and Twentieth Century Fox Television. Director: Will Mackenzie. Executive Producers: John Ritter, Robert Myman, David Kirschner, and Brian Levant. Producer: Lon Diamond. Writers: Lon Diamond and Brian Levant. Music: Andy Summers.

Stanley Poochinski is a tough, ill-mannered cop who has been gunned down in the line of duty and reincarnated as a talking, flatulent English bulldog, now fighting crime on all fours with his former partner, naïve, straight-arrow rookie detective Robert McKay. In the pilot, Poochinski is intent on putting the bite on his killer.

Cast: Peter Boyle (as Stanley Poochinski), George Newbern (Det. Robert McKay), Amy Yasbeck (Frannie Reynolds), Frank McRae (Capt. Ed Martin), Brian Haley (Sgt. Shriver).

156. Sniff. CBS 8/9/88. 60 minutes. Von Zerneck/Samuels Productions and New World Television. Director: James Quinn. Executive Producers: Stu Samuels, Frank Von Zerneck, and Robert M. Sertner.

Producers: Bruce Jay Friedman and Susan Weber-Gold. Writer: Bruce Jay Friedman. Music: Richard Elliot.

The adventures of a tabloid reporter (Robert Wuhl) and his bloodhound dog, Sniff, who is forever leading the reluctant hero into trouble.

Cast: Robert Wuhl (as Sid Barrows), Louis Guss (Nat Barrows), Tracie Lin (Sharon), Rebecca Holden (Vanessa), Robin Curtis (Barbara), Edward Power (Blaine Sterling), Richard Roat (Gormley), Nancy Fish (Liz Gertz), Michael Zand (Gaza), Christopher Thomas (Morosco), Gerry Black (Detective), P.R. Paul (Intern), Michael McNab (Guard).

157. **Turner and Hootch.** NBC 7/9/90. 30 minutes. Touchstone Television. Director: Donald Petrie. Executive Producer: Daniel Petrie, Jr. Producers: Raymond Wagner and Terry Morse. Writers: Jeffrey C. Sherman and Stephen Metcalfe, from a story by Metcalfe, based on characters created by Dennis Shryack and Michael Blodgett. Music: Charles Gross.

This pilot, based on the 1989 Tom Hanks movie about a cop whose partner is a slobbering dog, has Tom Wilson now playing detective Scott Turner, married to a veterinarian (Wendy Pratt), and still fighting crime with one ugly mutt named Hootch. Critically assailed (*Variety* called it "unbelievably boring"), this flop pilot was aired back-to-back with *Poochinski* under NBC's overall title "Two Dog Night." Dogs in more ways than one.

Cast: Tom Wilson (as Scott Turner), Wendy Pratt (Emily Turner), John Anthony (Derek), also Bradley Mott, Al Fann, Michael Rich, Ivy Bethune, Martin Casella, Jack Evans.

JOHNNY

Producers desperately want to convey their series concepts as quickly and decisively as possible—and the best way to do that is right up front, with the title.

Can there be any doubt what *Magnum, P.I.* is about? Or that *B.L. Stryker, Hunter,* and *Cannon* are action-adventure shows? It's all in the name.

And nothing proves that idea more than the spate of "Johnny" titles that ran rampant in the 1950s and early 1960s. Not only did they convey concepts (*Johnny Wildlife*) but played on the popularity of other TV characters, like Johnny Ringo and Johnny Yuma.

But it takes more than a catchy name, a name that just happens to match the character's profession and escapades, to sell a series, as the following pilots certainly prove.

158. Johnny Dollar. CBS 1962. 30 minutes. MCA/Revue. Producer: Blake Edwards.

William Bryant stars as the insurance investigator popularized in the radio series.

159. Johnny Eager. MGM Television, 1959. Producers: Wilbur Stark and Jerry Layton. Writer: Paul Monash.

A detective who lives in Detroit and operates a fleet of taxi cabs. The pilot is based on the 1941 movie, which starred Robert Taylor.

160. Johnny Garage. CBS 4/13/83. 30 minutes. Grosso-Jacobson Productions and Columbia Pictures Television. Director: Bill Persky. Producers: Sonny Grosso and Larry Jacobson. Writer: Gary Gilbert. Music: Elliot Lawrence and Bill Persky.

Ron Carey is Johnny "Garage" Antonizzio, the owner of a troubled gas station in Queens. Val Bisoglio is his partner Frankie, Carlin Glynn his landlord, and Timothy Van Patten his womanizing, not-too-bright mechanic.

Cast: Ron Carey (as Johnny Antonizzio), Val Bisoglio (Frankie), Carlin Glynn (Harriet), Timothy Van Patten (Mike), Christina Avis-Krauss (Brenda), William Smitrovich (Steve Enright), Jack Hallett (Paul Enright), Robert Cenedella (Mr. Freeze-It), Tony DiBenedetto (Mailman), Bill Marcus (Battery Man), Carol Levy (Girl).

161. Johnny Guitar. CBS 7/31/59. 30 minutes. Director: Robert Leeds. Producer: Robert Carney. Writer: Otis Carney.

Aired on *Stripe Playhouse* as "Ballad to Die By." Johnny Guitar is a carefree, singing cowboy roaming the West and helping people in trouble. In the pilot, he's hired to sing at a wedding and discovers the groom is a killer who is forcing the bride to marry him.

Cast: William Joyce (as Johnny Guitar), Fay Spain (Anna Carrick), Reg Parton (Harry Shay), Paul Burns (Gyte).

162. Johnny Hawk. MCA 1958.

Track and field star Floyd Simmons would play this modern-day sheriff who uses both a car and a horse in his efforts to fight crime.

163. Johnny Mayflower. CBS 1958.

The adventures of an orphan boy who comes to America as a stow-away on the *Mayflower*.

164. Johnny Moccasin. NBC 1956. NBC Productions.

Jody McCrea, son of Joel McCrea, stars as a white boy raised by Indians.

165. Johnny Nighthawk (aka Forced Landing). CBS 9/1/59. 30 minutes. Screen Gems. Director: Oscar Rudolph. Producer: Harold Greene. Writers: Sam H. Rolfe and Barney Slate, from a story by Lou Morheim.

Aired as an episode of *Geritol Adventure Showcase*. Scott Brady is an adventurous, free-lance pilot who likes to take on risky jobs.

Cast: Scott Brady (as Johnny Nighthawk). Richard Erdman (Matt Brent), Maggie Mahoney (Lorna Kendiss), Joe DeSantis (Mac Ustich).

166. Johnny Risk. NBC 6/16/58. 30 minutes. Four Star. Director: Don McDougall. Producer: Vincent Fennelly. Writer: Fred Freiberger.

Aired as an episode of *Alcoa Theatre*. Michael Landon starred as, he recalls, "a guy who owned a gambling ship in the Yukon in the late 1800s. I looked a solid fifteen or sixteen years old and wore a white lace shirt and tight, black pants. Alan Hale, Jr., was my sidekick, and Lew Ayres was my brother. It was nothing but shots being fired. It just went on for-ever. Needless to say, it didn't go." Guest stars included DeForest Kelley, Forrest Lewis, Robert Griffin, and Bonnie Holding.

167. Johnny Wildlife. Screen Gems, 1958.

The adventures of a wildlife cameraman and his young son.

BIG SCREEN TO SMALL SCREEN

PILOTS BASED ON MOVIES

Television is by nature imitative—the networks try to keep in step with the trends, the tastes, and the social changes of the world they seek to entertain.

But most of all, networks try to keep in step with success. Shamelessly. They will copy, remake, spin-off, and imitate their own success, or the successes of others. Networks have always been suckers for the myth of the "pre-sold" idea, concepts that have a built-in audience and a minimum of risk, whether it's the fourth spin-off of *Happy Days,* or an imitation of *Miami Vice.*

Nothing satisfies the desire for "pre-sold" ideas better than movie adaptations. And yet, almost nothing in television has as high a failure rate.

There have been well over one hundred television series based on movies, the vast majority of which were staggering failures. The box-office success of their inspirations were meaningless. But the few hits, like *M*A*S*H, The Odd Couple,* and *In the Heat of the Night,* and the lure of big syndication bucks they bring, have kept the adaptations coming.

Recent movie-based series include *Parenthood, Bagdad Cafe, Uncle Buck, Dirty Dancing, Working Girl, Alien Nation, True Believer,* and *Baby Boom.* Earlier ones were *Planet of the Apes, Logan's Run, Barefoot in the Park, 9 to 5, Beyond Westworld, Semi-Tough, Serpico, Shaft, Blue Thunder, The Bad News Bears,* even David Soul in *Casablanca.* And that ever-growing list of adaptations doesn't include the obvious, movie-inspired series like *BJ and the Bear* (from *Every Which Way But Loose*) and *Hunter* (from *Dirty Harry*).

Despite the overwhelming chance of failure, it's easier to sell a big-grossing movie as a series than the brilliant idea you came up with in the shower. A movie is a proven idea, its popularity measured in the enormous box-office dollars it reaped. And if they lined up to see it for six bucks, they ought to stay in their living rooms to see it for free.

Well, that's the theory anyway.

But there's a big difference between a $20 million, 70mm Dolby extravaganza starring an international celebrity, and the low-budget, nineteen-inch version starring the obscure stand-up comic or the former bit player. And some movies weren't meant to be repeated twenty-two times a year, for years on end. Some weren't meant to be repeated even once.

Here are some that never got the chance to find out.

Would America have watched *To Sir, With Love* every week? Or waited in suspense for each new episode of *The French Connection?* Would the studio have reaped untold millions off the further adventures of *The Doberman Gang?*

We'll never know.

168. **Adventures in Babysitting.** CBS 7/7/89. 30 minutes. Walt Disney Television. Director: Joel Zwick. Executive Producers: Greg Antoacci, Debra Hill, and Linda Obst. Producer: David Simkins. Writers: David Simkins and Greg Antonacci. Music: Dan Floriat and Howard Pearl.

Imagine seeing the popular movie again—and again—and again… the misadventures of a pert, conscientious babysitter rushing against the clock to get her mischievous charges out of trouble and back into the house before the parents get home. That's what would happen every week in this proposed series, which, in the pilot, stars Jennifer Guthrie as the babysitter and Susan Blanchard and Dennis Howard as the oblivious parents. The pilot was cowritten by David Simkins, who did the screenplay for the successful teen-oriented 1987 film on which it's based.

Cast: Jennifer Guthrie (Chris Parker), Susan Blanchard (Joanna-Anderson), Dennis Howard (Robert Anderson), Joey Lawrence (Brad-Anderson), Courtney Paldon (Sarah Anderson), Brian Green (Daryl-Anderson), Ariana Mohit (Brenda), Art Evans (Mr. Dukman), Rocky Giordani (Vince), Jason Tomlin (Rick).

169. **The Adventures of Pollyanna.** CBS 4/10/82. 60 minutes. Walt Disney Productions. Director: Robert Day. Executive Producer: William

Robert Yates. Producer: Tom Leetch. Writer: Ann Beckett, from the novel by Eleanor Porter. Music: Jerrold Immel.

Based on the 1960 Disney film *Pollyanna*. Patsy Kensit takes over for Hayley Mills as the energetic, twelve-year-old girl who, after her parents die, emigrates from England to live with her aunt (Shirley Jones) in a small American town, circa 1912. The stories would revolve around the relentlessly upbeat young girl's unique ability to enliven the people around her. Rossie Harris and Roxanna Zal are her two best friends, kids from the local orphanage.

Cast: Patsy Kensit (as Pollyanna Harrington), Shirley Jones (Aunt Polly), Edward Winter (Herman Chilton), Roxanna Zal (Mary Lee), Lucille Benson (Mrs. Leveler), Stacey Nelkin (Cora Spencer), Beverly Archer (Angelica), John Putch (Johnny Muller), John Randolph (Mr. Muller), Rossie Harris (Jimmy Bean), Mitzi Hoag (Mrs. Muller), Nicholas Hammond (Reverend Tull), Jay Macintosh (Widow Jean), James Collins (Thomas Jenn), Anne Haney (Miss Bess), Gretchen Wyler (Mrs. Tarkell).

170. African Queen (aka Safari). NBC 4/3/62. 60 minutes. Four Star. Executive Producer: Dick Powell. Writer: Juarez Roberts.

James Coburn and Glynis Johns recreate the roles of Charlie Allnot, a ragged riverboat captain, and Rosie Sayer, an African missionary, made famous by Humphrey Bogart and Katharine Hepburn in the motion picture *The African Queen*. This pilot was aired as an episode of *Dick Powell Theatre* and had the two heroes sabotaging the German war effort in World War I. Costarred Juano Hernandez, Oscar Beregi, and Ellen Corby.

171. The African Queen. CBS 3/18/77. 60 minutes. Mark Carliner Productions and Viacom Enterprises. Director: Richard Sarafian. Executive Producer: Mark Carliner. Producer: Len Kaufman. Writer: Irving Gaynor Neiman, based on the novel by C.S. Forester. Music: John Murtaugh.

The second attempt (the first was in the early 1960s) to turn the popular 1951 Bogart-Hepburn movie into a TV series. Warren Oates plays a steamboat captain to Mariette Hartley's missionary in an adventure set in World War I Africa. Shot on location in the Florida Everglades.

Cast: Warren Oates (as Charlie Allnot), Mariette Hartley (Rosie Sayer), Johnny Sekka (Jogana), Wolf Roth (Lt. Biedemeyer), Albert Paulsen (Major Strauss), Frank Schuller (Heinke), Clarence Thomas (Sgt. Abuto), Tyrone Jackson (Kaninu).

172. At Your Service (aka American in Paris). CBS 8/3/64. 30 minutes. MCA. Producer/Director: Gene Kelly. Writer: Cynthia Lindsay. Music: George Gershwin.

A comedy/adventure starring Van Johnson as a young American who owns a travel agency in France and helps tourists in trouble. Based on the 1951 movie *An American in Paris* starring Gene Kelly, this pilot, shot on location in 1961, sat on the shelf for several years before being aired.

Cast: Van Johnson (as James Devlin), Marcel Dalio (Michel), Jan Sterling (Gloria Miles), Judi Meredith (Penny Miles).

173. Barefoot in the Park. CBS 11/24/69. 30 minutes. Paramount Television. Director: Jerry Paris. Executive Producers/Writers: Garry Marshall and Jerry Belson. Producer: Charles Shyer. Music: Charles Fox.

After being rejected by CBS, this busted pilot was aired on *Love, American Style* as the episode "Love and the Good Deal," based on the Neil Simon play and the subsequent film starring Robert Redford and Jane Fonda about a young couple living on the top floor of a run-down Manhattan walk-up. The pilot episode deals with the problems the couple has with a cheap bed it bought. The proposed series, to have starred Skye Aubrey, Norman Fell, Hans Conried, Phil Clarke, Jane Wyatt, and Harvey Lembeck, would have featured stories in which the wife's blind faith and naïveté would get her into trouble that the husband must patiently work out.

The flop pilot was recast and reshot with an all-black cast and eventually aired as "The Bed" episode of the subsequent ABC series, which lasted twelve weeks. Marshall and Belson, who successfully brought Simon's *The Odd Couple* to TV, would later recast *that* for ABC with all-black actors (featuring Demond Wilson and Ron Glass) and redub it *The New Odd Couple*. That series lasted thirteen weeks.

174. Bates Motel. NBC 7/5/87. 2 hours. Universal Television. Director: Richard Rothstein. Executive Producer: Richard Rothstein. Producers: Ken Topolsky and George Linder. Writer: Richard Rothstein, from characters created by Robert Bloch. Music: J. Peter Robinson.

A sequel to the classic 1960 thriller *Psycho* that ignores events portrayed in the two theatrical sequels (released in 1983 and 1986 respectively). Bud Cort is a mental patient who inherits murderer Norman Bate's crumbling (and haunted) motel and reopens it, weekly, with the help of a runaway girl (Lori Petty) he finds living in the place. The proposed anthology would focus on the guests who stay at the motel and their supernatural experiences. The NBC ad campaign proclaimed: "Norman Bates may be gone, but his motel lives on!" In 2014, the A&E Network launched a series entitled *Bates Motel*, a prequel to *Psycho* rather than a continuation.

Cast: Bud Cort (as Alex West), Lori Petty (Willie), Moses Gunn (Henry), Gregg Henry (Tom), Kerrie Keane (Barbara), Jason Bateman (Tony), Khrystyne Haje (Sam), Robert Picardo (Dr. Goodman), Lee DeBroux (Sheriff), Kurt Paul (Norman Bates), Marla Frumkin (Dr. Phillips), Rick Lieberman (Architect), Roger Duffy (Young Alex), Greg Finley (Attorney), also Timothy Fall, Kelly Ames, Peter Dobson, Paula Irvine, Scot Saint James, Nat Bernstein, Buck Flower, Carmen Filpi, David Wakefield, Gart Ballard, Andy Albin, Dolores Albin, Hardy Rawls, Peter A. Stelzer, George J. Woods, Jack Ross Obney, John Kenton Schull, George Skinta, Pedro Gonzales-Gonzales, Robert Axelrod, Chad Jonas.

175. Bell, Book and Candle. NBC 9/8/76. 30 minutes. Columbia Pictures Television. Director: Hy Averback. Executive Producer: Bruch Lansbury. Writer: Richard DeRoy, from John Van Druten's 1950 play and the 1958 feature film.

Gillian Holroyd is a young witch who'd like to forget her supernatural abilities and just work in her art gallery with her bumbling Aunt Enid. Unfortunately, she is constantly hampered by her warlock brother Nicky and his get-rich-quick schemes—all of which depend for success on her superior ability at witchcraft. To make matters worse, Alex, a New York editor, moves into the apartment above the gallery—and falls in love with Gillian.

Cast: Yvette Mimieux (as Gillian Holroyd), Doris Roberts (Aunt Enid), Michael Murphy (Alex Brandt), John Pleshette (Nicky), Bridget Hanley (Lois), Susan Sullivan (Rosemary), Edward Andrews (Bishop Fairbarn), Dori Whittaker (Melissa).

176. Beyond Witch Mountain. CBS 2/20/82. 60 minutes. Walt Disney Productions. Director: Robert Day. Executive Producer: William Robert Yates. Producer: Jan Williams. Writers: Robert Malcolm Young, B.W. Sandefur, and Hal Kanter. Music: George Duning.

A sequel/pilot based on the Disney movies, *Escape From Witch Mountain* and *Return From Witch Mountain*. Tracey Gold and Andy Freeman are alien children with psychic powers who, with their families, crash-landed on Witch Mountain. They become separated from the survivors and befriend a man (Eddie Albert) who helps them elude a millionaire (Efrem Zimbalist, Jr.) hoping to exploit their incredible powers.

Cast: Eddie Albert (as Jason O'Day), Efrem Zimbalist, Jr. (Aristotle), Tracey Gold (Tia), Andy Freeman (Tony), J.D. Cannon (Deranian), Noah Beery, Jr. (Uncle Ben), Stephanie Blackmore (Dr. Adrian Molina), Peter Hobbs (Dr. Peter Morton), James Luisi (Foreman), William H. Bassett (Lowell Roberts).

177. Black Bart. CBS 4/4/75. 30 minutes. Warner Bros. Television. Director: Robert Butler. Executive Producer: Mark Tuttle. Producers: Michael Elias, Frank Shaw, and Robert Butler. Writers: Michael Elias and Frank Shaw. Creator: Mel Brooks.

Based on Brooks's *Blazing Saddles* of the year before. The adventures of a black sheriff and his quick-draw deputy working in a small, bigoted Arizona town in the Old West. Lou Gossett and Steve Landesberg played the roles originated by Cleavon Little and Gene Wilder.

Cast: Lou Gossett (as Black Bart), Steve Landesberg (Reb Jordan), Millie Slavin (Belle Buzzer), Noble Willingham (Mayor Fern B. Malaga), Ruben Moreno (Moonwolf), Ted Lehmann (Mr. Swenson), Gerritt Graham (Curley), Brooke Adams (Jennifer).

178. Captain Horatio Hornblower. ABC 2/28/63. 60 minutes. Director: John Newland. Producers: Julian Plowden and Collier Young. Writer: Donald Wilson, from the stories by C.S. Forester.

Aired as an episode of *Alcoa Premiere*. David Buck is Capt. Horatio Hornblower (played by Gregory Peck in the 1951 feature film), a British warship captain during the war between France and England in the early 1800s. Shot on location in England.

Cast: David Buck (as Capt. Horatio Hornblower), Terence Longdon (Lt. Bush), Peter Arne (Nathaniel Sweet), Nigel Green (Brown), Sean Kelly (Lt. Carlon), Jeremy Bulloch (Midshipman Bowser).

179. Captain Newman, M.D. NBC 8/19/72. 30 minutes. Thomas/ Crenna Productions. Producers: Danny Thomas and Richard Crenna. Writer/ Creator: Frank Tarloff.

Jim Hutton stars as an unorthodox Air Force psychiatrist along with Joan Van Ark and Bill Fiore, in this pilot based on the movie, which starred Gregory Peck and Tony Curtis.

180. Car Wash. NBC 5/29/79. 30 minutes. Universal Television. Director: Alan Myerson. Executive Producers: Leonard Stern and Arne Sultan. Producer: Bill Dana. Writers: Arne Sultan and Bill Dana. Music: Dave Fisher.

Based on the 1976 movie *Car Wash*. The exploits of a car wash owner (Danny Aiello) and his employees, including Rocky, a self-proclaimed ladies' man; Floyd and Lloyd, two aspiring singers; and Fingers, a skateboard expert. The other major character is Motor Mouth, a never-seen DJ whose radio show is always playing while they work.

Cast: Danny Aiello (as Frank Ravelli), Hilary Beane (Charlene Olson), Stuart Pankin (Last Chance), Sheryl Lee Ralph (Melba), Matt Landers (Rocky), John Anthony Bailey (Lloyd), T.K. Carter (Floyd), Lefty Pedroski (Fingers), Pepe Serna (Viva).

181. Cat Ballou. [Pilot # 1]. NBC 9/5/71. 30 minutes. Screen Gems. Director: Jerry Paris. Executive Producer: Harry Ackerman. Producer/ Writer: Aaron Ruben.

The first of two pilots based on the 1965 movie that starred Jane Fonda as a ranch owner who hires Lee Marvin, in his Oscar-winning role as a drunken ex-gunslinger. In the pilot, Cat (Lesley Ann Warren) hires Kid Sheleen (Jack Elam) and his friends, Jackson Two Bears (Tom Nardini) and Clay (Bo Hopkins), to help her set up a school and protect her ranch. This pilot, shot for the 1970–71 season, was rejected and wasn't aired until the following one, when the second pilot was offered to NBC.

Cast: Lesley Ann Warren (as Cat Ballou), Jack Elam (Kid Sheleen), Tom Nardini (Jackson Two Bears), Joel Higgins (The Sheriff), Laurie Main (Land Developer), Bo Hopkins (Clay).

181a. Cat Ballou. [Pilot #2]. NBC 9/6/71. 30 minutes. Screen Gems. Director: Bob Claver. Executive Producer: Bob Claver. Producer: Jon Epstein. Writer: William Blinn.

A completely revamped attempt to translate the film to TV and, aired the day after the first, was a sharp contrast that probably confused viewers who thought they'd be seeing more of the same. This time Forrest Tucker is Kid Sheleen, hired by Cat Ballou (Jo Ann Harris) to help her protect her recently inherited ranch, where she lives with her adopted, twelve-year-old Indian boy, Jackson Two Bears (Lee Casey). This was made for consideration in the 1971–72 season.

Cast: Jo Ann Harris (as Cat Ballou), Forrest Tucker (Kid Sheleen), Lee J. Casey (Jackson Two Bears), Harry Morgan (The Rancher), Bryan Montgomery (Clay), James Luisi (Spider Levinsky), Bill Calloway (Loopy), Jay Silverheels (Indian Chief).

182. Catch-22. ABC 5/21/73. 30 minutes. Paramount Television. Director: Richard Quine. Producer: Richard Bluel. Writer: Hal Dresden. Based on the book by Joseph Heller and inspired by the 1970 film, directed by Mike Nichols and written by Buck Henry.

Richard Dreyfuss plays Yossarian, Cast: Richard Dreyfuss (as Capt. Yossarian) assayed by Alan Arkin in the film, who in this pilot is a brash World War II Air Force flyer who finishes his tour of duty but, instead of returning home as he should, finds his rotation papers lost and ends up on a rear echelon base in the Mediterranean. Everywhere he turns he is confronted by insanity, and no matter how he schemes to get home, his plans always fail.

Cast: Richard Dreyfuss (as Capt. Yossarian), Dana Elcar (Col. Cathcart), Stewart Moss (Lt. Col. Kern), Andy Jarrell (Milo Minderbinder), Frank Welker (Lt. McWatt), Susan Zenor (Nurse Duckett).

183. Christmas Lilies of the Field (aka Lilies of the Field). NBC 12/16/79. 2 hours. Rainbow Productions and Osmond Television Productions. Director: Ralph Nelson. Executive Producer: Ralph Nelson. Producers: Jack N. Reddish and Toby Martin. Writers: John McGreevey and Ralph Nelson, from characters created by William E. Barrett. Music: George Aliceson Tipton.

Billy Dee Williams stars as carpenter Homer Smith, who is conned into building an orphanage adjacent to the chapel he built before—when he was played with Oscar-winning success by Sidney Poitier in the acclaimed 1963 movie *Lilies of the Field.* Williams wanders off in the end, but not before signing a contract to return if NBC opted for a series. Ralph Nelson directed the original and this sequel, which movie critic Leonard Maltin called a "joyous follow-up."

Cast: Billy Dee Williams (as Homer Smith), Maria Schell (Mother Maria), Faye Hauser (Janet Owens), Lisa Mann (Sister Gertrude), Hanna Hertelendy (Sister Albertine), Judith Piquet (Sister Agnes), Donna Johnson (Sister Elizabeth), Bob Hastings (Harold Pruitt), Jean Jenkins (Mrs. Constance Everett), Fred Hart (Father Brian Connor), Sam Di Bello (Dr. Mike Robles), Timmy Arnell (Josh), Oliver Nguyen (Trang), Regina Simons (Pokey), Julie Delgado (Felicia), Rachel Ward (Jenny), Danny Zapien (Joseph Owlfeather), Adolpho Flores (Rafael Serrano).

184. Crunch. ABC 1976. 90 minutes. Frankovich/Self Productions. Executive Producer: William Self. Producer: Robert Jacks. Writers: Cliff Gould and Charles Larson, from the novel and 1975 film *Report to the Commissioner.*

A proposed series based on the exploits of a real New York City undercover cop named Crunch, played in the movie and in this pilot by Yaphet Kotto, here partnered with a young detective (Stephen Nathan) and working for a tough lieutenant (Richard Venture).

185. **Diner.** CBS 8/8/83. 30 minutes. Weintraub/Levinson Productions and MGM/UA Television. Director/Writer/Creator: Barry Levinson. Executive Producers: Jerry Weintraub and Barry Levinson. Producer: Mark Johnson. Music: Harry Lojewski.

Based on Levinson's 1982 hit movie, set in 1960 Baltimore, that focused on five young men who are making the awkward transition into adulthood and who gather nightly at a local diner to hash out their problems and grapple with their new responsibilities. The characters include a hairdresser with big dreams, an appliance salesman in his first year of marriage, a sports-addicted newlywed, and a college dropout flirting with alcoholism. Paul Reiser reprises his film role as Modell, an insecure man with a motormouth.

Cast: Paul Reiser (as Modell), James Spader (Fenwick), Michael Binder (Eddie), Max Cantor (Shrevie), Michael Madsen (Boogie), Alison LaPlaca (Elyse), Mady Kaplan (Beth), Robert Pastorelli (Turko), Arnie Mazer (The Gipper), Ted Bafaloukos (George).

186. **Doberman Gang.** [Pilot #1] **Alex and the Doberman Gang.** NBC 4/11 /80. 60 minutes. Bennett-Katleman Productions and Columbia Pictures Television. Director: Byron Chudnow. Executive Producers: Harve Bennett and Harris Katleman. Producer: Ralph Sariego. Writers: James D. Parriott and Richard Chapman. Music: Earle Hagen.

Jack Stauffer is a private eye who inherits five trained dobermans from a carnival and uses them to help him solve cases. In the pilot, the dogs sniff out some stolen art treasures. *Variety* felt this pilot "bordered on being infantile" and "only the well-trained dogs were impressive." Byron Chudnow, who directed this, also directed the three *Doberman Gang* feature films.

Cast: Jack Stauffer (Alexander Parker), Taureen Blacque (Barney), Lane Binkley (Denise), Jerry Orbach (Rogers), Martha Smith (Susan

Hamilton), Alan Gibbs (Myers), Don Starr (Preacher), Sari Price (Valley Woman).

186a. [The Dobermans] [Pilot #2] **Nick and the Dobermans.** NBC 4/25/80. 60 minutes. Bennett-Katleman Productions and Columbia Pictures Television. Director: Bernard L. Kowalski. Executive Producers: Harve Bennett and Harris Katleman. Producers/Writers: James D. Parriott and Richard Chapman. Music: Jerrold Immel.

Michael Nouri is a private eye who uses three dobermans to help him solve crime.

Cast: Michael Nouri (as Nick Macazie), Robert Davi (Lt. Elbone), Judith Chapman (Barbara Gatson), John Cunningham (Roger Vincent), Vivian Bonnell (Speed Queen), Chris Hayward (Speedy Man).

187. Egan. ABC 9/18/73. 30 minutes. Miller-Milkis Productions and Paramount Television. Director: Jud Taylor. Producers: Tom Miller and Ed Milkis. Writer: Abram S. Ginnes. Music: Lalo Schifrin.

A pilot based on the true exploits of N.Y.P.D. detective Eddie Egan, dramatized in 1971 in *The French Connection.* Gene Hackman won an Oscar for his portrayal of Egan, whose name was changed to Popeye Doyle in the film. Egan later began an acting career of his own, appearing in such series as *Eischied* and *Police Story.* This time, Eugene Roche is Egan, now an L.A.P.D. detective who defies authority and does things his way. The Egan character was revived again in 1986 as *Popeye Doyle,* with Ed O'Neill starring.

Cast: Eugene Roche (as Eddie Egan), Dabney Coleman (Capt. Jones), Glenn Corbett (Det. Burke), John Anderson (J.R. King), John Carlin (Deveaux), Marian Geller (Woman), Michael Bell (Bobby), Fred Holliday (Clerk), Ian Sander (Cab Driver).

188. The Flamingo Kid. ABC 6/11/89. 30 minutes. Viacom Enterprises, Sweetum Productions, and Mercury Entertainment Corp. Director: Tom Moore. Executive Producers: Michael Phillips, Richard Rosenstock, and Michael Vittes. Writer: Richard Rosenstock, based on a character created by Neal Marshall for the popular 1984 film.

Sasha Mitchell stars as Jeffrey, a sixteen-year-old whose blue-collar father (Dan Hedaya) expects his son to follow in his work-a-day footsteps. But when Jeff takes a job at a beach club, he meets a fun-loving car salesman who introduces him to a different life-style and another perspective on life. The series would depict Jeff's attempts to reconcile what his father wants with what he is learning about the world.

Cast: Sasha Mitchell (as Jeffrey Willis), Dan Hedaya (Arthur Willis), Jerry Orbach (Phil Brody), Todd Graff (Hawk), Carol Locatel (Ruth), Patty McCormack (Mrs. Brody), Robert Costanzo (Angry Man), Carmine Caridi (Harvey), Kellie Martin (Lauren Brody), Taryn Smith (Ellen Brody), Madelyn Cates (Mrs. Gaskin), Jill Klein (Angry Man's Wife), Myra Turley (The Chickenfat Lady).

189. **The Flim-Flam Man.** NBC 9/1/69. 30 minutes. Twentieth Century Fox Television. Director: Alan Rafkin. Executive Producer: Lawrence Turman. Producer: Herman Saunders. Writer: James Bridges. Music: Don Scardino.

Based on the 1967 motion picture. Forrest Tucker has George C. Scott's movie role of Mordecai Jones, a con man roaming the backwoods of the North and deep South with his able assistant, Curley Treadway (Don Scardino). Together, they swindle the greedy, the dishonest, the gullible—but never an honest man.

Cast: Forrest Tucker (as Mordecai Jones), Don Scardino (Curley Treadway), James Gregory (Packard), Elena Verdugo (Mrs. Packard), Gene Evans (Sheriff Slade), Dub Taylor (Weehunt), Lada Edmond, Jr. (Bonnie Lee), Guy Raymond (Buck), Bob Hastings (Meeshaw), Hope Summers (Debbie Packard).

190. **Full House (aka Author! Author!).** CBS 9/20/83. 60 minutes. Brownstone Productions and Twentieth Century Fox Television. Director: Tony Bill. Executive Producer: Marc Merson. Producer: Paul Waigner. Writer/Creator: Israel Horovitz. Music: Fred Karlin.

Based on the 1982 motion picture *Author! Author!* Dennis Dugan assumes Al Pacino's role as a harried New York playwright who has acquired five children—one of whom is his, the four others are from his runaway wife's first three failed marriages. The disorganized, financially troubled father often has to rely on his children to keep the chaotic household—and his life—together.

Cast: Dennis Dugan (as Ivan Travalian), Ari Meyers (Debbie Travalian), Shelby Balik (Bonnie Travalian), Eric Gurry (Igor Travalian), Scott Nemes (Spike Travalian), Danny Ponce (Geraldo Travalian), Kenneth Mars (Arthur Krantz), Miriam Flynn (Bobbie Hall), Roberta Picardo (Mary), James Murtaugh (Eugene), Julie Payne (Mrs. Knopf), Ray Girardin (Ken Adams), Sam J. Cooper (Tony).

191. Friendly Persuasion (aka Except for Me and Thee). ABC 5/18/75. 2 hours. ITC Entertainment and Allied Artists. Producer/ Director: Joseph Sargent. Executive Producers: Emmanuel Wolf and Herbert B. Leonard. Writer: William Wood, from the books by Jessamyn West and the 1956 motion picture. Music: John Cacavas. Theme: Dimitri Tiomkin.

Richard Kiley and Shirley Knight (assuming the roles played by Gary Cooper and Dorothy McGuire) are Quaker farmers who, during the Civil War, help runaway slaves reach freedom. Real-life brothers Michael and Kevin O'Keefe portray the couple's eldest sons.

Cast: Richard Kiley (as Jess Birdwell), Shirley Knight (Eliza Birdwell), Michael O'Keefe (Josh Birdwell), Kevin O'Keefe (Labe Birdwell), Tracie Savage (Mattie Birdwell), Sparky Marcus (Little Jess Birdwell), Clifton James (Sam Jordon), Paul Benjamin (Swan Stebeney), Erik Holland (Enoch), Maria Grimm (Lily Truscott), Bob Minor (Burk).

192. Goodbye Charlie. ABC 6/4/85. 30 minutes. Twentieth Century Fox Television. Director: Charlotte Brown. Executive Producer: Pat Nardo. Writer: Pat Nardo, from the play by George Axelrod and the motion picture screenplay by Harry Kurnitz. Music: Charles Fox. Lyrics: Al Kasha and Joel Hirschorn.

Based on the 1959 play starring Lauren Bacall and the 1964 Debbie Reynolds-Tony Curtis movie. In the play and movie, a skirt-chasing mobster named Charlie, killed by a jealous husband, returns to earth as a woman. In the sitcom, a womanizing advertising executive falls to his death—and comes back as Suzanne Somers, a fate worse than death. The reincarnated Charlie...now Charlene...goes to work as the secretary for the guy (Ray Buktenica) who replaced her when she was a he. But she's still very much a he, and best friend John Davidson is the only one who knows the truth.

Cast: Suzanne Somers (as Charlie/Charlene), John Davidson (George), Ray Buktenica (Ray), Kathleen Wilhoite (Victoria).

193. The Goodbye Girl (aka Goodbye Doesn't Mean Forever). [Pilot #1]. NBC 5/28/82. 30 minutes. MGM Television, Rastar Television, and Warner Bros. Television. Director: James Burrows. Executive Producer/ Writer: Allan Katz. Producer: Charles Raymond. Creator: Neil Simon. Music: Harry Lojewski. Theme song: David Gates.

Based on the 1977 movie *The Goodbye Girl*, which starred Marsha Mason as a widowed dancer, raising a young girl (Quinn Cummings), who reluctantly shares an apartment with a struggling actor (Richard Dreyfuss) and falls in love with him. Karen Valentine, Lili Haydn and Michael Lembeck assume the roles as Paula McFadden, Elliott Garfield, and Lucy McFadden in this pilot (filmed in 1980), which *Variety* felt "comes off several notches higher than the usual tryouts" and that "as a series, it could be a pleasure."

193a. The Goodbye Girl. [Pilot #2]. NBC 1981. 30 minutes. MGM Television. Director: Charlotte Brown. Executive Producer: Gerald Isenberg. Producers/Writers: Charlotte Brown and Pat Nardo, based on characters created by Neil Simon.

A second pilot based on the movie *The Goodbye Girl*, the story of an out-of-work dancer and her nine-year-old daughter, who share their New York apartment with a struggling actor. Although the two adults fight constantly, they are held together by the clear-thinking girl. New characters include the dancer's middle-aged boyfriend and the actor's uptight, business executive brother. JoBeth Williams was slated to star, taking over from Karen Valentine, from the earlier pilot.

194. Guess Who's Coming to Dinner. ABC 7/4/75. 30 minutes. Columbia Pictures Television. Producer/Director: Stanley Kramer. Writers: Richard DeRoy and Bill Idelson.

A situation comedy, inspired by the 1967 film that starred Katharine Hepburn, Spencer Tracy, and Sidney Poitier, revolving around what happens when a socially prominent white girl marries an upper class black man and the two families become one.

Cast: Leslie Charleson (as Joanna Prentiss), Bill Overton (John Prentiss), Eleanor Parker (Christine Drayton), Richard Dysart (Matt Drayton), Lee Weaver (Ralph Prentiss), Madge Sinclair (Sarah Prentiss), Rosetta Le Noir (Tillie), William Calloway (Joe Delaney), Joseph R. Sicari (Orville Peacock).

195. A Guide for the Married Man. ABC 1969. 30 minutes. Twentieth Century Fox Television. Director: James Frawley. Executive Producer/Writer: Frank Tarloff. Producer: Frank McCarthy.

Based on the 1967 motion picture. Episodes would explore such topics as how to hire a secretary, how to explain an old girlfriend and how to be a girl-watcher. The characters included a conservative, thirty-five-year-old, recently married man and his friend Ed, who has been married for six years. This starred Hal Buckley, Anthony Roberts, Pat Delaney, and Sally Ann Richards.

196. Gulliver. NBC 1963. Screen Gems. Producer: Charles Schneer.

Based on the story by Jonathan Swift and adapted from the movie *The Three Worlds of Gulliver,* made in 1960 by Schneer and effects wizard Ray Harryhausen. John Cairny steps in for Kerwin Mathews as Gulliver, the sailor who lands on Lilliput, an island populated by miniature people. In this retelling, he lands with his girlfriend, played by Christina Gregg. Filmed in *Dynamation,* Harryhausen's animation process.

197. Hearts of the West (aka Riding High). NBC 8/25/77. 30 minutes. MGM Television. Director: Lee Phillips. Producer: Marc Merson. Writer: Larry Gelbart.

Based on the 1975 movie *Hearts of the West*, which was set in Hollywood in the 1930s and starred Jeff Bridges as a would-be Western writer who works as an extra in cowboy serials. Charles Frank takes over in the pilot, which also features Lonny Chapman as a has-been star who is now an extra, Allan Miller as the cheap producer, Allen Case as the Western star, and Wendy Phillips as a production assistant.

Cast: Charles Frank (as Lewis Tater), Wendy Phillips (Wendy Trout), Lonny Chapman (Howard Pike), Allan Miller (Bert Kessler), Don Calfa (Sid), Bill Hart (Wally), Allen Case (Lyle Montana), Pat Crenshaw (Bear).

198. Holly Golightly. ABC 1969. 30 minutes. Twentieth Century Fox Television. Producer/Director: James Frawley. Writer: James Henerson.

Based on the 1961 Paramount film *Breakfast at Tiffany's*, adapted from Truman Capote's book. In the pilot, Holly (Stefanie Powers) moves into a new apartment—and accidentally sparks an all-night party filled with dozens of strange people doing weird things. Also featured are George Furth, Jack Kruschen, and Jean-Pierre Aumont.

199. Honky Tonk. NBC 4/1/74. 90 minutes. MGM Television. Director: Don Taylor. Executive Producer/Writer: Douglas Heyes. Producer: Hugh Benson. Music: Jerry Fielding.

An attempt to turn the 1941 Western *Honky Tonk*, starring Clark Gable and Lana Turner, into a TV series. Richard Crenna is now Candy Johnson, a con man in the Old West, and Margot Kidder is Lucy Cotton, his partner, a judge's daughter. Douglas Heyes knows how to write Western con men—he did it best for several years on *Maverick*.

Cast: Richard Crenna (as Candy Johnson), Margot Kidder (Lucy Cotton), Stella Stevens (Gold Dust), Will Geer (Judge Cotton), John Dehner (Brazos), Geoffrey Lewis (Roper), Gregory Sierra (Slade), James Luisi (Blackie), Robert Casper (Doc Goodwin), Richard Stahl (Mr. Arnold), Stephen Coit (Mr. Bennett).

200. House of Wax (aka Chamber of Horrors). ABC 1966. 99 minutes. Warner Bros. Television. Director: Hy Averback. Writer: Stephen Kandel. Music: William Lava.

Wilfrid Hyde-White starred in this pilot (based on the 1953 motion picture) that, once it was rejected as a series, was also released as a feature film, faring no better. Despite such cinematic gimmicks as the "Horror Horn and Fear Flasher," it was quickly (and justifiably) forgotten. Steven Scheuer says in *Movies on TV* that viewers will "laugh in the wrong places" and that "Patrick O'Neal rolls his eyes a great deal as the notorious madman," killing people in Baltimore circa 1880.

Cast: Patrick O'Neal (Jason Cravette), Cesare Danova (Anthony Draco), Wilfrid Hyde-White (Harold Blount), Laura Devon (Marie Champlain), Patrice Wymore (Vivian), Suzy Parker (Barbara Dixon), Tun Tun (Sr. Pepe de Reyes), Philip Bourneauf (Inspector Strudwick), Jeanette Nolan (Mrs. Ewing Perryman), Marie Windsor (Mme. Corona), Wayne Rogers (Sgt. Albertson), Vinton Hayworth (Judge Randolph), Richard O'Brien (Dr. Cobb), Berry Kroeger (Chun Sing).

201. If I Had a Million. NBC 12/31/73. 60 minutes. Universal Television. Director: Daryl Duke. Executive Producer: David Levinson. Producer: James McAdams. Writers: Various.

Based on the all-star 1932 movie of the same name. Peter Kastner is a wealthy man who goes to the local library, randomly chooses a phone book from some American city, flips the pages, and picks a name. Then he anonymously gives that person a million dollars. The pilot was divided into four short stories about four different recipients.

#1. The Good Boy. Writers: Lionel E. Siegel and Herbert Wright, from a story by Siegel. *Cast:* John Schuck, Louis Zorich, Val Biscoglio, and Doolie Brown.

#2. The Searchers. Writer: Robert Van Scoyk. *Cast:* Joseph Wiseman, Ruth McDevitt, Gerald Hiken, and Rae Allen.

#3. Three. Writer: M. Charles Cohen. *Cast:* Kenneth Mars, Elayne Helveil, and Melendy Britt.

#4. First the Tube, and Now You, Darling. Writer: Oliver Hailey. *Cast:* Brett Somers, Ted Gehring.

202. The Jerk, Too (aka Another Jerk). NBC 1 /6/84. 2 hours. 40 Share Productions and Universal Television. Director: Michael Schultz. Executive Producer: Steve Martin. Producers: Ziggy Steinberg and Al Burton. Writers: Ziggy Steinberg and Rocco Urbisci. Creators: Steve Martin and Carl Gottlieb. Theme: John Sebastian.

A sequel/adaptation of the 1979 Steve Martin movie *The Jerk*. Mark Blankfield is Navin Johnson, a naive, good-natured, clumsy oaf, a white orphan raised by a family of black sharecroppers whom he leaves to go on a cross-country trek to prevent his truelove (Stacey Nelkin) from marrying an unscrupulous, European aristocrat (Barrie Ingham). Along the way, Navin befriends Diesel (Ray Walston), a hobo who wants to exploit Navin's skill at cards. In the proposed series, Navin would settle with Diesel in Los Angeles, screw up at various odd jobs, and court his truelove, to the consternation of her snobbish parents.

Cast: Mark Blankfield (as Navin Johnson), Ray Walston (Diesel), Stacey Nelkin (Marie Van Buren), Barrie Ingham (Carl), Jean LeClerc (Count Marco del Belvedere), Thalmus Rasulala (Crossroads), Mabel King (Mama Johnson), Al Fann (Papa Johnson), Robert Sampson (Gilbert Van Buren), Patricia Barry (Helen Van Buren), Todd Hollowell (Damon Johnson), Larry B. Scott (Harold Johnson), Stacy Harris (Carmen Johnson), Lina Raymond (Cheetah Johnson), Pat McCormick (Dudley), Bill Saluga (Shoes), William Smith (Suicide), Peter Schrum (Ugly Eddie), Lainie Kazan (Card Player), Martin Mull (Card Player), Jimmie Walker (Card Player), Gwen Verdon (Bag Lady), Jack O'Leary (Porter), Benny Baker (Pop), Frank Birney (Priest).

203. Kissin' Cousins. NBC 1965. 30 minutes. MGM Television. Director: Don Weis. Producer: Sam Katzman.

Based on the 1964 movie starring Elvis Presley. Edd Byrnes plays an Army officer from the Ozarks who goes back to the mountains to scout a location for a missile site. The locals are suspicious and untrusting of him, so he uses his "kissin' cousins" to help him out. Stanley Adams costars in this completed pilot.

204. The Last Detail. ABC 1975. 30 minutes. Columbia Pictures Television. Director: Jackie Cooper. Producer: Gerry Ayres. Writers: Gerry Ayres and Bill Kirby.

This is a whistle-clean sitcom version of the 1973 movie, which starred Jack Nicholson and Otis Young. Robert F. Lyons and Charles Robinson now portray career men Buddusky and Mulhall in the peacetime Navy who, as much as they may like civilian life, can't seem to fit in and really need the dull routine of the military to be happy.

205. The Main Event. NBC 1980. Warner Bros. Television.

Based on the previous year's movie, which starred Barbra Streisand as a woman who manages a boxer, played by Ryan O'Neal—though most of the fights happen between them, and not in the ring.

206. The Man Who Fell to Earth. ABC 8/23/87. 2 hours. MGM Television. Director: Bobby Roth. Executive Producer: David Gerber. Producers: Lewis Chesler and Richard Kletter. Writer: Richard Kletter, from the screenplay by Paul Mayersberg, based on the book by Walter Tevis. Music: Doug Timm.

Lewis Smith takes over the role, originated by David Bowie in director Nicolas Roeg's 1976 movie, of an extraterrestrial from a drought-stricken planet who crash-lands on Earth. He infiltrates our society and, teamed with a shrewd businessman (James Laurenson), uses his advanced knowledge to create inventions and build a successful company, hoping to use his money to build a craft to take him home—and lead his people back here. But a government agent (Robert Picardo) uncovers him, and he flees, forced to find another way to build his craft before his people perish—and before he is caught. Lewis Chesler produced HBO's *Hitchhiker* anthology.

Cast: Lewis Smith (as Thomas Newton), James Laurenson (Felix Hawthorne), Robert Picardo (Agent Richard Morse), Beverly D'Angelo (Eva), Bruce McGill (Dr. Vernon Gage), Wil Wheaton (Billy), Annie Potts (Louise), also Bobbi Jo Lathan, Henry Sanders, Carmen Argenziano, Chris DeRose, Richard Shydner, Bob Neilsen, Steve Natole, Michael Fontaine, Albert Owens, Anne O'Neill, Amy Sawaya, Carl Parker, Hank Stratton.

207. Meet Me in St. Louis. CBS 9/2/66. 30 minutes. MGM Television. Executive Producer: Alan Courtney. Producer: Paul West. Writer: Sally Benson, based on her story.

Adapted from the 1944 Judy Garland musical set at the turn of the century at the World's Fair. The pilot stars Shelley Fabares as Esther, a girl from Missouri who has just arrived in New York. It was ultimately rejected, says Courtney, when a network executive decided "he didn't want anything on his network with an ice wagon rattling down the street."

Cast: Shelley Fabares (as Esther Smith), Celeste Holm (Anne Smith), Larry Merrill (Glenn Smith), Judy Land (Faye Morse), Reta Shaw (Katie), also Susanne Cupito and Tommy Locke.

208. Mother, Juggs and Speed. ABC 8/17/78. 30 minutes. Twentieth Century Fox Television. Director: John Rich. Producer: Bruce Geller. Writer/Creator: Tom Mankiewicz.

Based on the 1976 movie, which starred Raquel Welch, Bill Cosby, Harvey Keitel and was written by Mankiewicz. The proposed series, like the film, is about the reckless paramedic team driving a rundown ambulance for a ramshackle company.

Cast: Ray Vitte (as Mother), Joanne Nail (Jennifer "Juggs" Juggston), Joe Penny (Speed), Harvey Lembeck (Harry Fishbine), Shay Duffin (Whiplash Moran), Barbara Minkus (Mrs. Fishbine), Rod McCary (Murdock), Jan Shutan (Mrs. Barry), Charlotte Stewart (Iris), Marcus Smythe (Tom).

209. Miss Bishop (aka Cheers for Miss Bishop). NBC 9/1/61. 30 minutes. Paramount Television.

A sitcom based on the 1941 movie *Cheers for Miss Bishop*, a drama which starred Martha Scott as a teacher at a midwestern college. Like the movie, this pilot was based on the book by Bess Streeter. Jan Clayton stars as Miss Bishop, who finds herself attracted to one of her adult students (Tom Helmore), a middle-age gentleman she's tutoring on the side. Also in the cast was Julie Payne.

210. Mr. Mom. ABC 11/30/84. 30 minutes. Sherwood Productions and Twentieth Century Fox Television. Director: Terry Hughes. Executive

Producers/Writers: Frank Dungan and Jeff Stein. Producer: Pat Rickey. Creator: John Hughes. Music: Dave Fisher. Singers: Gary Portnoy and Judy Hart Angelo.

Based on the previous year's hit movie, which starred Michael Keaton as an unemployed auto worker who takes over running the household when his wife, played by Teri Garr, goes to work at an advertising agency. Barry Van Dyke and Rebecca York assume the roles in the TV version. Aaron Spelling, who produced the movie, is billed on the pilot as executive consultant.

Cast: Barry Van Dyke (as Jack Butler), Rebecca York (Caroline Butler), Brendon Blincoe (Curtis Butler), Sean de Veritch (Kenny Butler), Heidi Zeigler (Megan Butler), Phyllis Davis (Joan Hampton), Howard Honig (Darryl Fetty), Pat McNamara (Vernon Wesley), Sam Scarber (Sgt. Preston), Dimitri Michas (Marine).

211. Mrs. Sundance. ABC 1/15/74. 90 minutes. Twentieth Century Fox Television. Director: Marvin J. Chomsky. Producer: Stan Hough. Writer: Christopher Knopf. Music: Patrick Williams.

A sequel to the movie *Butch Cassidy and the Sundance Kid.* Elizabeth Montgomery takes over for Katharine Ross as Etta Place, the fugitive lover of the outlaw Sundance Kid—who, she thinks, may still be alive. She's relentlessly pursued by Charles Siringo, a Pinkerton agent. Katharine Ross returned to the role in a subsequent pilot from producer Stan Hough, *Wanted: The Sundance Woman*, in 1976, in which she still was chased by the Pinkerton man—played by Steve Forrest—and became a gunrunner for Pancho Villa.

Cast: Elizabeth Montgomery (as Etta Place), Robert Foxworth (Jack Maddox), L.Q. Jones (Charles Siringo), Arthur Hunnicutt (Walt Putney), Lorna Thayer (Fanny Porter), Lurene Tuttle (Mrs. Lee), Claudette Nevins (Mary Lant), Byron Mabe (Merkle), Robert Donner (Ben Lant), Dean Smith (Avery), Jack Williams (Davis), Todd Shelhorse (David).

212. Nevada Smith. NBC 5/3/75. 90 minutes. MGM Television. Director: Gordon Douglas. Producers/Writers/Creators: John Michael Hayes and Martin Rackin, based on the character created by Harold Robbins. Music: Lamont Dozier.

This Western pilot has a long lineage. It's based on Harold Robbins's book *The Carpetbaggers*, the 1964 movie of the same name, and the 1966 celluloid sequel *Nevada Smith*. Cliff Potts and Lorne Greene star as Nevada Smith, a half-breed gunslinger, and his mentor Jonas Cord, roles portrayed earlier by Steve McQueen and Brian Keith, who carried on where Alan Ladd and Leif Erickson had left off. In the pilot, Cord and his family open the first munitions factory in the West and hire Smith to help run the operation and escort a shipment of explosives to Utah. Filmed on location in Durango, Mexico, this marks the return of Adam West to the genre in which he made his name prior to *Batman*.

Cast: Cliff Potts (as Nevada Smith), Lorne Greene (Jonas Cord), Adam West (Frank Hartlee), Warren Vanders (Red Fickett), Jorge Luke (Two Moon), Jerry Gatlin (Brill), Eric Cord (Davey), John McKee (McLane), Roger Cudney (Perkins), Alan George (MacBaren), Lorraine Chanel (Belva).

213. **Norma Rae.** NBC 11/21/81. 60 minutes. McKeand Productions and Twentieth Century Fox Television. Director: Ed Parone. Executive Producers: Alex Rose and Tamara Asseyev. Producer: Nigel McKeand. Writer: Carol McKeand. Music: David Shire.

Based on the 1979 movie that earned Sally Field an Academy Award. Cassie Yates takes over the role of Norma Rae, an outspoken millworker, union organizer, and mother of two who lives with her father in a small southern town.

Cast: Cassie Yates (as Norma Rae Webster), Nancy Jarnagin (Willie Webster), Keith Mitchell (Craig Webster), Barry Corbin (Vernon Witchard), Jane Atkins (Alma Woodruff), Jordan Clarke (Frank Osborne), Ernest Hardin, Jr. (William Poole), Gary Frank (Reuben), Mickey Jones (Emery), Richard Dysart (Judge Elvin Allen), James T. Hall (Clay Johnson), Enid Kent (Waitress), Jon Van Ness (Process Server), Ed Call (Boss Man), Jack Garner (Bailiff).

214. **Our Man Flint (aka Our Man Flint: Dead on Target).** ABC 3/17/76. 90 minutes. Twentieth Century Fox Television. Director:

Joseph Scanlon. Executive Producer: Stanley Colbert. Producer: R.H. Anderson. Writer: Norman Klenman.

Ray Danton takes over as superspy Derek Flint, originally portrayed by James Coburn in the theatrical 007 spoofs *Our Man Flint* and *In Like Flint*. This time, Flint, an agent for Z.O.W.I.E. (Zonal Organization for World Intelligence and Espionage), searches for a kidnapped scientist.

Cast: Ray Danton (as Derek Flint), Sharon Acker (Sandra), Gaye Rowan (Benita), Donnelly Rhodes (LaHood), Lawrence Dane (Runzler), Fran Russell (Delia Cieza).

215. **The Owl and the Pussycat.** NBC 12/29/75. 30 minutes. Rastar Productions and Screen Gems. Director: Paul Bogart. Producer: Marc Neufield. Writer: Buck Henry. Music: Lennie Stark.

A sitcom adaptation of Bill Manhoff's 1964 play and the 1970 motion picture starring George Segal and Barbra Streisand. Buck Henry and Bernadette Peters take over the roles of a frustrated writer and a frustrated actress who become friends.

Cast: Buck Henry (Felix), Bernadette Peters (Doris), Liam Dunn (Mr. Crumley), Dorothy Neuman (Mrs. Crumley), Val Basiglio (The Man).

216. **Pete 'n' Tillie.** CBS 3/28/74. 30 minutes. Universal Television. Director: Jerry Belson. Producer/Writer: Carl Kleinschmitt, based on the novel *Witch's Milk* by Peter de Vries. Music: Michael Melvoin.

An adaptation of the 1972 movie, which starred Walter Matthau as a forty-eight-year-old school teacher who marries a thirty-eight-year-old social worker, played by Carol Burnett. It's the first marriage for both, and adjusting to living with someone else after such a long single life takes some getting used to. Carmine Caridi and Cloris Leachman are the couple in this sitcom adaptation.

Cast: Cloris Leachman (as Tillie Schaefer), Carmine Caridi (Pete Schaefer), Mabel Albertson (Norma Jean Ryerson), Dick Balduzzi (Alan Kipeck).

217. **Popeye Doyle.** ABC 9/7/86. 2 hours. Twentieth Century Fox Television. Director: Peter Levin. Executive Producer: Robert Singer.

Producer: Richard Dilello. Technical Consultant: Eddie Egan. Writer: Richard Dilello. Music: Brad Fiedel.

Another attempt to turn the adventures of real-life cop Eddie (*The French Connection*) Egan into a TV series. Now Ed O'Neill is Popeye Doyle, a tough narcotics detective absorbed in his job. Matthew Laurance is his partner, and James Handy is his boss.

Cast: Ed O'Neill (as Popeye Doyle), Matthew Laurance (Tony Párese), James Handy (Lt. Gregory Paulus), Audrey Landers (Jill Anneyard), Elias Zarou (Fahoud Nazzin), Candy Clark (Corrine), Nicholas Kadi (The Weasel), George de la Peña (The Shadow), Gary Tacon (Deli Bandit #1), Phil Neilson (Deli Bandit #2), Elizabeth Lennie (Toni), Richard Monette (Patrick Henley), Peter Virgile (Pretty Boy), S.J. Fellows (Nurse #1), Guy Sanvido (Sammy), Phillip Williams (Patrolman #1), Linda Gambell (Nurse #2), Chick Roberts (Detective Bender), Jonathan Simmons (Park Patrolman), Richard McMillan (Apartment Manager), Joanna Perica (Connie Parese), Alexandria Innes (Maria Rodriquez), Tony Rosato (Wiseass Reporter), Todd Postlethwaite (Club Manager), Susan Diol (The Blonde).

218. Returning Home (aka The Best Years of Our Lives). ABC 4/29/75. 90 minutes. Samuel Goldwyn Productions and Lorimar Productions. Director: Daniel Petrie. Executive Producer: Lee Rich. Producer: Herbert Hirschman. Writers: Bill Svanoe and John McGreevey. Music: Ken Lauber.

A TV-movie pilot based on 1946's Oscar-winning *The Best Years of Our Lives*, about three World War II soldiers—a married banker with two children, an air force hero with a bride he hardly knows, and an infantryman who lost both his arms (roles played by Fredric March, Dana Andrews, and Harold Russell respectively in the film)— who return home to a small town and try to adjust to civilian life. Dabney Coleman is the banker, Tom Selleck the flying ace, and new-comer James Miller, handicapped in Vietnam, plays the permanently disabled soldier.

Cast: Dabney Coleman (as Al Stephenson), Tom Selleck (Fred Derry),

James Miller (Homer Parrish), Whitney Blake (Millie Stephenson), Joan Goodfellow (Peggy Stephenson), Sherry Jackson (Marie Derry), Laurie Walters (Wilma Parrish), James A. Watson, Jr. (Capt. Will Tobey), Lenka Peterson (Mrs. Parrish), Patricia Smith (Mrs. Cameron), Booth Colman (Vern Milton), Lou Frizzell (Butch Cavendish), Jim Antonio (Avery Novak), Don Keefer (Mr. Parrish), James Beach (Henry "Wimpy" Jergens), Paul Lambert (Mike Harris), Tom Blank (Dave), Joseph DiReda ATC Sergeant), Ed Call (Hank), Allen Price (Rob Stephenson), Eileen McDonough (Luella).

219. **The Seven Little Foys.** NBC 1/24/64. 60 minutes. Universal Television. Director: Jack Laird. Executive Producer: Gordon Oliver. Music: Johnny Mandel.

Aired as an episode of *Bob Hope Chrysler Theatre* and based on the 1955 movie which starred Bob Hope as Eddie Foy, a widower vaudevillian raising seven performing kids, and James Cagney as George M. Cohan. In the pilot, Eddie Foy, Jr., plays his real-life father, and Mickey Rooney plays Cohan, with the Osmonds portraying the Foy sons.

Cast: Eddie Foy, Jr. (as Eddie Foy), Mickey Rooney (George M. Cohan), George Tobias (Barney Green), Naomi Stevens (Aunt Clara), Christy Jordan (Mary Foy), Alan Osmond (Bryan Foy), Wayne Osmond (Charley Foy), Merrill Osmond (Richard Foy), Donny Osmond (Irving Foy), Jay Osmond (Eddie Foy, Jr.), Elaine Edwards (Miss Williams).

220. **Shamus (aka A Matter of Wife and Death).** NBC 4/10/76. 90 minutes. Columbia Pictures Television. Director: Marvin J. Chomsky. Executive Producer: David Gerber. Producer: Robert M. Weitman. Writer: Don Ingalls. Music: Richard Shores.

Rod Taylor is the womanizing, freewheeling private eye Burt Reynolds played in producer Weitman's 1973 movie *Shamus*. Convenient name. He's lucky his name wasn't "Bricklayer." Shamus works out of a pool hall run by Dick Butkus and has a friend-on-the-force (Shamus *is* a lucky guy) played by Joe Santos, who became James Garner's friend-on-the-force in *The Rockford Files*. In the pilot, Shamus investigates the murder of a small-time private eye whose office was bombed.

Cast: Rod Taylor (as Shamus), Joe Santos (Lt. Vince Promuto), Eddie Firestone (Blinky), Luke Askew (Snell), John Colicos (Joe Ruby), Tom Drake (Paulie Baker), Anita Gillette (Helen Baker), Charles Picerni (Bruno), Anne Archer (Carol), Larry Block (Springy), Dick Butkus (Heavy), Marc Alaimo (Angie), Cesare Danova (Dottore), Lynda Carter (Zelda).

221. **Six Pack (aka Brewster's Brood).** CBS 7/24/83. 60 minutes. Twentieth Century Fox Television. Director: Rod Amateau. Executive Producer/ Writer: Gy Waldron. Producers: Rod Amateau and James Heinz. Music: Lance Rubin.

Based on the 1982 movie *Six Pack* starring Kenny Rogers as a race car driver who takes in five orphaned kids as his pit crew. Don Johnson takes over the role for the TV version. Markie Post is his girlfriend, and Mae Marmy is the prim English nanny he hires to teach the kids on the road.

Cast: Don Johnson (as Brewster Baker), Markie Post (Sally Leadbetter), Jennifer Runyon (Heather Akins), Billy Warlock (Duffy Akins), Bubba Dean (Rebel Akins), Con Martin (Hank Akins), Leaf Phoenix (Tad Akins), Mae Marmy (Sybil Cadbury), Ralph Pace (Joe Apple), Terry Beaver (JoJo), Jerry Campbell (Red Lyles), Cliff Brand (D.C. Dempsey), Julian Bond (Judge), Wallace Wilkinson (Superintendent), C. Pete Munro (Luther).

222. **Sidekicks (aka The Skin Game).** CBS 3/21/74. 90 minutes. Warner Bros. Television. Producer/Director: Burt Kennedy. Writer: William Bowers. Creator: Richard Alan Simmons. Music: David Shire.

A television sequel to the 1972 movie *Skin Game,* which starred James Garner and Lou Gossett as two con men roaming the pre-Civil War West posing as master and slave. Gossett repeats his film role, and Larry Hagman steps in for Garner in the pilot, which aimed for a style reminiscent of the old *Maverick* series. Unfortunately, the charm of both *Skin Game* and *Maverick* was Garner, and he's missing from this.

Cast: Larry Hagman (as Quince), Lou Gossett (Jason), Blythe Danner (Prudy), Jack Elam (Boss), Harry Morgan (Sheriff Jenkins),

Gene Evans (Sam), Noah Beery (Tom), Hal Williams (Max), Dick Peabody (Ed), Denver Pyle (Drunk), John Beck (Luke), Dick Haynes (Man), Tyler McVey (Jones), Billy Shannon (Carl).

223. Slither. CBS 3/21/74. 30 minutes. MGM Television. Director: Daryl Duke. Producer: Jack Shea. Writer/Creator: W.D. Richter.

Based on the 1973 film, which starred James Caan as Dick Kanipsia, a friendly, slightly hapless ex-con who has a tendency to meet strange people and get in over his head in outlandish schemes. Barry Bostwick has the role in this sitcom version.

Cast: Barry Bostwick (as Dick Kanipsia), Patti Deutsch (Ruthie), Cliff Emmich (Fat Stranger), Michael C. Gwynne (Stranger), Seamon Glass (Farmer), Louis Quinn (Seller #1), Robert Stiles (Seller #2), John Delgado (Driver).

224. Sounder. CBS 1975. Robert Radnitz-Mattel Productions. Producer: Robert Radnitz. Writer: Lonne Elder, based on his motion picture screenplay.

The folks who brought you the much-admired 1972 film *Sounder* adapted it as a one-hour television drama about a black family living in Depression-oppressed Louisiana. Harold Sylvester, Eboney Wright, Darryl Young, Ronnie Bolden, and Ericha Young star.

225. State Fair. CBS 5/14/76. 60 minutes. Twentieth Century Fox Television. Director: David Lowell Rich. Executive Producers: M.J. Frankovich and William Self. Producer: Robert L. Jacks. Writers: Richard Fielder and Richard DeRoy, based on the novel by Phillip Strong and the three feature films it inspired. Music: Laurence Rosenthal. Songs: "Carousel Love" and "Wind in the Trees" by Harriet Schock; "Everything Reminds Me of You" by Mitch Vogel.

The story of a family—a mother and father with a divorced daughter raising her child, a daughter studying to be a veterinarian, and a son in high school who dreams of being a country music star—living on a dairy farm set against the backdrop of the annual State Fair that is the big event in their lives. This pilot was designed to launch a "family hour" series.

Cast: Vera Miles (as Melissa Bryant), Tim O'Connor (Jim Bryant), Mitch Vogel (Wayne Bryant), Julie Cobb (Karen Bryant Miller), Dennis Redfield (Chuck Bryant), Linda Purl (Bobby Jean Shaw), Jeff Cotler (Tommy Miller), W.T. Zacha (Catfish McKay), Jack Garner (Mr. Grant), Virginia Gregg (Miss Detweiler), Harry Moses (Ben Roper), Joel Stedman (David Clemmans), Dina K. Ousley (Marnie), Ranee Howard (Deputy), Ivor Francis (Judge).

226. **The Sunshine Boys.** NBC 6/9/77. 60 minutes. MGM Television. Director: Robert Moore. Executive Producer: Michael Leves. Producer: Sam Denoff. Writer/Creator: Neil Simon.

Simon scripted this adaptation of his 1972 play, which became a hit movie in 1975 starring Walter Matthau and George Burns as Willie Clark and Al Lewis, two ex-vaudevillians who dislike each other but, deep down, have a great deal of affection for one another. In the proposed TV series version, Red Buttons and Lionel Stander are a geriatric odd couple forced by circumstances to share an apartment together. Michael Durrell is Willie's nephew and agent, Sarina Grant is Willie's nurse, Barra Grant is Al's daughter, and George Wyner is his son-in-law.

Cast: Red Buttons (as Willie Clark), Lionel Stander (Al Lewis), Michael Durrell (Ben Clark), Bobbie Mitchell (Myrna Navazio), Sarina Grant (Muriel Green), George Wyner (Ray Banks), Barra Grant (Sylvia Banks), Philip Tanzini (Gary Banks), Danny Mora (Julio), Belle Bruck (Mrs. Kraise), Ann Cooper (Anita DeVane).

227. **Supercops.** CBS 3/21/75. 30 minutes. MGM Television. Director: Bernard L. Kowalski. Executive Producer: Bruce Geller. Producers: James David Buchanan and Ronald Austin. Writers: Austin Kalish and Irma Kalish. Music: Jack Urbont.

Based on the true-life exploits of N.Y.P.D. cops Greenberg and Hantz, known on the force and on the streets as "Batman and Robin." Their adventures filled two L.H. Wittemore books and were dramatized in the previous year's movie *Supercops*, starring Ron Leibman and David Selby. In the pilot, cut from sixty minutes, these unorthodox officers hunt down a brutal thief.

Cast: Steven Keats (as Dave Greenberg), Alan Feinstein (Bobby Hantz), Cliff Osmond (Dawson), Dick O'Neill (Capt. McLain), Peggy Rea (Bessie), Byron Morrow (Lt. Gorney), Tony Brande (Lt. Vanesian), Lou Tiano (Sgt. Falcone), George Loros (Delgado).

228. **Take Her, She's Mine.** ABC 1965. 30 minutes. Twentieth Century Fox Television. Producer: Richard Murphy. Based on the 1961 play— and subsequent 1963 Jimmy Stewart movie—by Henry and Phoebe Ephron.

Van Johnson is a widower trying to raise his mischievous daughter, a college freshman, who always has one scheme after another—and gets her dad involved in all of them.

229. **Three Coins in the Fountain.** NBC 8/10/70. 30 minutes. Twentieth Century Fox Television and General Foods. Director: Hal Kanter. Executive Producer: Hal Kanter. Producer: Robert L. Jacks. Writers: Hal Kanter and Melville Shavelson. Music: Jeff Alexander.

This 1967 pilot, based on the popular 1954 film, sat on the shelf for several years before being aired. Cynthia Pepper, Joanna Moore, and Yvonne Craig star as three American girls living in Rome.

Cast: Cynthia Pepper (as Maggie Wilson), Yvonne Craig (Dorothy), Joanna Moore (Ruth), Antony Alda (Gino), Nino Castelnuovo (Count Giorgio).

230. **Three-Way Love (aka Handle With Care; aka Citizen's Band).** CBS 1978. 30 minutes. Paramount Television. Producer/Writer: Gail Parent. Creator: Paul Brickman.

Based on the 1977 movie *Handle With Care*, which was originally released as *Citizen's Band*, with Ann Wedgeworth and Marcia Rodd recreating their roles as two women, one from Texas and one from South Dakota, who discover that they are married to the same man when he is hurt in an auto accident in Portland, Oregon. He deserts them both, so, pooling their resources and their children (Robbie Rist, Shannon Terhune, and Poindexter), the women decide to live together. Alix Elias reprises her role as their neighbor and friend.

231. To Sir, With Love. CBS 4/19/74. 30 minutes. David Gerber Productions and Screen Gems. Director: Jay Sandrich. Executive Producer: David Gerber. Producer: Ronald Rubin. Writers: Ronald Rubin and Michael Zagor, from the screenplay by James Clavell, based on the book by E.R. Braithwaite.

The 1967 movie starred Sidney Poitier as a high school teacher who, as part of a foreign exchange program, ends up in a school in a working-class section of London. Hari Rhodes assumes the role in the pilot.

Cast: Hari Rhodes (as Paul Cameron), James Grout (Headmaster Hawthorne), Rosemary Leach (Philippa), Roddy Maude-Roxby (Walter), Jane Anthony (Cheryl), Jane Carr (Ruby), Marc Harris (Trevor), Leonard Brockwell (Terry), Brinsley Forde (Charles), Paul Eddington (Moran).

232. Topper. ABC 11/9/79. 2 hours. Cosmo Productions and Robert Papazian Productions. Director: Charles S. Dubin. Executive Producers: Andrew Stevens and Kate Jackson. Producer: Robert A. Papazian. Writers: George Kirgo, Mary Anne Kascia and Michael Scheff, from the novel by Thorne Smith. Music: Fred Karlin.

An attempt to update *Topper* for television. It already had been a series in the 1950s, and there was an earlier pilot in 1973 with Roddy McDowall as Cosmo Topper and Stefanie Powers and John Fink as Marion and George Kerby. This time, Kate Jackson and her then-husband Andrew Stevens are Marion and George Kerby, two carefree ghosts who haunt their lawyer, Cosmo Topper (Jack Warden), to bring some fun into his life.

Cast: Kate Jackson (as Marion Kerby), Andrew Stevens (George Kerby), Jack Warden (Cosmo Topper), Rue McClanahan (Clara Topper), James Karen (Fred Korbel), Macon McCalman (Wilkins), Charles Siebert (Stan Oglivy), Larry Gelman (Mechanic), Gloria LeRoy (Saleswoman), Lois Areno (Charlene), Jane Wood (Nurse), Mary Peters (Marsha), Marsha Ray (Mrs. Quincy), Gregory Chase (Steve), Ellen Marsh (Hostess), Marshall Teague (Man at Disco), Tom Spratley (Jailer).

233. True Grit (aka True Grit: A Further Adventure). ABC 5/19/78. 2 hours. Paramount Television. Director: Richard T. Heffron. Producer/

Writer: Sandor Stern, from characters created by Charles Portis. Music: Earle Hagen.

Based on the book *True Grit*, a Western which inspired the 1969 movie of the same name and the 1975 sequel *Rooster Cogburn*, both of which starred John Wayne as a rough, grizzled, hard-drinking, one-eyed U.S.

Marshal. Warren Oates, who the previous season attempted stepping into Bogart's shoes for *The African Queen*, has the equally uncomfortable task of sitting in the Duke's saddle. In the pilot, Cogburn agrees to take an orphaned, free-spirited teenage girl named Mattie Ross from Arkansas to her relatives in California. The proposed series would follow their adventures along the way.

Cast: Warren Oates (as Rooster Cogburn), Lisa Pelikan (Mattie Ross), Lee Meriwether (Annie Sumner), James Stephens (Joshua Sumner), Jeff Osterhage (Chris Sumner), Lee Montgomery (Daniel Sumner), Ramon Bieri (Sheriff Ambrose), Jack Fletcher (Clerk), Parley Baer (Rollins), Lee DeBroux (Skorby), Fredric Cook (Chaka), Redmond Gleeson (Harrison), Gregg Palmer (Slatter), Derrel Maury (Creed), Roger Frazier (Moses Turk), John Perak (Tom Lacey), Dom Spencer (Doc Wade), Burt Douglas (Bast), Simon Tyme (Udall), Charles Burke (Hopkins).

234. **Used Cars.** CBS 5/15/84. 30 minutes. Can't Sing, Can't Dance Productions and Columbia Pictures Television. Director: Victor Lobl. Executive Producer: Barbara Corday. Producer/Writer: Bob Gale. Creators: Robert Zemeckis and Bob Gale. Music: Norman Gimbel and Charles Fox. Singer: Roy Clark.

Based on the 1980 movie that starred Kurt Russell and Jack Warden. Deborah Harmon inherits a struggling Las Vegas used car lot, run by Fred McCarren, who will resort to just about any outlandish scheme to outsell her unscrupulous Uncle Roy (Pat Corley), owner of every other car lot in town. Clayton Landey is McCarren's assistant, and Frank McRae is a mechanic learning to be a fast-talking salesman.

Cast: Deborah Harmon (as Barbara Fuchs), Fred McCarren (Rudy Russo), Clayton Landey (Jeff Kirkwood), Frank McRae (Jim), Pat Corley (Uncle Roy Fuchs), Michael Talbott (Mickey), Robert Costanza (Irving), David Wyley (Claude Wiggins), J.P. Bumstead (Sam), Don Maxwell (Sergeant).

235. What's Up, Doc? ABC 5/27/78. 30 minutes. Warner Bros. Television. Director: E.W. Swackhamer. Executive Producer: Hal Kanter. Producers: Charles B. Fitzsimons and Michael Norell. Writer: Michael Norell. Music: Ian Fairbain-Smith.

Based on the 1972 movie, which starred Ryan O'Neal as a stiff geology professor who, although engaged to an uptight woman (Madeline Kahn), falls in love with a wild, carefree, fun-loving incarnation of Bugs Bunny (Barbra Streisand) while on a trip to San Francisco. In the pilot version, Barry Van Dyke is the professor, Caroline McWilliams is his former fiancée, and Harriet Hall is his free-spirited new love.

Cast: Barry Van Dyke (as Howard Bannister), Harriet Hall (Judy Maxwell), Caroline McWilliams (Claudia), Don Porter (Urban Wyatt), Neva Patterson (Amanda Wyatt), Jeffrey Kramer (Fabian Leek).

236. Where's Poppa? ABC 7/17/79. 30 minutes. Marvin Worth Productions. Director: Richard Benjamin. Producers: Marvin Worth and Robert Klane. Writer/Creator: Robert Klane. Music: Ken Lauber.

Based on director Carl Reiner's cult 1970 feature, which screenwriter Klane adapted from his book about a New York lawyer (Steven Keats) constantly nagged by his selfish, overprotective mother (Elsa Lanchester), who demands—and gets—more of his time than his clients do. When all else fails, she pretends to be senile and helpless just to get him to do her bidding. And as much as he begs his older, married brother (Allan Miller) for help, he never gets any. George Segal, Ruth Gordon, and Ron Leibman played the roles in the motion picture.

Cast: Elsa Lanchester (as Momma Hockheiser), Steven Keats (Gordon Hockheiser), Judith-Marie Bergan (Louise Hamelin), Allan Miller (Sid Hockheiser).

STAR VEHICLES

SHOWS CREATED FOR A "NAME"

Sometimes, a star makes the show.

Mary Tyler Moore was already beloved for her five years on *The Dick Van Dyke Show* when a new series was fashioned for her. *The Mary Tyler Moore Show* ran for seven years, was showered with honors, and begat three other series.

Sometimes, a show makes the star.

Tom Selleck was nobody. He did seven pilots before one sold, and that one he was written out of. But with *Magnum, P.I.*, the producers found a concept that revealed his hidden talents, and made him a star.

The right match can create magic. Unknown Robin Williams as Mork. Star James Garner as Rockford. They call it packaging—the art of matching the personality with a concept, the star with the vehicle that both the actor and the network can ride to success.

In many ways, the star is more important than the series concept. Networks often give stars on-air commitments without an idea, a title, or anything...except the actor's pretty face and bankable name. A concept that is less than scintillating suddenly becomes a hot property if the right star is attached.

Would ABC have bought the concept of *Life With Lucy*, and given it a thirteen-episode guarantee, if Lucille Ball wasn't attached? Would *B.L. Stryker* have been passed over as just another private eye show if Burt Reynolds wasn't the star?

Networks are always on the lookout for movie stars on the way down, nobodies on the way up, and proven television personalities ready to transfer their success into a new show. Of course, it doesn't always work.

The art of packaging is a tricky thing. Why will people watch James Arness as a frontier marshal and not as a tough L.A. cop? Why does Ted Danson fail as a spy but succeed as a bartender? Or, for that matter, why is Patty Duke better suited to play identical twins than Ginger Rogers? Why would the networks gamble on Robert Urich as a Las Vegas private eye and not Peter Graves?

Chemistry. Timing. Instinct.

Television, at its heart, is a business of personalities, getting viewers to make the indelible connection between an actor and a character, and between the character and themselves. And when that happens, they stop being television shows, they become institutions, cultural icons, and, ultimately, members of the family.

And when it doesn't, they become unsold pilots.

237. Acres and Pains. CBS 5/12/62. 30 minutes. ZIV/United Artists. Producer/Director: Perry Lafferty. Writers: Harvey Yorkin and Dave Schwartz, based on material by S.J. Perelman.

Aired as an episode of *G.E. Theatre*. A writer (Walter Matthau) and his wife (Anne Jackson) leave the big city to live in Bucks County, Pennsylvania. The house they rent turns out to be a wreck, so they move into a motel/bowling alley full of strange tenants. It was originally planned as a pilot for Tom Poston.

Cast: Walter Matthau (Tom Dutton), Anne Jackson (Jenny Dutton), Edward Andrews (Paul Goodlove), Alice Pearce (Mrs. Ledbetter), Philip Coolidge (Mr. Ledbetter), Jerry Stiller (Harold), David Doyle (Burton Fairbanks).

238. Alexander the Great. ABC 1/26/68. 60 minutes. Selmur Productions. Director: Phil Karlson. Producer: Albert McCleary. Writers: William Robert Yates and Robert Pirosh.

Aired as an episode of *Off to See the Wizard*. William Shatner starred in the title role in this dramatization of the Battle of Issus between the Greeks and the Persians in 333 B.C. Costar Adam West recalls: "We did it in the desert outside St. George, Utah. I played Alexander's associate, General Cleander, the wine, women, and song general, who rode his

Arabian stallion across the desert, dressed in a loin cloth. Man, it was cold. It just didn't work. The audience and Madison Avenue just weren't ready for orgies with Shatner and West lying there on their backs, eating grapes, with belly dancers beside them." No loss. Shatner says "the nine months I spent working on *Alexander the Great* came in handy for *Star Trek.* Capt. Kirk is, in many ways, the quintessential hero, and the Greek heroes in literature have many of the same qualities I wanted to explore."

Cast: William Shatner (as Alexander), John Cassavetes (General Karonos), Joseph Cotten (General Antigonus), Simon Oakland (Attalos), Cliff Osmond (General Memnon), Ziva Rodann (Ada), Adam West (Cleander).

239. The Bette Davis Show (aka The Decorator). ABC 1965. 30 minutes. Four Star. Producer: Aaron Spelling.

Bette Davis is an interior decorator who lives with her clients in order to fit her designs to their personalities—which she usually adjusts by helping them with their problems.

240. Collectors Item. CBS 1958. 30 minutes. TCF Television Productions and CBS Productions. Director: Buzz Kulik. Producer/Writer: Herb Meadow.

A detective pilot, subtitled *The Left Hand of David,* featuring Vincent Price as Henry Prentiss, an art gallery owner, and Peter Lorre as Mr. Munsey, a forger with underworld ties, who works for him. Guest stars included Whitney Blake, Thomas Gomez, Eduard Franz, Dick Ryan, Dick Winslow, Harvey Parry.

241. Dark Mansions. ABC 7/23/86. 2 hours. Aaron Spelling Productions. Director: Jerry London. Executive Producers: Aaron Spelling and Douglas Cramer. Supervising Producer: E. Duke Vincent. Producers: Jerry London and Robert H. Justman. Writer: Robert McCullough. Music: Ken Harrison.

Loretta Young was to have been the star of this proposed serial set in San Francisco. She was later replaced by Joan Fontaine as Margaret Drake, matriarch of a family made rich by shipbuilding, a business now fought over by her two sons, Paul Shenar and Michael York, now that her husband (Dan O'Herlihy) is struck dead by lightning. But there are other problems—her secretary Linda Purl bears a haunting resemblance to her grandson Grant Aleksander's dead wife; her blind granddaughter Melissa Sue Anderson struggles to make it in the world; and her grandson Yves Martin lusts for his cousin Nicollette Sheridan. All in the family live on the same block in side-by-side mansions, hence the title.

Cast: Joan Fontaine (as Margaret Drake), Paul Shenar (Charles Drake), Michael York (Bryan Drake), Melissa Sue Anderson (Noelle), Linda Purl (Shellane), Yves Martin (Cody Drake), Grant Aleksander (Nicholas), Nicollette Sheridan (Banda), Lois Chiles (Jessica), Raymond St. Jacques (Meadows), Dan O'Herlihy (Alexander Drake), Brian Morrow (David Forbes), Steve In wood (Mills), Vincent Pandoliano (Chef), Lee Corrigan (Capt. Hemmings).

242. **The Claudette Colbert Show (aka Welcome to Washington; aka Francy Goes to Washington).** NBC 9/30/58 (NBC) and 8/23/60 (CBS). 30 minutes. Producer/Director: Norman Tokar. Writers: Inez Asher and Whitfield Cook.

Initially aired as an episode of *Colgate Theatre* on NBC and then offered on CBS as part of a showcase of flops entitled *Comedy Spot.* Claudette Colbert is elected to Congress, moves to Washington, D.C., with her family, and tries to cope.

Cast: Claudette Colbert (Elizabeth Harper), Leif Erickson (Paul Harper), Shelley Fabares (Susie Harper), Eric Anderson (Billy Harper), also Maudie Pritchard, Herb Butterfield, Herb Ellis, Malcolm Cassell, Elvia Allman, Tony Henning.

243. **The Elizabeth McQueeny Story.** NBC 10/28/59. 60 minutes. Universal Television. Director/Writer: Allen H. Miner. Producer: Howard Christie. Music: Jerome Moross.

Aired as an episode of *Wagon Train.* Bette Davis stars as the leader of an all-female dance troupe that travels through the Old West. The cast included Robert Strauss, Terry Wilson, Frank McGrath, Maggie Pierce, John Wilder, Meg Wyllie, Marjorie Bennett, Daniele Aubry, Joseph Mell.

244. Fear No Evil (aka Bedeviled). NBC 3/3/69. 2 hours. Universal Television. Director: Paul Wendkos. Producers: Richard Alan Simmons and David Levinson. Writer: Richard Alan Simmons, from the story by Guy Endore. Music: Billy Goldenberg.

The first of two critically acclaimed, truly chilling pilots featuring Louis Jourdan as psychiatrist and occult expert Dr. David Sorrell and Wilfrid Hyde-White as Harry Snowden. One of Sorrell's patients says she's brought her husband back from the dead through an antique mirror. And she has. Universal continued to dabble with this concept until finally selling *The Sixth Sense*—about a parapsychologist—to NBC in 1972. The series only lasted a few months and utilized some of the score from *Ritual of Evil*, the sequel to this pilot.

Cast: Louis Jourdan (as Dr. David Sorrell), Carroll O'Connor (Myles Donovan), Bradford Dillman (Paul Varney), Lynda Day (Barbara Varney), Marsha Hunt (Mrs. Varney), Wilfrid Hyde-White (Harry Snowden), Kate Woodville (Ingrid Dome), Harry Davis (Wyant).

245. For the Defense. Independent 1956. 30 minutes. Director: James Nielsen. Producer: Samuel Bischoff. Writer: Donn Mullally.

Edward G. Robinson, in his only stab at a TV series, plays a hardened cop-turned-defense-attorney named Matthew Considine. In the pilot, Robinson takes on "The Case of Kenny Jason"—the episode's title—with Glen Vernon as Jason and Ann Doran as his mother. John Hoyt would have the recurring role of police captain Thomas Hardy.

Cast: Edward G. Robinson (Matthew Considine), Glen Vernon (Kenny Jason), Ann Doran (Mrs. Jason), John Hoyt (Captain Thomas Hardy), Robert Osterloh (Duke), Vic Perrin (Barney), Herbert Hayes (Judge), Morris Ankrum (District Attorney), Tom Dugan (Desk Sergeant).

246. The Frontier World of Doc Holliday. ABC 1959. 60 minutes. Warner Bros. Television. Director: Leslie H. Martinson. Producer: Roy Huggins.

Scheduled to air as an episode of *Cheyenne* entitled "Birth of a Legend." Adam West, described by Warners as a "traditional western star, tall and good looking, suggesting great strength and good breeding," played the title role. Warners planned to play down Holliday's tuberculosis, but it would, nonetheless, provide the impetus for the series concept—a doctor tells Holliday he has six months to live. In the pilot episode, Holliday kills for the first time but doesn't care because he is doomed anyway. Adam West says "I played him as an alcoholic with a consumptive cough. It isn't too attractive when you kiss your horse, and the horse dies. I don't think ABC, Warners, or Madison Avenue appreciated it at the time. And probably rightly so."

247. Everything Is Coming Up Roses (aka You're Gonna Love It Here). CBS 6/1/77. 30 minutes. S/K Productions and Warner Bros. Television. Director/Writer: Bruce Paltrow. Executive Producer: Frank Königsberg. Producer: Mel Färber. Music: Peter Matz.

Ethel Merman plays an out-of-work Broadway star with a talent agent son (Austin Pendleton) and a wisecracking, eleven-year-old grandson (Chris Barnes), whose parents are temporarily in jail.

Cast: Ethel Merman (as Lolly Rogers), Chris Barnes (Peter Rogers), Austin Pendleton (Harry Rogers), Dianne Kirksey (Neighbor), also Glenn Scarpelli, Jerome Dempsey, Mathew Anton, Tony Holmes.

248. The Ginger Rogers Show (aka A Love Affair Just for Three). CBS 7/22/63. 30 minutes. Director: Norman Z. McLeod. Executive Producer: William Self. Producers: Sidney Sheldon and Roy Huggins. Writer: Valentine Davies.

Ginger Rogers plays identical twin sisters—one a fashion designer and one a magazine writer—and Charles Ruggles costars as their befuddled uncle. Rogers designed her own wardrobe for this pilot, which had been in the works since the 1961–1962 season. In the pilot, Rogers is one sister posing as the other to discover why an Italian playboy jilted her (them).

Cast: Ginger Rogers (Elizabeth/Margaret Harcourt), Charles Ruggles (Eli Harcourt), Cesare Danova (Mario Cellini), Gardner McKay (Himself), Maureen Leeds (Girl), Warren Parker (Boy).

249. The Gypsy Warriors. CBS 5/12/78. 60 minutes. Universal Television. Director: Lou Antonio. Executive Producer: Stephen J. Cannell.

Producer: Alex Beaton. Writers/Creators: Stephen J. Cannell and Phil DeGuere. Music: Mike Post and Pete Carpenter.

The first of two unsold pilots Cannell developed to showcase the talents of James Whitmore, Jr., and Tom Selleck. This time, they play two espionage agents, posing as gypsies roaming France and Germany, who take on unusual missions during World War II. The relationship between Cannell, Whitmore and Selleck predated this pilot and lasted long afterward. Whitmore and Selleck had both previously appeared frequently on *The Rockford Files*, and Whitmore would later have roles in Cannell's *Black Sheep Squadron* and *Hunter*, as well as Selleck's *Magnum, P.I.*, on which even Cannell showed up as a guest star.*Cast:* James Whitmore, Jr. (as Capt. Shelley Alhern), Tom Selleck (Capt. Ted Brinkerhoff), Joseph Ruskin (Ganault), Lina Raymond (Lela), Michael Lane (Androck), Albert Paulsen (Bruno Schlagel), Kenneth Tigar (Shulman), William Westley (Ramon Pierre Cammus), Hubert Noel (Henry), Kathryn Leigh Scott (Lady Britt Austin-Forbes).

250. **Harry's Battles.** ABC 6/8/81. 30 minutes. Marble Arch Productions. Director: Alan Rafkin. Executive Producer: Martin Starger. Producer/Writer: Charlie Hauck.

Based on the BBC series *A Sharp Intake of Breath*. Dick Van Dyke is a Pittsburgh supermarket manager who always seems to be embroiled in bureaucracy and red tape, to the consternation of wife Connie Stevens. Danny Wells and Marley Sims are their neighbors.

Cast: Dick Van Dyke (as Harry Fitzsimmons), Connie Stevens (Mary Carol Fitzsimmons), Danny Wells (Herb), Marley Sims (Diane), Brooke Alderson (Nurse Hewitt), Joe Regalbuto (Dr. Harwood), David Ruprecht (Sands), Florence Halop (Patient).

251. **Higher and Higher, Attorneys-at-Law.** CBS 9/9/68. 60 minutes. Clovis Productions. Director: Paul Bogart. Producers: Tony Ford and Jacqueline Babbin. Writer: Irving Gaynor Nieman.

This "whodunit" comedy, modeled after *The Thin Man*, would have been shot in New York and would chronicle the adventures of a husband and wife attorney team (Sally Kellerman and John McMartin) who solve murders. Dustin Hoffman, just before hitting it big on the big screen, plays one of their clients.

Cast. Sally Kellerman (as Liz Higher), John McMartin (John Higher), Dustin Hoffman (Arthur Greene), Robert Forster (Doug Pay son), Alan Alda (Frank St. John), Barry Morse (Colin St. John), Ruth White (Ellen St. John), Marie Masters (Paula), George Wallace (Charlie), Billy Dee Williams (David Arnold), Gunilla Hutton (Astrid), Eugene Roche (McElheny).

252. **Higher Ground.** CBS 9/4/88. 2 hours. Green/Epstein Productions and Columbia Pictures Television. Director: Robert Day. Executive Producers: Jim Green, Allen Epstein, and John Denver. Producers: Steve Barnett and Jim Green. Writer: Michael Eric Stein. Music: Lee Holdridge. Title Song: John Denver.

John Denver stars as Jim Clayton, a former FBI agent who moves to Alaska to operate an air charter with his old partner (Martin Kove). When the latter is murdered, Clayton hunts down the killers, and continues operating the charter with his partner's widow (Meg Wittner) and her son (Brandon Marsh).

Cast. John Denver (as Jim Clayton), Martin Kove (Rick Loden), John Rhys-Davies (Lt. Smight), Meg Wittner (Ginny Loden), Brandon Marsh (Tommy Loden), David Renan (Line Holmes), Richard Masur (Bill McClain).

253. **Jarrett.** NBC 8/11/73. 90 minutes. David Gerber Productions and Screen Gems. Director: Barry Shear. Executive Producer: David Gerber. Producer/Writer/Creator: Richard Maibaum. Music: Jack Elliott and Allyn Ferguson.

Glenn Ford is an ex-prize-fighter-turned-private-eye specializing in cases associated with the arts. His constant nemesis is Bassett Cosgrove, an eccentric, villainous art collector. Richard Maibaum, writer of most of the 007 scripts, said he created the character for a younger, more physical actor and that casting Ford was the pilot's death knell.

Cast: Glenn Ford (as Sam Jarrett), Anthony Quayle (Bassett Cosgrove), Forrest Tucker (as Reverend Vocal Simpson), Laraine Stephens (Sigrid Larsen), Yvonne Craig (Luluwa), Richard Anderson

(Spenser Loomis), Herb Jeffries (Karoufi), Elliot Montgomery (Dr. Carey), Lee Kolima (Kara George), Joseph Paul Herrara (I Knooh), Bob Schott (Gordon), Peter Brocco (Arnheim), Jody Gilbert (Sawyer), Robert Easton (Toby), Stack Pierce (Prison Guard), Read Morgan (Casimin), Ted White (Arthur), Frank Arno (Motor Man).

254. **The Judge and Jake Wyler.** NBC 12/2/72. 2 hours. Universal Television. Director: David Lowell Rich. Executive Producers/Writers: Richard Levinson and William Link. Producer: Jay Benson. Music: Gil Melle.

Bette Davis stars as a retired judge who becomes a private eye and lures Doug McClure, an ex-con serving his probation with her, to be her legman. In the pilot, they help a girl prove her father's suicide was actually murder. Davis was previously committed to *Madame Sin*, and could only star in a series as Judge Meredith if the ABC pilot failed. As it turned out, both pilots died—though this one didn't go quietly. It was pitched again the following year as *Partners in Crime*, starring Lee Grant as a judge who goes into the private detective business with ex-con legman, Lou Antonio.

Cast: Bette Davis (as Judge Meredith), Doug McClure (Jake Wyler), Eric Braeden (Anton Granicek), Joan Van Ark (Alicia Dodd), Gary Conway (Frank Morrison), Lou Jacobi (Lt. Wolfson), James McEachin (Quint), Lisabeth Hush (Caroline Dodd), Kent Smith (Robert Dodd), Barbara Rhoades (Chloe Jones), John Randolph (James Rockmore), Milt Kamen (Mr. Gilbert), John Lupton (Senator Joseph Pritchard), Michael Fox (Dr. Simon), Eddie Quillan (Billy Lambert), Celeste Yarnall (Ballerina), Ray Ballard (Harvey Zikoff), Virginia Capers (Mabel Cobb), Myron Natwick (Lyle Jefferson), Harriet E. MacGibbon (Hostess), Stuart Nisbet (Doctor), Rosanna Huffman (Receptionist), Steven Peck (Paul), Don Diamond (Workman), Margarita Cordova (Woman), Khalil Ben Bezaleel (African Diplomat).

255. **Las Vegas Beat.** NBC 1961. 60 minutes. Fenady/Kowalski Corp., Goodson-Todman Productions, and NBC Productions. Director: Bernard L. Kowalski. Executive Producers: Mark Goodson and Bill

Todman. Producer/Writer/Creator: Andrew J. Fenady. Music: Richard Markowitz.

Peter Graves is Bill Ballin, an ex-cop-turned-private-eye who works for the casinos and occasionally helps out the police through his friend, Lt. Bernard McFeety (Richard Bakalyan). He's aided by a wisecracking assistant (Jamie Farr) and a crusty, cynical reporter (William Bryant). This pilot wasn't cheap. It was shot on location in Las Vegas and featured a helicopter chase and a climax at Hoover Dam. The unusually violent story pits Ballin against a gang plotting to rob an armored car loaded with casino cash.

"I played a kind of public relations guy who also worked as a detective for some of the casinos," recalls Graves. "It was going to be a mystery, but it would incorporate Las Vegas shows." The pilot ended with a sales pitch from Graves to would-be sponsors: "Well, that's it. The pilot. The Beginning. Now it's a well known fact-for the great majority of pilots, the beginning and the ending are one in the same. Quite unashamedly, we don't think that's so for *Las Vegas Beat*.... We think we have a chemistry that adds up to a tubeful of excitement." Of course, Graves was wrong. Today, he still doesn't know what happened. "We had a very hot line to NBC, and then, all of a sudden, we weren't hearing anything anymore."

Cast: Peter Graves (as Bill Ballin), Jamie Farr (Gopher), William Bryant (R.G. Joseph), Richard Bakalyan (Lt. Bernard McFeety), Diane Millay (Cynthia Raine), Lawrence Dobkin (Fredericks), Maggie Mahoney (Helen Leopold), Jay Adler (Duke Masters), Tom Drake (Leopold), Jim Sutton (Martin Scott), also Harry Harvey, Jr., Ralph Moody, Beau Hickman, Jimmy Cavanaugh, Lisa Seagram, Bill Couch.

256. **Lassiter.** CBS 7/8/68. 60 minutes. Filmways. Director: Sam Wanamaker. Producer/Writer: Richard Alan Simmons.

Burt Reynolds played a free-lance writer who specializes in exposing underworld crime for *Contrast* magazine.

Cast: Burt Reynolds (as Pete Lassiter), Cameron Mitchell (Stan Marchek), Sharon Farrell (Joan Mears), James Mac Arthur (Russ Faine),

Nicholas Colasanto (Charlie Leaf), Stanley Waxman (Pat), Lloyd Haynes (Kramer), Lawrence Haddon (Jerry Burns).

257. **Luxury Liner.** NBC 2/12/63. 60 minutes. Four Star. Executive Producer: Dick Powell. Producer: Aaron Spelling. Music: Herschel Burke Gilbert.

Aired as an episode of *Dick Powell Theatre*. An anthology / drama, which would be hosted by James Stewart, about the lives of the people who travel on a cruise ship commanded by Rory Calhoun, who would be the only regular. Over a decade later, producer Aaron Spelling would take the same concept, add a touch of *Love, American Style*, and title it *The Love Boat*.

Cast: Rory Calhoun (as Capt. Victor Kihlgren), Jan Sterling (Selena Royce), Michael Davis (Digo), Carroll O'Connor (Dr. Lyman Savage), Ludwig Donath (Jan Veltman), Ed Kemmer (Sam Barrett), Oscar Beregi (La Guerne), Danny Scholl (Mr. Marion).

258. **The Man From Everywhere.** CBS 4/13/61. 30 minutes. Four Star. Producer: Hal Hudson. Writer: Fred S. Fox.

Aired as an episode of *Zane Grey Theatre*. Burt Reynolds is a saddle tramp wandering through the Old West, picking up odd jobs as he goes.

Cast: Burt Reynolds (as Branch Taylor), Cesar Romero (Tom Bowdry), King Calder (Sheriff Jed Morgan), Peter Whitney (Moose), Ruta Lee (Jenny Aldrich).

259. **The Mouse That Roared.** CBS 1967. 30 minutes. Screen Gems. Producer: Jack Arnold.

Sid Caesar plays three different roles in this pilot based on the Leonard Wibberly novel and the 1959 Peter Sellers movie about a mythical kingdom declaring war on the United States in order to lose—and then receive foreign aid. Arnold directed the original movie version. Costars include Joyce Jameson and Richard Deacon.

260. **Murder in Music City (aka Music City Murders; aka Country Music Murders; aka Sonny and Sam).** NBC 1/16/79. 2 hours. Frankel Films/

Gank Inc. Director: Leo Penn. Executive Producer: Ernie Frankel. Producer: Jimmy Sangster. Writers: Ernie Frankel and Jimmy Sangster. Music: Earle Hagen.

Sonny Bono is a Nashville songwriter who buys a detective agency as a tax shelter and ends up taking over the business—with his bride, a model (Lee Purcell)—when the private eye is killed. Country singers Charlie Daniels, Larry Gatlin, Barbara Mandrell, Ronnie Milsap, Ray Stevens, and Mel Tillis all make cameo appearances as themselves.

Cast. Sonny Bono (as Sonny Hunt), Lee Purcell (Samantha Hunt), Lucille Benson (Mrs. Bloom), Claude Akins (Billy West), Belinda J. Montgomery (Peggy Ann West), Morgan Fairchild (Dana Morgan), Michael MacRae (Chigger Wade), Harry Bellaver (Jim Feegan), Jim Owen (Sam Prine), T. Tommy Cutrer (Lt. Culver).

261. The Oprah Winfrey Show (aka Natalie). ABC 1988. 30 minutes. Reeves Entertainment and Mort Lachman Productions. Director: Barnet Kellman. Executive Producer: Mort Lachman. Writers: Winifred Hervey and Mort Lachman.

ABC hoped to capitalize on the phenomenal success of syndicated talkshow host Oprah Winfrey by giving her a thirteen-episode commitment for a sitcom loosely based on her own life. However, Winfrey scuttled the deal after filming the pilot, which she publicly decried as horrible, and chose instead to concentrate on her fledgling movie career.

262. The Orson Welles Show. NBC 9/16/58. 30 minutes. Desilu Productions. Producer/Director/Writer: Orson Welles.

Aired as an episode of *Colgate Theatre.* The series would have been comprised of dramatizations of classic tales, including books by Kipling and H.G. Wells, as well as episodes devoted to magic, interviews, readings, and whatever else Welles wanted to do. For the pilot, Welles directed and narrated an adaptation of John Collier's *Fountain of Youth,* about a scientist who invents a secret elixir that keeps people young. Before the pilot was even completed, the proposed series was doomed. Welles went over budget, took four weeks instead of the allotted ten days to shoot it, and threw an expensive wrap party that he billed to Desilu. The pilot, though hailed by critics for its inventive directing and honored with the Peabody Award of Excellence, was rejected by the networks because they felt it was too sophisticated. It was, according to *Variety*, "unceremoniously dumped. Welles was never hired again to direct anything in Hollywood."

Cast: Orson Welles (as Dr. Humphrey Baxter), Joi Lansing (Caroline Coates), Rick Jason (Alan Broadie), Nancy Kulp (Stella Morgan), Billy House (Albert Morgan).

263. Return of the Original Yellow Tornado. NBC 1967. 30 minutes. Universal Television. Producer/Creator: Jack Laird. Writers: George Balzar, Hal Goldman, and Al Gordon.

In the year 1987, two famous superheroes have retired but return to active duty when the Yellow Tornado, their arch enemy whom they put in prison in 1967, is set free—and vows to wreak havoc on the world. Mickey Rooney and Eddie Mayehoff played the not-so-young good guys.

264. Savage. NBC 3/31/73. 90 minutes. Universal Television. Director: Steven Spielberg. Executive Producers/Creators: Richard Levinson and William Link. Producer: Paul Mason. Writers: Mark Rodgers, Richard Levinson, and William Link. Music: Gil Melle.

Martin Landau is Savage, an investigative reporter with his own television show that examines the political world. Landau's then-wife Barbara Bain plays his producer. In the pilot, they investigate a scandal involving a Supreme Court nominee. This was the last TV movie Spielberg directed before going into motion pictures and becoming an industry unto himself. "It needed work, no question about it, but it was a good beginning," Landau says. "It was ahead of its time. That show was a platform to do intelligent television. It was television doing television, and it was innovative as hell and we got shot down for the wrong reasons. It was clearly political. The network news department took exception to our show. I got a call from [Universal president] Sid Sheinberg and he said 'it's the best thing we've got, NBC is crazy about it, it's on-the-air.' And it went from there to being buried in a week's time."

Cast: Martin Landau (as Paul Savage), Barbara Bain (Gail Abbott), Will Geer (Joel Ryker), Paul Richards (Phillip Brooks), Michele Carey

(Allison Baker), Barry Sullivan (Judge Daniel Stern), Louise Latham (Marion Stern), Dabney Coleman (Ted Seligson), Pat Harrington, Jr. (Russell), Susan Howard (Lee Reynolds), Jack Bender (Jerry).

265. The Sheriff and the Astronaut. CBS 5/24/84. 60 minutes. Warner Bros. Television. Director: E.W. Swackhamer. Producers: Gerald DiPego and Robert Lovenheim. Writer: Gerald DiPego. Music: Basil Poledouris.

Alec Baldwin is a Florida county sheriff in love with a lady astronaut (Ann Gillespie) and at odds with the space center's security chief (Kene Holliday).

Cast: Ann Gillespie (as Dr. Ellen Vale), Alec Baldwin (Sheriff Ed Cassaday), Don Hood (Deputy Tom Cassaday), Kene Holliday (Al Stark), Gregg Berger (John Fitch), Tuck Milligan (Deputy Billy LaPantier), Scott Paulin (Robert Malfi), Ruth Drago (Felice Winter), John Randolph (Hank Bashaw), Steve Franken (Agent Henley), Bruce Fischer (Axel Soames), Stanley Kamel (Phillip Tabbet), Bill Morey (Charles Tabbet), Mark Schubb (Tim Hillman).

266. The Shirley Temple Show. ABC 1965. 30 minutes. Twentieth Century Fox Television. Producer/Director: Vincent Sherman.

Shirley Temple stars as a San Francisco social worker who gets involved in the lives of the people she works with.

267. Tom Selleck Project. NBC 11/16/79. 60 minutes. Cherokee Productions and Universal Television. Director: John Patterson. Executive Producer: Meta Rosenberg. Producers: Stephen J. Cannell, Chas. Floyd Johnson, David Chase, and Juanita Bartlett. Writer/Creator: Stephen J. Cannell. Music: Mike Post and Pete Carpenter.

Aired as the "Nice Guys Finish Dead" episode of *The Rockford Files*. Tom Selleck stars as mediocre private eye Lance White, who does everything wrong but still gets more glory than Jim Rockford (James Garner), who does everything right. Lance White is a spoof of *Mannix* and the epitome of the private-eye cliche *The Rockford Files* set out to debunk. (The White character first appeared in the "White on White and Nearly

Perfect" episode, which was written and directed by Cannell and aired on 10/20/78.)

Cast: Tom Selleck (as Lance White), James Luisi (Lt. Chapman), Simon Oakland (Vernon St. Cloud), Larry Manetti (Larry St. Cloud), James Whitmore, Jr. (Fred Beemer), Joseph Bernard (Carmine DeAngelo), Fritzi Burr (Mrs. DeAngelo), Roscoe Born (TV Commentator), Steve James (Newsman), Al Berry (Ed Fuller), Gregory Norman Cruz (Attendant), Larry Dunn (Norm Cross), John Lombardo (Police Clerk).

THE NEW OLD

TELEVISION SERIES REVIVALS

Old is the newest thing on television these days. You only have to crack open the latest *TV Guide* to see that for yourself...*Kojak, The Bradys, Star Trek, Dark Shadows,* and the *Mission: Impossible* team are all back, even if they are a bit older and fatter than you remember them.

Television series revivals and remakes are exploding across the big and small screen—a trend that began with *Rescue From Gilligan's Island* in 1978 and has continued, unabated, through the eighties and into the nineties with resurrections of such favorites as *Perry Mason* and *Columbo* and such losers as *That's My Mama.*

It's a trend that has reached insane proportions. *Maverick* was revived three times in three years on three networks, while in syndication, independent stations revived a revival of *The Twilight Zone.* With a hundred revivals done already, there aren't many "old favorites" left.

Why this mad rush to remake the old shows?

Sheer desperation.

The television marketplace has radically changed in the last ten years. The three networks once dominated television, but now they are running scared, looking over their shoulders at the likes of HBO, Lifetime, MTV, and the coalition of independent stations that are producing their own network-quality programming, as well as made-for-home video.

The good old days are gone, but the networks are hoping to regain some of their lost glory by recreating them. And, to some degree, it's working.

Rescue From Gilligan's Island, which started the whole trend, copped a staggering 30.4 rating, 52 share. More recently, *A Very Brady Christmas* stomped the competition with a 25.1 rating, 39 share.

Now, NBC routinely trots out *Perry Mason* specials during the crucial "sweeps" periods to stoke ratings, while other networks ravage their old *TV Guides*, searching for the few ancient hits left to exhume. While the "one-shot" reunion specials may shore up sagging audience shares, the series that spin off from them aren't so lucky. *The Bradys, Sanford, Kojak, Bret Maverick, Dobie Gillis*, and *Mission: Impossible*, to name a few, all bombed.

Yet cable producers, not to be outmaneuvered, are willing to feed on nostalgia, too. Showtime revived *The Paper Chase*, the Disney Channel mounted *Still the Beaver*, and independent stations have turned *Star Trek—The Next Generation* into a bigger hit than the original series. Even the movie industry, feeling the pinch from cable and home video, has gotten into the act, recruiting *Star Trek, Get Smart, The Jetsons, The Twilight Zone, Dragnet, The Addams Family, Car 54—Where Are You?* and *The Untouchables* to lure patrons to the box office.

And more are on the way.

All this nostalgia makes the studios very happy. It's a way to tack on additional episodes to tired syndication packages, a way to make old series look more attractive as reruns and to rekindle interest in forgotten shows. It's also easier to sell a network or station consortium a revived older series than a new one, the theory being if they liked it once, maybe they'll like it all over again.

But there's something more at work here than network panic and studio greed.

We've grown up with television. There's something comforting about seeing those familiar faces again, even if the hair is gray, the paunches pronounced, and the smiles not as sparkling.

Because, for that hour or two, we aren't just anonymous TV viewers sitting alone in our living rooms—we're plugging into a big, cultural, family reunion, sharing fond memories and old friends.

And despite the crass manipulation of it all, that's still pretty special.

268. Aliens Are Coming (aka The Aliens; aka The New Invaders). NBC 3/2/80. 2 hours. Quinn Martin Productions. Director: Harvey Hart. Executive Producer: Quinn Martin. Producer: Philip Saltzman. Writer: Robert W. Lenski. Music: William Goldstein.

A new version of *The Invaders*, Quinn Martin's 1967–68 series about an architect who knows Earth is being invaded by humanoid aliens—but only a handful of people believe him. In this remake/pilot, Dr. Scott Dryden tries to stop invading aliens who possess earthlings to achieve their evil ends. But Dr. Dryden isn't fighting alone—he works with the Nero Institute, where he gets help from Leonard Nero and Gwen O'Brien.

Cast: Tom Mason (as Dr. Scott Dryden), Melinda Fee (Gwen O'Brien), Eric Braeden (Leonard Nero), Max Gail (Russ Garner), Caroline McWilliams (Sue Garner), Matthew Laborteaux (Timmy Garner), Fawne Harriman (Joyce Cummings), Ron Masak (Harve Nelson), John Milford (Eldon Gates), Lawrence Haddon (Bert Fowler), Hank Brandt (John Sebastian), Richard Lockmiller (Officer Strong), Sean Griffin (Dr. Conley), Gerald McRaney (Norman), Curtis Credel (Frank Foley).

269. Dobie Gillis [Pilot #1]. **Whatever Happened to Dobie Gillis?** CBS 5/10/77. 30 minutes. Komack Company. Directors: James Komack and Gary Shimokawa. Executive Producers: James Komack and Paul Mason. Producer: Michael Manheim. Writers: Peter Meyerson and Nick Arnold. Creator: Max Shulman. Music: Randy Newman.

An update of the 1959–63 sitcom *Dobie Gillis*. Dobie (Dwayne Hickman) has married Zelda (Sheila James), has a sixteen-year-old son (Steven Paul), and runs his father's (Frank Faylen) grocery store. Maynard (Bob Denver) is now a successful entrepreneur, and Chatsworth (Steve Franken) has become town banker. Another revival, entitled *Bring Me the Head of Dobie Gillis* was mounted by Hickman in 1988 for CBS, where he is a program executive.

Cast: Dwayne Hickman (as Dobie Gillis), Bob Denver (Maynard G. Krebs), Sheila James (Zelda Gilroy), Frank Faylen (Herbert T. Gillis), Steven Franken (Chatsworth Osborne, Jr.), Steven Paul (Georgie Gillis), Lorenzo Lamas (Lucky), Wynn Irwin (Henshaw), Alice Backes (Mrs. Lazlo), Susan Davis (Mrs. Tucker).

269a. Dobie Gillis [Pilot #2]. **Bring Me the Head of Dobie Gillis.** CBS 2/21/88. 2 hours. Twentieth Century Fox Television. Director: Stanley

Z. Cherry. Executive Producer: Stanley Z. Cherry. Producers: Dwayne Hickman, Stan Hough, Marc Summers, and Steve Clements. Writers: Deborah Zoe Dawson, Victoria Johns, and Stanley Z. Cherry, from a story by Max Shulman. Creator: Max Shulman. Music: Jimmy Haskell. Theme: Lionel Newman and Max Shulman.

A second attempt to revive *Dobie Gillis* as a half-hour comedy. Dobie and his wife Zelda run the family store, while their son Georgie follows in his dad's footsteps in high school.

Cast: Dwayne Hickman (as Dobie Gillis), Sheila James (Zelda Gillis), Bob Denver (Maynard G. Krebs), Steve Franken (Chatsworth Osborne, Jr.), Scott Grimes (Georgie Gillis), Connie Stevens (Thalia Menninger), William Schallert (Mr. Promfritt), Lisa Wilcox (Bonnie Bascomb), Tricia Leigh Fisher (Chatsie Osborne), Nicholas Worth (Max the Chauffeur), Kathleen Freeman (Marie), Joey D. Viera (Sheriff Billy Pervis Ward), Dody Goodman (Ruth Knedelman), Hank Rolike (Andy Spunk), James Staley (Donald Snardmann), Lisa Fuller (Eloise).

270. **Escapade.** CBS 5/19/78. 60 minutes. Quinn Martin Productions. Director: Jerry London. Executive Producer: Quinn Martin. Producer: Philip Saltzman. Writer/Creator: Brian Clemens. Music: Patrick Williams.

This was an attempt to do an Americanized version of *The Avengers*, an outlandish, stylized spoof of spy movies, which was made in England and ran on ABC from 1966–1969, becoming a cult classic, starring Patrick Macnee as debonair spy John Steed and Diana Rigg as his sexy, and dangerous, partner Emma Peel (and later Linda Thorson as Tara King). Brian Clemens, who created, wrote, and produced *The Avengers*, penned this lighthearted pilot, about two San Francisco-based spies (Granville Van Dusen and Morgan Fairchild) who take their orders from an uppity computer named OZ. It was made shortly after Clemens finished producing twenty-six episodes of a European-produced revival called *The New Avengers*, which starred Macnee, Joanna Lumley, and Gareth Hunt, and aired late-night on CBS during the 1978–79 season.

Cast: Granville Van Dusen (as Joshua Rand), Morgan Fairchild (Susie), Len Birman (Arnold Tulliver), Janice Lynde (Paula), Alex

Henteloff (Wences), Gregory Walcott (Seaman), Dennis Rucker (Charlie Webster).

271. **The Father Knows Best Reunion.** [Pilot #1]. NBC 5/15/77. 90 minutes. Columbia Pictures Television. Director: Norman Abbott. Producer: Hugh Benson. Writer: Paul West. Music: George Duning.

Jim and Margaret Anderson mark their thirty-fifth anniversary, and everyone comes back together for the celebration. Betty is now a widow with two kids; Bud is a married motorcycle racer with a young son; and Kathy is single but dating a doctor ten years older than she is. Two more pilots followed this one.

Cast: Robert Young (as Jim Anderson), Jane Wyatt (Margaret Anderson), Elinor Donahue (Betty), Billy Gray (Bud), Lauren Chapin (Kathy), Hal England (Dr. Jason Harper), Jim McMullan (Frank Carlson), Susan Adams (Jeanne), Cari Anne Warder (Jenny), Christopher Gardner (Robbie Anderson), Kyle Richards (Ellen), Nellie Bellflower (Mary Beth), Noel Conlon (Reverend Lockwood).

271a. **Father Knows Best: Home for Christmas.** [Pilot #2]. NBC 12/18/77. 90 minutes. Columbia Pictures Television. Director: Marc Daniels. Executive Producer: Rene Valentee. Producer: Hugh Benson. Writer: Paul West. Music: George Duning.

Jim and Margaret Anderson are depressed about having to spend Christmas alone and the possibility they may have to sell their home. *Cast:* Robert Young (as Jim Anderson), Jane Wyatt (Margaret Anderson), Elinor Donahue (Betty), Lauren Chapin (Kathy), Billy Gray (Bud), Hal England (Dr. Jason Harper), Jim McMullan (Frank Carlson), Susan Adams (Jeanne), Cari Anne Warder (Jenny), Christopher Gardner (Robbie Anderson), Kyle Richards (Ellen), Stuart Lancaster (George Newman), June Whitley Taylor (Jan Newman), Priscilla Morrill (Louise).

272. [Gilligan's Island] [Pilot #1]. **Rescue From Gilligan's Island.** NBC 10/14/78 and 10/21/78. 2 hours. Redwood Productions and Paramount Television. Director: Leslie H. Martinson. Executive Producer/Creator: Sherwood Schwartz. Producer: Lloyd J. Schwartz. Writers: Sherwood

Schwartz, Elroy Schwartz, Al Schwartz, and David P. Harmon. Music: Gerald Fried. Theme: Sherwood Schwartz and George Wylie.

This revival pilot of the 1964—67 CBS series *Gilligan's Island* was the surprise smash hit of the 1979–80 season (30.4 rating/52 share), prompting a rash of series revivals and "reunion" shows—over fifty in all—that continued virtually unabated when the success of *Perry Mason Returns* in 1986 sparked a whole new wave of resurrections. In this, the first of three *Gilligan's Island* revival pilots, the castaways are swept out to sea by a tidal wave, are rescued, and return home to Hawaii, only to get shipwrecked on the same uncharted island during a reunion cruise a year later.

Cast: Alan Hale, Jr. (as the Skipper), Bob Denver (Gilligan), Jim Backus (Thurston Howell, III), Natalie Schafer (Lovey Howell), Dawn Wells (Mary Ann Summers), Russell Johnson (the Professor), Judith Baldwin (Ginger Grant), Vincent Schiavelli (Dimitri), June Whitley Taylor (Miss Ainsworth), Martin Ashe (Butler).

272a. [Gilligan's Island] [Pilot #2]. Castaways on Gilligan's Island. NBC 5/3/79. 90 minutes. Redwood Productions and Paramount Television. Director: Earl Bellamy. Executive Producer/Creator: Sherwood Schwartz. Producer: Lloyd J. Schwartz. Writers: Sherwood Schwartz, Elroy Schwartz, and Al Schwartz. Music: Gerald Fried. Theme: Sherwood Schwartz and George Wylie.

The hapless castaways find the remains of two planes and (a la *The Flight of the Phoenix*) use the parts from both to make one working aircraft. They once again leave their uncharted island. But this time, they intentionally return once more and, with millionaire Thurston Howell's money, open a resort hotel that purposefully lacks many of the modern amenities. The proposed series would spring, not unlike *The Love Boat*, from the interaction between the castaways and their many guests.

Cast: Alan Hale, Jr. (as the Skipper), Bob Denver (Gilligan), Jim Backus (Thurston Howell, III), Natalie Schafer (Lovey Howell), Dawn Wells (Mary Ann Summers), Russell Johnson (the Professor), Constance Forslund (Ginger Grant), David Ruprecht (Thurston Howell, IV), Tom Bosley (Henry Elliot), Marcia Wallace (Myra Elliot), Ronnie Scribner

(Robbie), Rod Browning (Tom Larsen), Lanna Saunders (Mrs. Sloan), Mokihana (Naheete), Joan Roberts (Laura Larsen).

272b. **[Gilligan's Island]** [Pilot #3], **Harlem Globetrotters on Gilligan's Island.** NBC 5/15/81. 2 hours. Redwood Productions and Paramount Television. Director: Peter Baldwin. Executive Producer/Creator: Sherwood Schwartz. Producer: Lloyd J. Schwartz. Writers: Sherwood Schwartz, Al Schwartz, David P. Harmon, and Gordon Mitchell. Music: Gerald Fried. Theme: Sherwood Schwartz and George Wylie.

The castaways and the Harlem Globetrotters battle an evil scientist (Martin Landau) and his army of robots who are after a rare mineral found only on the island. Originally, this was intended to feature the Dallas Cowboy Cheerleaders. The castaways later reappeared in animated form on the 1982–83 CBS Saturday morning series *Gilligan's Planet* and showed up in the flesh in 1987 on episodes of *The New Gidget* and *ALF.* A new incarnation, *Gilligan's Island II*, in which the children of the original castaways are themselves stranded on the island, was in the works in 1987 by Sherwood Schwartz for Superstation WTBS.

Cast: Alan Hale, Jr. (as the Skipper), Bob Denver (Gilligan), Jim Backus (Thurston Howell, III), Natalie Schafer (Lovey Howell), Dawn Wells (Mary Ann Summers), Russell Johnson (the Professor), Constance Forslund (Ginger Grant), David Ruprecht (Thurston Howell, IV), Dreama Denver (Lucinda), Rosalind Chao (Manager), Martin Landau (J.J. Pierson), Barbara Bain (Olga Schmetner), Whitney Rydbeck (George), Scatman Crothers (Dewey Stevens), Chick Hearn (Sportscaster), Bruce Biggs (Referee), Cindy Appleton (Linda), Wendy Hoffman (Jackie).

273. **Gunsmoke: Return to Dodge.** [Pilot #1]. CBS 9/26/87. 2 hours. CBS Entertainment. Director: Vincent McEveety. Executive Producer: John Mantley. Supervising Producer: Stan Hough. Writer: Jim Byrnes. Music: Jerrold Immel.

After twelve years, Matt Dillon is back—only now he's a former marshal, a mountain man urged back to action when an old adversary, Will Mannon, returns to Dodge City seeking vengeance. Miss Kitty has sold the Long Branch Saloon to Miss Hannah and Newly O'Brien is the new marshal, but it's still the *Gunsmoke* we know and love. And it's only fitting that the longest running series in TV history should also be the basis for the best of all the television revival shows, vividly enhanced with flashbacks to episodes (from 1969 and 1970) involving earlier encounters between Matt Dillon and the villainous Mannon, as well as Kitty's decision to leave Dodge City. This revival, unlike most, was mounted by the series' original creative team—producer Mantley, director McEveety, and frequent *Gunsmoke* writer Jim Byrnes. The one change: shooting was done in Calgary—TV's "new" Old West.

Cast: James Arness (Matt Dillon), Amanda Blake (Kitty Russell), Buck Taylor (Newly O'Brien), Fran Ryan (Miss Hannah), Steve Forrest (Will Mannon), Earl Holliman (Jake Flagg), Ken Olandt (Lt. Dexter), Patrice Martinez (Bright Water), Tantoo Cardinal (Little Doe), W. Morgan Sheppard (Digger), Mickey Jones (Oakum), Frank M. Totino (Logan), Robert Koons (Warden Brown), Walter Kaasa (Judge Collins), Tony Epper (Farnum), Louie Ellias (Bubba), Ken Kirzinger (Potts), Denny Arnold (Clyman), Alex Green (The Flogger).

273a. Gunsmoke: The Last Apache. [Pilot #2]. CBS 3/19/90. 2 hours. CBS Entertainment. Director: Charles Correll. Executive Producer: John Mantley. Producer: Stan Hough. Writer: Earl Wallace. Music: Bruce Rowland.

James Arness saddles up again and goes on the warpath with tough Army scout Chalk Brighton when a renegade Apache named Wolf abducts the daughter Matt Dillon never knew he had—the result of a longago love affair with Mike Yardner (Michael Learned, repeating her role from a 1973 *Gunsmoke* episode). Once again, flashbacks from the earlier episode give this one (as with the 1987 revival pilot) a unique poignancy, thanks to old hands like Mantley, Stan Hough (who died just before this one aired) and former *Gunsmoke* story editor Wallace, who wrote this one. Missing from this episode, sadly, was Amanda Blake, who had died since the earlier pilot and to whom this one was dedicated. It was nice, however, to see Hugh O'Brian, TV's erstwhile Wyatt Earp, turning up as a guest star with pal Jim Arness. Three more *Gunsmoke* revival movies were made: *Gunsmoke: To The Last Man* (1992), *The Long Ride* (1993) and *One Man's Justice* (1994).

Cast: James Arness (Matt Dillon), Richard Kiley (Chalk Brighton), Michael Learned (Mike Yardner), Joe Lara (Wolf), Amy Stock-Poynton (Beth Yardner), Geoffrey Lewis (Bodine), Joaquin Martinez (Geronimo), Peter Murnik (Lt. Davis), Sam Vlahos (Tomas), Ned Bellamy (Capt. Harris), Robert Covarrubias (Bartender), David Florek (Smiley), Kevin Sifuentes (Nachite)

274. The Incredible Hulk Returns (aka Thor). NBC 5/22/88. 2 hours. B&B Productions and New World Television. Director/Writer: Nicholas Corea. Executive Producers: Nicholas Corea and Bill Bixby. Producer: Daniel McPhee. Creator: Kenneth Johnson, based on the Marvel Comics character. Music: Lance Rubin.

New World Pictures and NBC used a revival of *The Incredible Hulk* (CBS 1978–82) as a ploy to launch *Thor*, a proposed series starring Steve Levitt as an anthropology student who discovers a magic hammer which allows him to conjure up Thor (Eric Kramer), a Viking warrior, with whom he teams to fight crime. Thor comes crashing into Banner's life just as he, now working for a high-tech corporation, is about to cure himself with a new bolt of gamma radiation. ("He's been seething for six long years," blared the ads, "tonight, the incredible explosion!") But bad guys kidnap Banner's girlfriend (Lee Purcell), dogged reporter McGee (Jack Colvin) comes snooping, and Banner finds himself back on the run again. Although this pilot didn't sell, the stellar ratings of this revival prompted NBC to buy several sequel movies also designed to spin-off Marvel Comics characters. A second revival/pilot, *Trial of the Incredible Hulk*, was directed by star Bill Bixby, who costarred with Rex Smith as Daredevil, a blind attorney by day and a caped crime-fighter by night. A third pilot, *Death of the Incredible Hulk*, aired on NBC in 1990. ABC commissioned a *She-Hulk* pilot script from writer Jill Donner, but later abandoned the project over casting difficulties.

Cast: Bill Bixby (as David Banner), Lou Ferrigno (Hulk), Jack Colvin (Jack McGee), Steve Levitt (Donald Blake), Eric Kramer (Thor), Lee Purcell (Maggie Shaw), Tim Thomerson (Jack LeBeau), also Charles

Napier, William Riley, Tom Finnegan, Donald Willis, Carl Nick Ciafalio, Bobby Travis McLaughlin, Burke Denis, Nick Costa, Peisha McPhee, William Malone, Joanie Allen.

275. Kung Fu: The Movie (aka The Return of Kung Fu). [Pilot #1]. CBS 2/1/86. 2 hours. Lou-Step Productions and Warner Bros. Television. Director: Richard Lang. Executive Producer: Paul R. Picard. Producers: Skip Ward and David Carradine. Writer: Durrell Royce Crays, from the TV series created by Ed Spielman and developed by Herman Miller. Music: Lalo Schifrin.

An attempt to revive *Kung Fu*, the 1972–75 ABC series. David Carradine once again is Kwai Chang Caine, the soft-spoken Shaolin priest who fled 19th century China after being forced to kill an Imperial Manchu's son. Caine became a loner, roaming the Old West, pursued by Chinese assassins and American bounty hunters. He hated violence, but when necessary, he relied on the deadly art of Kung Fu and other teachings of Master Po (Keye Luke), his blind mentor in China. In the pilot, Caine's framed for murder, accidentally uncovers an opium smuggling ring, and the assassins he's eluded in the series catch up with him—The Manchu Lord and his deadly servant Chung Wang. CBS and producer Paul Picard later updated *Kung Fu* to the present day for 1987–88's unsold pilot *Way of the Dragon* (aka *Kung Fu: The Next Generation* and *Warriors*), which focused on Caine's Chinese-American namesake and descendant, played by David Darlow. The two concepts would be combined in *Kung Fu: The Legend Continues*, a 1993-1997 syndicated series that starred David Carradine as a modern-day descendent of Caine who teams up with his estranged son, a cop played by Chris Potter, to fight crime.

Cast: David Carradine (as Kwai Chang Caine), Kerrie Keane (Sarah Perkins), Mako (The Manchu), William Lucking (Wyatt), Luke Askew (Sheriff Mills), Keye Luke (Master Po), Benson Fong (The Old One), Brandon Lee (Chung Wang), Martin Landau (John Martin Perkins), Ellen Geer (Old Wife), Robert Harper (Prosecutor), Paul Rudd (Rev. Lawrence Perkins), John Alderman (Well-Dressed Man), Michael Paul Chan (Ching), Patience Cleveland (Maid), Roland Harrah, III (Liu), Jim Haynie (Federal Marshal), Roy Jenson (Foreman).

275a. Kung Fu: The Next Generation (aka Way of the Dragon; aka Warriors). [Pilot #2]. CBS 6/19/87. 60 minutes. Warner Bros. Television. Director: Tony Wharmby. Executive Producers: Paul Picard and Ralph Riskin. Producers/Writers: Paul DiMeo and Danny Bilson, from the series *Kung Fu*, created by Ed Spielman and developed by Herman Miller. Music: Stanley Clarke.

Aired as a segment of *CBS Summer Playhouse*. David Darlow stars as the modern-day descendant of the character David Carradine played in the Western series *Kung Fu*. Like his ancestor, this Caine is a gentle man who espouses inner peace and lives modestly-he teaches Kung Fu, sells herbs, and helps people in trouble. Perhaps the person needing help most is his estranged son Johnny (Brandon Lee), who became a gang member, served a short jail term for burglary, and, in the pilot, hooks up with some dangerous criminals. But thanks to a ghostly visit from the original Caine, Johnny turns away from crime and adopts his father's altruistic life-style.

Cast: David Darlow (as Kwai Chang Caine), Brandon Lee (Johnny Caine), Miguel Ferrer (Mick), Paula Kelly (Lt. Lois Poole), Marcia Christie (Ellen), Victor Brandt (Buckley), Dominic Barto (Carl Levin), John C. Cooke (Cliff), Aaron Heyman (Sid), Eddie Mack (Rob), Michael Walter (Dave), Richard Duran (Raul), Michael Gilles (Security Cop), Neil Flynn (L.A.P.D. Officer), Mark Everett (Student), Oscar Dillon (Darnell).

276. Lassie: A New Beginning. ABC 9/17/78 and 9/24/78. 2 hours. McDermott/Wrather Productions. Director: Don Chaffey. Executive Producer: Tom McDermott. Producers: Jack Miller and William Beaudine, Jr. Writer/Creator: Jack Miller. Music: Jerrold Immel.

This attempt to fashion a new *Lassie* series has a complicated back-story. There were two brothers in love with the same woman—and she chose one of them. The other moves west and cuts himself off from his family. Now, years later, the couple is killed in an accident, leaving orphaned their fourteen-year-old son (Shane Sinutko), nine-year-old daughter (Sally Boyden), and their pet dog Lassie. The grandmother takes the two kids and their pet to live with their bachelor uncle (John Reilly), editor of a small-town newspaper, but she dies on the way.

Cast: John Reilly (as Stuart Stratton), Sally Boyden (Sally Stratton), Shane Sinutko (Chip Stratton), Lee Bryant (Kathy McKendrick), David Wayne (Dr. Amos Rheams), Gene Evans (Sheriff Marsh), Jeff Harlan (Buzz McKendrick), Jeanette Nolan (Ada Stratton), John McIntire (Dr. Spreckles), Charles Tyner (Asa Bluel), Jim Antonio (Mr. Waldrop), Gwen Van Dam (Mrs. Waldrop), Woodrow Chambliss (Victor Turley), Lucille Benson (Juno), Logan Ramsey (Flannagan), Helen Page Camp (Miss Tremayne).

277. The Losers. NBC 1/15/63. 60 minutes. Four Star. Director/Creator: Sam Peckinpah. Executive Producer: Dick Powell. Producers: Sam Peckinpah, Bruce Geller, and Bernard L. Kowalski. Associate Producer: Stanley Kallis. Writer: Bruce Geller, from a story by Geller and Sam Peckinpah. Music: Herschel Burke Gilbert.

Aired as an episode of *Dick Powell Theatre,* which was guest-hosted by Charles Boyer. An attempt to update and revive Peckinpah's shortlived series *The Westerner,* which survived for a mere thirteen episodes in 1960 and starred Brian Keith as Dave Blassingame, a footloose cowboy who wandered the Old West with his dog Brown and—sometimes—cowardly con man Burgundy Smith (John Dehner). It's become something of a cult classic, its demise blamed on its violence and "adult" attitude. The same production team that produced the series was responsible for this pilot, set in the present with a light tone reminiscent of *Maverick.* Lee Marvin is Dave Blassingame, a drifter who wanders the country accompanied by his dog Brown and con man Burgundy Smith, played by Keenan Wynn. In the pilot, they are pursued by thugs they bilked in a poker game and, while on the move, befriend a blind gospel singer and his orphan companion and hide out with an ornery farmer and his shy daughter.

Cast: Lee Marvin (as Dave Blassingame), Keenan Wynn (Burgundy Smith), Rosemary Clooney (Melissa), Adam Lazarre (Blind Johnny), Michael Davis (Tim), Mike Mazurki (Mr. Anston), Dub Taylor (Gregory), Carmen Phillips (Jeen), Elaine Walker (Diedre), Jack Perkins (Farr), Charles Horvath (Mulana), Paul Stader (Monroe), Kelly Thordsen (Frank Davis), Russ Brown (Isaiah).

278. Make More Room for Daddy. NBC 11/6/61. 60 minutes. Danny Thomas Productions. Director: Sheldon Leonard. Producer: Danny Thomas. Writers: Jack Elinson and Norman Paul. Music: Earle Hagen.

Aired as an episode of the *Danny Thomas Hour*. A pilot for a proposed continuation of the hit series *Make Room for Daddy* for the one network the show had never run on—NBC. The original series ran on ABC from 1953–57, then jumped to CBS, where it stayed until 1964. In this pilot, Danny Thomas returns as nightclub entertainer Danny Williams, and Marjorie Lord again plays his second wife, Kathy. Danny's son Rusty (Rusty Hamer) gets married to the daughter (Jana Taylor) of an Army colonel, while Kathy's daughter Linda (Angela Cartwright) begins college. Oddly, two years after this pilot was junked, Thomas did another for a continuation for CBS, which passed on it as a series. A year later, though, the series turned up on ABC as *Make Room for Granddaddy* (with Sherry Jackson returning as daughter Terry, a role she played on the original series for the first few seasons) and managed to limp through one season.

Cast: Danny Thomas (as Danny Williams), Marjorie Lord (Kathy Williams), Rusty Hamer (Rusty Williams), Angela Cartwright (Linda Williams), Jana Taylor (Susan McAdams Williams), Sid Melton (Charlie Halper), Amanda Randolph (Louise), Edward Andrews "(Col. McAdams).

279. Man on a String. CBS 2/18/72. 90 minutes. Screen Gems. Director: Joseph Sargent. Producers: Douglas Cramer and Joseph Goodson. Writer: Ben Maddows.

A revamped version of *Tightrope*, a short-lived 1960 series the production company won't let die. They tried reviving it several times (see *The New Tightrope* and *The Expendables*) in the two or three seasons that followed the cancellation and then let it die—until 1972. Christopher George is an undercover agent working for William Schallert, the leader of a super-secret government organization.

Cast: Christopher George (as Pete King), William Schallert (William Connaught), Michael Baselson (Mickey Brown), Keith Carradine (Danny

Brown), Joel Grey (Big Joe Brown), Kitty Winn (Angela Canyon), Paul Hampton (Cowboy), Jack Warden (Jake Moniker), J. Duke Russo (Carlo Buglione), Jack Bernardi (Counterman), Lincoln Demyan (Billy Prescott), Bob Golden (Motor Officer), Jerome Guardino (Scarred Man), Byron Morrow (Judge), Carolyn Nelson (Anita), James Sikking (Pipe Smoker), Richard Yniguez (Officer Jack), Garry Walberg (Sergeant).

280. The Munsters' Revenge. NBC 2/27/81. 2 hours. Universal Television. Director: Don Weis. Executive Producer: Edward J. Montagne. Producers/Writers: Don Nelson and Arthur Alsberg. Music: Vic Mizzy.

A plodding revival of *The Munsters*, with Herman, Lily, and Grandpa. The family is wanted for crimes committed by a mad scientist's (Sid Caesar) robots, which look just like them. A new version of the sitcom, entitled *The Munsters Today*, with an entirely new cast, was launched in 1988 by Universal Television and the Arthur Company for first-run syndication.

Cast: Fred Gwynne (as Herman Munster), Yvonne DeCarlo (Lily Munster), Al Lewis (Grandpa), Jo McDonnell (Marilyn Munster), K.C. Martel (Eddie Munster), Sid Caesar (Dr. Diablo/Emil Hornshymier), Bob Hastings (Phantom of the Opera), Howard Morris (Igor), Herbert Voland (Chief Harry Boyle), Peter Fox (Detective Glen Boyle), Charles Macauley (Commissioner McClusky), Colby Chester (Michael), Michael McManus (Ralph), Joseph Ruskin (Pizza Man), Ezra Stone (Dr. Licklider), Billy Sands (Shorty), Gary Vinson (Officer Leary), Barry Pearl (Warren Thurston), Al C. White (Prisoner), Tom Newman (Slim), Anita Dangler (Elvira), Dolores Mann (Mrs. Furnston).

281. Murder in Peyton Place. NBC 10/3/77. 2 hours. Twentieth Century Fox Television and Peter Katz Productions. Director: Bruce Kessler. Producer: Peter Katz. Writer: Richard DeRoy. Creator: Grace Metalious. Music: Laurence Rosenthal.

An attempt to revive the 1964—69 serial. In this pilot, Rodney Harrington (played originally by Ryan O'Neal) and Alison MacKenzie (Mia Farrow)—in clips from the original series—are killed and everyone wants to know why. Another attempt was made to continue the series in 1986's *Peyton Place: The Next Generation.*

Cast. Christopher Connelly (as Norman), Tim O'Connor (Elliot Carson), Ed Nelson (Dr. Rossi), Dorothy Malone (Constance), Joyce Jillson (Jill), Janet Margolin (Betty), David Hedison (Steven Cord), Stella Stevens (Stella Chernak), Marj Dusay (Ellen), James Booth (Crimpton), Jonathan Goldsmith (Stan), Charlotte Stewart (Denise Haley), Kaz Garas (Springer), Linda Gray (Carla Cord), Kimberly Beck (Bonnie Buehler), Royal Dano (Bo Buehler), Priscilla Morrill (Mae Buehler), David Kyle (Billie Kaiserman), Norman Burton (Jay Kamens), Charles Siebert (Kaiserman), Chris Nelson (Andy Considine), Robert Deman (Tristan), Gale Sladstone (Ruth), Catherine Bach (Linda), Edward Bell (David Roerich).

282. **The New Maverick.** ABC 9/3/78. 2 hours. Warner Bros. Television and Cherokee Productions. Director: Hy Averback. Executive Producer: Meta Rosenberg. Producer: Bob Foster. Writer: Juanita Bartlett, based on characters created by Roy Huggins. Music: John Rubinstein.

A revival of ABC's old *Maverick* series, which ran from 1957–62 and featured James Garner and Jack Kelly as two brothers who are crafty gamblers roaming the West in the 1880s. Both are on hand to introduce young Ben Maverick (Charles Frank), the Harvard-educated son of their Cousin Beau (played by Roger Moore in the original series). In the pilot, the Mavericks become involved in a plot by a larcenous judge to steal a shipment of rifles. ABC turned it down, but CBS later reworked the concept as *Young Maverick* and commissioned a new pilot, which spawned a disastrously short-lived series. That didn't stop NBC from trying its own *Maverick* sequel—*Bret Maverick*, which starred James Garner and lasted one season.

Cast: Charles Frank (as Ben Maverick), Susan Blanchard (Nell McGarrahan), James Garner (Bret Maverick), Jack Kelly (Bart Maverick), Eugene Roche (Judge Crupper), Susan Sullivan (Poker Alice), Jack Garner (Homer), Graham Jarvis (Lambert), Helen Page Camp (Flora Crupper), George Loros (Vinnie), Woodrow Parfrey (Levesque), Gary Allen (Dobie).

283. The New Millionaire. CBS 12/19/78. 2 hours. Don Fedderson Productions. Director: Don Weis. Producer/Creator: Don Fedderson. Writer: John McGreevey. Music: Frank DeVol.

An attempted revival of *The Millionaire* (1955–60) with Robert Quarry taking over Marvin Miller's role as Michael Anthony, the executive secretary who delivers million-dollar cashier's checks to unsuspecting people picked at random by the unseen, mysterious tycoon John Beresford Tipton. This pilot, like the original series, follows the fortunes of people once they get a million tax-free dollars.

Cast: Robert Quarry (as Michael Anthony), Martin Balsam (Arthur Haines), Edward Albert (Paul Matthews), Bill Hudson (Eddie Reardon), Mark Hudson (Mike Reardon), Brett Hudson (Harold Reardon), Pat Crowley (Maggie Haines), Pamela Toll (Kate Matthews), Allan Rich (George Jelks), John Ireland (Marshall Wayburn), Ralph Bellamy (George Matthews), Jane Wyatt (Mrs. Matthews), William Demarest (Oscar Pugh), Talia Balsam (Doreen), Michael Minor (Clark), Milt Kogan (Parker), Sally Kemp (Judge), Patricia Hindy (Dorothy), P.R. Paul (Alan), Ann Greer (Cory).

284. The New Tightrope. [Pilot #1]. ABC 1961 60 minutes. Producers: Clarence Greene and Russell Rouse.

An hour-long revamp of the half-hour CBS series. Mike Connors would again star as undercover agent Nick Stone. Quinn Reddecker would costar. The producers and Connors tried this once more the following season under the title *The Expendables*.

284a. The Expendables. [Pilot #2]. CBS 9/27/62. 60 minutes. Screen Gems. Producers: Clarence Greene and Russell Rouse.

Yet another attempt to revive the old CBS series *Tightrope*, this time with original star Mike Connors and costars Zachary Scott and Dina Merrill.

285. Peter Gunn. ABC 4/23/89. 2 hours. Blake Edwards Company and New World Television. Director/Writer/Creator: Blake Edwards.

Executive Producers: Blake Edwards and Tony Adams. Music: Henry Mancini.

It looked at the outset like a blueprint for disaster: revive a classic television series and have not a single member of the original cast. The late 1980s *Peter Gunn* would be Peter Strauss, taking over for Craig Stevens as the suave private eye whose "office" is a cocktail lounge known as Mother's. Happily, Strauss more than ably fills the bill. He plays the urbane Gunn with all the expected debonair charm—a sly attitude and even a little self-parody as he hunts down a vigilante group of rogue cops. One of its memorable moments is an unusually realistic, refreshingly amusing fight scene that's anything but the smoothly choreographed interludes of fisticuffs that television—and Peter Gunn—are known for. Aided by a tight, humor-filled script by Blake Edwards, who put his stamp on television with the original show; the memorable Mancini music, for what would an Edwards project be without Mancini; and strong performances by Peter Jurasik in the late Herschel Bernardi's part of Lt. Jacoby, Barbara Williams as Gunn's chanteuse girlfriend Edie (the old Lola Albright part), and Pearl Bailey in a rare TV acting role—her last (inspired casting in the late Hope Emerson's trademarked "Mother" part), *Peter Gunn* was a winning hand. ABC made the mistake of passing on it.

Cast. Peter Strauss (Peter Gunn), Peter Jurasik (Lt. Jacoby), Barbara Williams (Edie), Jennifer Edwards (Maggie), Pearl Bailey (Mother), Charles Cioffi (Tony Amatti), Richard Portnow (Spiros), Debra Sandlund (Sheila), David Rappaport (Speck), Leo Rossi (Det. Russo), Tony Longo (Sgt. Holmstead), Jeffrey Allan Chandler (Abe Greenspan), Eddie Zammit (Johnny Stefano), J. J. Johnson (Barney), Jeremy Roberts (Slick), Vito D'Ambrosio (Futsy)

286. **Police Story (aka Police Story: The Freeway Killings).** NBC 5/3/87. 3 hours. David Gerber Productions, MGM/UA Television, and Columbia Pictures Television. Director: William A. Graham. Executive Producer: David Gerber. Producer: Charles B. FitzSimons. Writer: Mark Rodgers. Creator: Joseph Wambaugh, developed by E. Jack Neuman. Music: John Cacavas. Theme: Jerry Goldsmith.

An attempt to revive the 1973–77 NBC anthology *Police Story*, which continued as a series of TV movies for a season after its cancellation. Following the proven concept, the pilot mixed internal police politics, the troubled personal lives of police officers, and the hunt for a serial killer, with a cast comprised of frequent *Police Story* guest stars. Several more *Police Story* movies, remakes of the old episodes, were produced for ABC during the 1988 Writers Guild strike.

Cast: Richard Crenna (as Deputy Chief Bob Devers), Angie Dickinson (Officer Anne Cavanaugh), Ben Gazzara (Capt. Tom Wright), Tony Lo Bianco (Detective DiAngelo), Don Meredith (Detective Foley), James B. Sikking (Major Cameron), Gloria Loring (Kate Devers), Scott Paulin (Lt. Todd Bannion), Frances Lee McCain (Clare Wright), Vincent Baggetta (Paul Harris), Michael C. Gywnne (Calvin), Joan McMurtrey (Joan Manning), Julie Phillips (Carrie Wright), Rob Knepper (Karl Jones), Marc Alaimo (Morello), Sam Vlahos (Diaz), Javier Graieda (Garcia), Ken Hixon (Hallett), Louise Shaffer (Laura Henley), Freddye Chapman (Mary Morris), Michael Griswold (Al Nader), Julie Ariole (Test Examiner), Carlos Cervantes (Chico), Hawthorn James (Reverend Johnson), Kamala Lopez (Lydia Chacon), Murray Leward (Max), Susie Chan (Kim), Steve Kahan (Paulis), Tony Perez (Capt. Rodriquez), Wendy Cooke (Marna), James Hess (Chairman), Charles FitzSimons, Jr. (Tony).

287. The Return of Frank Cannon. CBS 11/1/80. 2 hours. Quinn Martin Productions. Director: Corey Allen. Executive Producer: Quinn Martin. Producer: Michael Rhodes. Writers: James David Buchanan and Ronald Austin. Music: Bruce Broughton. Theme: John Parker.

An attempt to revive *Cannon*, the 1971–76 CBS series about overweight private eye Frank Cannon (William Conrad), who tooled around Los Angeles in a Lincoln Continental and had a taste for gourmet food. Now Cannon has opened up his own restaurant, and instead of chasing crooks, he hits the high seas to catch fish for his cook (James Hong) to prepare. But Cannon becomes a detective once again (hunting down clues in his Lincoln convertible) when an old C.I.A. buddy's suicide looks more like murder. In the proposed series, Cannon would double as restaurateur and P.I. *People* magazine said the plot of this pilot "lumbers along as heavily as its star."

Cast: William Conrad (as Frank Cannon), James Hong (Yutong), Diana Muldaur (Sally Bingham), Joanna Pettet (Alana Richardson), Ed Nelson (Mike Danvers), Burr DeBenning (Charles Kirkland), Arthur Hill (Curtis McDonald), Allison Argo (Jessica Bingham), Taylor Lacher (Lew Garland), William Smithers (William Barrett), Hank Brandt (Pearson).

288. **Kojak: The Belarus File (aka The Return of Kojak).** [Pilot # 1]. CBS 2/15/85. 2 hours. Universal Television. Director: Robert Markowitz. Executive Producer: James McAdams. Producer/Writer: Albert Ruben. Creator: Abby Mann, from a book by Selwin Raab. Music: Joseph Conlan and Barry DeVorzon.

An attempt to revive the series *Kojak*, which ran from 1973–78. He's still a tough N.Y.P.D. detective bucking bureaucrats while baring down on his hard-working staff, which once again includes Stavros (George Savalas), Rizzo (Vince Conti), and Saperstein (Mark B. Russell). Even Capt. McNeil (Dan Frazer) shows up. Notably absent is Crocker, Theo Kojak's young protégé, played by Kevin Dobson, who was tied up as a regular on *Knots Landing* when this was made. In the pilot, Kojak's friend (Max Von Sydow) may be involved in the murders of three suspected Nazi war criminals living in New York. Suzanne Pleshette is a concerned State Department official who helps Kojak obtain crucial information—contained in the so-called Belarus file—that the agency won't reveal. John Loftus, author of *The Belarus Secret*, was technical advisor. A second pilot, *Kojak: The Price of Justice*, was made in 1987, and a new series of two-hour TV movies was commissioned for ABC in 1989. Both pilots were shot in New York.

Cast: Telly Savalas (Lt. Theo Kojak), Max Von Sydow (Peter Barak), Suzanne Pleshette (Dana Sutton), Betsy Aidem (Elissa Barak), Alan Rosenberg (Lustig), Herbert Berghof (Buchardt), Charles Brown (Julius Gay), David Leary (Chris Kennert), George Savalas (Stavros), Mark B. Russell (Saperstein), Vince Conti (Rizzo), Dan Frazer (Capt. Frank McNeil), Clarence Felder (Kelly), Adam Klugman (Morgan), Rita Karin (Mrs. Fitzev), Harry Davis (Rabbi), Margaret Thomson (Secretary),

Otto Von Wernherr (Bodyguard), James Handy (First Federal Agent), Dan Lauria (Second Federal Agent).

288a. Kojak: The Price of Justice (aka The Return of Kojak). [Pilot #2]. CBS. 2/21/87. 2 hours. Universal Television. Director: Alan Metzger. Executive Producer: James McAdams. Producer: Stuart Cohen. Writer: Albert Ruben, from the book by Dorothy Uhnak. Creator: Abby Mann, from a book by Selwin Raab. Music: Patrick Williams.

A second attempt to revive *Kojak*, this time melding the character to a crime book based vaguely on New York's notorious Alice Crimmins case. Theo is now an inspector heading an N.Y.P.D. Major Crime Unit. In the pilot, Kojak investigates charges that a woman (Kate Nelligan) murdered her children while they slept. John Bedford-Lloyd is Kojak's new protégé. Shot on location in New York.

Cast: Telly Savalas (as Inspector Theo Kojak), Kate Nelligan (Kitty Keeler), Pat Hingle (George Keeler), Jack Thompson (Aubrey Dubose), Brian Murray (Tim Neary), John Bedford-Lloyd (Milton Bass), Jeffrey DeMunn (Marsucci), Tony DiBenedetto (Det. Catalano), Ron Frazier (J.T. Williams), Stephen Joyce (Chief Brisco), Earl Hindman (Danny), James Rebhorn (Quibro), Martin Shakar (Arnold Nadler), Joseph Carberry (Lorenzo), Fausto Bara (Benjamin), Novella Nelson (Mrs. Silverberg), Kenneth Ryan (Johnson), Candace Savalas (Anna).

289. The Return of Marcus Welby, M.D. (aka Jennings and Jennings: A Family Practice). ABC 5/16/84. 2 hours. Marstar Productions and Universal Television. Director: Alexander Singer. Executive Producer: Martin Starger. Producers: Dennis Doty, Michael Braverman, and Howard Alston. Writers: John McGreevey and Michael Braverman. Creator: David Victor. Music: Leonard Rosenman.

A revival of *Marcus Welby, M.D.* aimed at launching a different but similarly themed show, entitled *Jennings and Jennings: A Family Practice*, in which Robert Young would occasionally appear. In the pilot, Marcus Welby fights to retain his accreditation at the hospital where he now works. The proposed series would focus on Dr. David Jennings (Darren McGavin), a doctor who believes, as Dr. Welby does, that he has a responsibility to his patients that extends beyond mere diagnosis and treatment. Jennings opens a practice with his son (Morgan Stevens) and hires Welby's nurse (Elena Verdugo). On some cases, Jennings would work with a husband-and-wife team of pediatricians (Dennis Haysbert and Cyndi James-Reese). In 1989, *Marcus Welby: A Holiday Affair* was broadcast on NBC to lackluster ratings.

Cast: Robert Young (as Dr. Marcus Welby), Elena Verdugo (Nurse Consuelo Lopez), Darren McGavin (Dr. David Jennings), Morgan Stevens (Dr. Matt Jennings), Dennis Haysbert (Dr. Hoover Beaumont), Cyndi James-Reese (Phaedra Beaumont), Jessica Walter (Astrid Carlisle), Yvonne Wilder (Dr. Nina Velasquez), Cristina Raines (Nikki St. Hilliare), Joanna Kerns (Pamela Saletta), Katherine DeHetre (Francine Parnell), Milt Kogan (Perry McMasters), Robert Carnegie (Dr. Ingram), Milt Oberman (Joel Silvers), Nicholas Hormann (Kevin Saletta), Fran Ryan (Millie Clark), Jacqueline Hyde (Fanny Glickman).

290. The Return of Mod Squad. ABC 5/18/79. 2 hours. Spelling/ Thomas Productions. Director: George McCowan. Executive Producers: Aaron Spelling and Danny Thomas. Producer: Lynn Loring. Writer: Robert Janes. Music: Mark Snow, Shorty Rogers, and Earle Hagen.

An attempt at reviving the 1968–73 ABC series *The Mod Squad,* which followed the adventures of Pete Cochran (Michael Cole), Julie Barnes (Peggy Lipton), and Line Hayes (Clarence Williams III)— three young people of the "Flower Power" generation who are arrested and drafted into a special unit of the police department, headed by no-nonsense cop Adam Greer (Tige Andrews), that infiltrates hippie organizations. In the new pilot, businessman Pete, housewife-and-mother Julie, and school teacher Line reunite to find a hit man who is after Greer, who is now deputy police commissioner.

Cast: Michael Cole (as Pete Cochran), Peggy Lipton (Julie Barnes-Bennett), Clarence Williams, III (Line Hayes), Tige Andrews (Deputy Commissioner Greer), Simon Scott (Commissioner Metcalf), Roy Thinnes (Dan Bennett), Todd Bridges (Jason Hayes), Ross Martin (Buck Prescott), Victor Buono (Johnny Starr), Mark Slade (Richie Webber), Tom Bosley (Frank Webber), Tom Ewell (Cook), John Karlen (Marty),

Jess Walton (Kate Kelsey), Taylor Lacher (Jake), Rafael Campos (Johnny Sorella), Byron Stewart (Bingo), Hope Holliday (Willie).

291. The Return of Sam McCloud. CBS 11/12/89. 2 hours. Michael Sloan Productions and Universal Television. Director: Alan J. Levi. Executive Producers: Michael Sloan and Dennis Weaver. Producers: Nigel Watts and Bernadette Joyce. Writer: Michael Sloan. Creator: Herman Miller. Music: Steve Dorff

Sam McCloud, the country cop from Taos, New Mexico, who found himself a member of the N.Y.P.D., returns as a homespun United States Senator, enlisting the aid of his old colleague Joe Broadhurst, now chief of detectives, and their cantankerous former boss Peter Clifford, now police chief, to help bring down the corrupt chemical company that had his niece killed. (Even Diana Muldaur returned from the earlier series, now as a *London Times* correspondent.) Most of the action in this pilot takes place in London, where location filming was done. The charm of the original series was completely lost in this reprise, a victim of the baffling decision to scrap the old show's homespun premise in favor of making McCloud a crime-fighting politician. Patrick Macnee (John Steed from *The Avengers*) and David McCallum (Ilya Kuryakin from *The Man From U.N.C.L.E.*) guest star.

Cast: Dennis Weaver (Sam McCloud), Terry Carter (Chief Joe Broadhurst), J.D. Cannon (Peter B. Clifford), Diana Muldaur (Chris Coughlin), Kerrie Keane (Ashley Stevens), Patrick Macnee (Tom Jamison), David McCallum (Inspector Craig), Melissa Anderson (Colleen), Roger Rees (Jason Cross), Simon Williams (Simon Langton), Sondra Currie (Rachel), Robert Beatty (William Maitland), Michael Cochrane (Geraint Davies), Patrick Monckton (Jack Barron), John Turner (McFarland), Ricco Ross (Rifkin), Linda Hay den (Nancy Cratchett), Mel Cobb (John Bishop), also Simon Tudor Owen, Hilary Crane, Ian Taylor, Raymond Marlowe, Alan Polonsky, Adam Richardson, Maxine Howe, Keith Nichols, Paul Stanton.

292. Return of the Beverly Hillbillies (aka Beverly Hillbillies Solve the Energy Crisis). CBS 10/6/81. 2 hours. CBS Entertainment. Director:

Robert Leeds. Executive Producers: Albert J. Simon and Ron Beckman. Producer/Writer: Paul Henning. Music: Billy May.

The Clampetts, the hillbilly family that struck oil in the Ozarks and moved to Beverly Hills, return pretty much intact (Irene Ryan, the original Granny, had died, and Max Baer, the original Jethro, had gotten out of acting to become a producer/director) to solve the energy crisis for Energy Department Official Jane Hathaway (Nancy Kulp) with Granny's moonshine. Ray Young steps in as the new Jethro, and Imogene Coca guest stars as Granny's one-hundred-year-old mother.

Cast: Buddy Ebsen (as Jed Clampett), Donna Douglas (Elly May), Nancy Kulp (Jane Hathaway), Ray Young (Jethro Bodine), Imogene Coca (Granny), Werner Klemperer (C.D. Medford), Linda Henning (Linda), King Donovan (Andy Miller), Lurene Tuttle (Mollie Heller), Charles Lane (Chief), Shug Fisher (Judge Gillum), Howard Culver (Veterinarian), Heather Locklear (Heather), also Shad Heller, Earl Scruggs, Nancy Gayle, Dana Kimmell, Fenton Jones, John Hartford, Rodney Dillard, Buddy Van Horn.

293. The Return of the Greatest American Hero (aka Another Great American Hero; aka A New Great American Hero; aka Greatest American Heroine). NBC. 20 minutes. Stephen J. Cannell Productions. Director: Tony Mordente. Executive Producers: Stephen J. Cannell and Babs Greyhosky. Producer: Jo Swerling, Jr. Writer: Babs Greyhosky. Creator: Stephen J. Cannell. Music: Mike Post and Pete Carpenter.

A demonstration film aimed at sparking a revamped version of the ABC series *The Greatest American Hero* for the 7:00–8:00 Sunday evening time slot (that eventually went to *Our House*). The original series followed schoolteacher Ralph Hinkley (William Katt), who was given a superhero suit by benevolent aliens he had stumbled upon and fought crime with conservative F.B.I. agent Bill Maxwell (Robert Culp). Now, the aliens give the suit to a young woman (Mary Ellen Stuart), also a schoolteacher and a foster parent (to Mya Akerling), and she, too, fights baddies with Maxwell's help. The demo film was later combined with excerpts from previous episodes, dubbed *Greatest American Heroine*, and added to the syndication package. Jerry Potter and John Zee guest starred.

294. The Return of Man From U.N.C.L.E.: The Fifteen Years Later Affair. CBS 4/5/83. 2 hours. Michael Sloan Productions and Viacom Enterprises. Director: Ray Austin. Executive Producer/Writer: Michael Sloan. Producer: Nigel Watts. Creators: Norman Felton and Sam H. Rolfe. Music: Gerald Fried. Theme: Jerry Goldsmith.

Retired superspies Napoleon Solo, now a computer company chief with a taste for gambling, and Ilya Kuryakin, now a fashion designer, are called back to service by the new U.N.C.L.E. boss (Patrick Macnee) to battle an old T.H.R.U.S.H. foe (Anthony Zerbe) who has escaped from prison. The veteran, albeit rusty, agents are teamed with Benjamin Kowalski (Tom Mason), a brash, new U.N.C.L.E. operative. George Lazenby, one-time 007, made a cameo appearance as a thinly veiled James Bond named J.B. Michael Sloan would later oversee the revival of *McCloud* as well as *The Six Million Dollar Man* and *The Bionic Woman*.

Cast: Robert Vaughn (as Napoleon Solo), David McCallum (Ilya Kuryakin), Patrick Macnee (Sir John Raleigh), Tom Mason (Benjamin Kowalski), Gayle Hunnicutt (Andrea Markovich), Geoffrey Lewis (Janus), Anthony Zerbe (Justin Sepheran), Simon Williams (Nigel Pennington Smythe), John Harkins (Alexi Kemp), Jan Triska (Vaselievitch), Susan Woolen (Janice Friday), Carolyn Seymour (Actress), George Lazenby (J.B.), Judith Chapman (Z), Lois De Banzie (Ms. Delquist), Dick Durock (Guido), Randi Brooks (Model), Jack Somack (Tailor), Eddie Barker (Card Dealer).

295. The Return of the Six Million Dollar Man and the Bionic Woman. NBC 5/17/87. 2 hours. Michael Sloan Productions and Universal Television. Director: Ray Austin. Executive Producer: Michael Sloan. Producer: Bruce Lansbury. Writer: Michael Sloan, from a story by Sloan and Bruce Lansbury, based on the book *Cyborg* by Martin Caiden. Music: Marvin Hamlisch.

An attempt to mount a spin-off of *The Six Million Dollar Man* (ABC 1973–78) and *The Bionic Woman* (ABC 1976–77, NBC 1977–78). The bionic duo of Steve Austin (Lee Majors) and Jaime Sommers (Lindsay Wagner) are called out of retirement and reunited by Oscar Goldman (Richard Anderson) to battle a maniacal villain (Martin Landau). In the midst of it all, they relive (via flashbacks) and rekindle their ill-fated romance. But the real story revolves around Steve's (never before mentioned) estranged son Michael (Tom Schanley), an Air Force test pilot who, like his father, is nearly killed in a catastrophic crash. He's fitted with bionic parts, helped through feelings of freakishness by shrink Jaime, and reconciles with his father—all before being kidnapped by the evil baddie. Although this pilot earned big ratings, a Schanley bionic series didn't happen, and a second pilot, *The Bionic Showdown*, featuring a young, female bionic spy, was made in 1989. That new bionic woman was played by Sandra Bullock who, of course, went on to much bigger and better things. In 2007, NBC tried 'rebooting' *The Bionic Woman* as a new series starring Michelle Ryan as Jaime Sommers. It was cancelled after only nine episodes.

Cast: Lee Majors (as Steve Austin), Lindsay Wagner (Jaime Sommers), Richard Anderson (Oscar Goldman), Tom Schanley (Michael Austin), Martin E. Brooks (Dr. Rudy Wells), Martin Landau (Charles Stenning), Lee Majors, II (Jim Castillian), Gary Lockwood (John Praiser), Deborah White (Sally), Robert Hoy (Kyle), Patrick Pankhurst (Duke Rennecker), Terry Kiser (Santiago).

296. **Return to Green Acres.** CBS 5/18/90. 2 hours. Jaygee Productions and Orion Television. Director: William Asher. Executive Producer: Jerry Golod. Producer: Anthony Santa Croce. Writers: Craig Heller, Guy Shulman, based on characters created by Jay Sommers. Music: Dan Foliart. Theme: Vic Mizzy. Sung by Eddie Albert and Eva Gabor.

Just about everyone from the beloved sitcom of the 1960s is back for this bloated, witless revival that's a rarity—a two-hour pilot with a laugh track. Oliver Douglas, once the sensible and certainly the most intelligent citizen of Hooterville, has apparently softened over the years, mainly in the head, so that now he is as daffy as his neighbors. If only he were as funny, too. Wife Lisa remains, well, Lisa. Otherwise, Hooterville is as we left it, but not for long—a greedy real estate tycoon (played by Henry Gibson) is about to bulldoze the entire town to make way for a parking lot. The new theme, sung by the two stars, began with the familiar "Green Acres" lyrics, then segued into:

OLIVER: "Seems time has been just rollin' on/
Made a lot of friends who've come and gone/
Some things change as years go by/
On other things you can rely."
LISA: "I never thought you'd hear me say/
Milking cows is how I start my day."
OLIVER: "We're happy with this life we've found/
Who needs the city, we're on solid ground."
OLIVER/LISA: "We'll take the country/
It's fresh and clear/
Green Acres, we live here."

Thankfully, Arnold the Pig had the sense not to join in.

Cast: Eddie Albert (Oliver Douglas), Eva Gabor (Lisa Douglas), Alvy Moore (Hank Kimball), Mary Grace Canfield (Ralph Monroe), Sid Melton (Al Monroe), Tom Lester (Ed Dawson), Frank Cady (Sam Drucker), Pat Buttram (Mr. Haney), Mary Tanner (Daisy Ziffel), Henry Gibson (E. Mitchell Armstrong), John Scott Clough (Brad Armstrong), Mark Ballou (Jeb Dawson), Lucy Lee Flippin (Flo Dawson), John Asher (Chill), Jeff Rochlin (Lester), Lycia Naff (B.B.), John Alvin (E. Wilfred), Tom Simmons (Sheriff Bedford), Sally Kemp (Ruthie), Tippi Hedren (Arleen).

297. The Saint (aka The Saint in Manhattan). CBS 6/12/87. 60 minutes. D.L. Taffner Productions and Television Reports International, Ltd. Director: James Frawley. Executive Producers: Dennis E. Doty and Robert S. Baker. Producer: George Manasse. Writers: Peter Gethers and David Handler. Creator: Leslie Charteris. Music: Mark Snow.

Aired as a segment of *CBS Summer Playhouse.* Andrew Clarke, a mustachioed Australian actor, assumes the role of Simon Templar, the handsome rogue, thief, and dapper adventurer who, in this flop pilot, moves from London to New York, where he and his manservant Woods reside in a luxurious Waldorf Astoria suite, to the consternation of N.Y.P.D. Inspector Fernack. Clarke winked, mugged, and wiggled his eyebrows across Manhattan, but he failed to capture the charm of his predecessors in the role. In the pilot, he becomes the prime suspect when the ballerina he's been protecting finds her diamond tiara missing. Robert S. Baker also served as executive producer of the original *Saint* TV series starring Roger Moore and its short-lived sequel, *Return of the Saint*, which starred Ian Ogilvy and aired on CBS late-night during the late 1970s. Undaunted by CBS' rejection, the producers took the project to syndication for a series of TV movies starring Simon Dutton.

Cast: Andrew Clarke (as Simon Templar), George Rose (Woods), Kevin Tighe (Inspector John Fernack), Christopher Mercantel (Joey), Holland Taylor (Fran Grogan), Caitlin Clarke (Jessica Hildy), Liliana Komorowska (Margot Layne), Michael Lombard (Wally Grogan), Raymond Serra (Carmine), Robert LuPone (Jeffrey Sinclair), Peter Maloney (The Fixer), Ben Vereen (Nightclub Singer), Kevin O'Rourke (Detective), Kelly Connell (Elevator Man), Brian Evers (Bartender), Mick Muldoon (Doorman), Elyse Knight (Stewardess), Katie Anders (Nanny), Ellis E. Williams (Willie the Con), Mary Lou Picard (Desk Clerk), Frank Ferrara (Goon #1), Valentino Diaz (Goon #2), Al Cerullo (Helicopter Pilot), Ray Iannicelli (Toy Store Clerk).

298. **Still Crazy Like a Fox.** CBS 4/5/87. 2 hours. Shulman/Baskin/Schenk/Cardea Productions and Columbia Pictures Television. Director: Paul Krasny. Executive Producers/Writers: George Schenk and Frank Cardea. Producer: Bill Hill. Based on characters created by Roger Shulman, John Baskin, George Schenk, and Frank Cardea. Music: Mark Snow.

An attempt to pump new life into the 1984—86 series *Crazy Like a Fox,* with rumpled private investigator Harry Fox vacationing in London with his uptight, button-down lawyer son Harrison, daughter-in-law Cindy, and grandson Josh, and finding himself accused of murdering a duke. The pilot, which the production company referred to simply as "episode #36," was filmed entirely on location in England. Plans were to offer the revival series into first-run syndication if the network turned it down. Apparently, the fickle independent stations were not interested, having also rejected Columbia's newly proposed *The Return of Ben Casey* and *That's My Mama Now!*

Cast: Jack Warden (Harry Fox), John Rubinstein (Harrison Fox), Penny Peyser (Cindy Fox), Robby Kiger (Josh Fox), Catherine Oxenberg (Nancy Church), Graham Chapman (Inspector Palmer), Michael Jayston (Randall Perry), James Faulkner (William Church), Rosemary

Leach (Mrs. Eleanor Trundle), also Colin Stinton, Moray Watson, John Moffatt, Maxine Howe, Matt Zimmerman, Allan Cuthbertson, John Cater, Paul Brooke, C. J. Allen, Stephen Churchett, Alberto Morris.

299. Still the Beaver. CBS 3/19/83. 2 hours. Bud Austin Productions and Universal Television. Director: Steven Hilliard Stern. Executive Producer: Bud Austin. Producer: Nick Abdo. Writer: Brian Levant, from a story by Levant and Nick Abdo. Creators: Joe Connelly and Bob Mosher. Music: John Cacavas. Theme: Melvin Lenard, Mort Greene, and Dave Kahn.

A nostalgic, bittersweet pilot that reunites the cast of the beloved comedy *Leave It to Beaver*. Beaver Cleaver, now a divorced father of two kids, returns to Mayfield to raise his kids with the help of his widowed mother. His brother Wally is a married lawyer with a daughter of his own, and his friend Eddie Haskell is married, too, and has a son who's the mirror image of himself as a kid. Although CBS passed on it, *Still the Beaver* went on to become (with some cast changes) a successful series on the Disney Channel cable network. It then jumped to Superstation WTBS, where it was redubbed *The New Leave It to Beaver* and continued for several seasons before going into syndication.

Cast: Barbara Billingsley (as June Cleaver), Tony Dow (Wally Cleaver), Jerry Mathers (Beaver Cleaver), Ken Osmond (Eddie Haskell), Frank Bank (Clarence "Lumpy" Rutherford), Ed Begley, Jr. (Whitey Whitney), Corey Feldman (Corey Cleaver), John Snee (Oliver Cleaver), Richard Correll (Richard Rickover), Rusty Stevens (Larry Mondello), Janice Kent (Mary Ellen Cleaver), Joanna Gleason (Kimberly Cleaver), Diane Brewster (Miss Canfield), Luke Fafara (Tooey Brown), Damon Hines (Marcus Garvey), Eric Osmond (Eddie Haskell, Jr.).

300. The Wild Wild West Revisited. [Pilot #1]. CBS 5/9/79. 2 hours. CBS Entertainment. Director: Burt Kennedy. Executive Producer: Jay Bernstein. Producer: Robert L. Jacks. Writer: William Bowers. Creator: Michael Garrison. Music: Richard Markowitz.

The first of two unsold pilots reuniting secret service agents James West (Robert Conrad) and Artemus Gordon (Ross Martin), who traveled the frontier in the 1860s and the airwaves on CBS from 1965–69.

They are brought out of retirement (West owns a bordertown saloon, Gordon is a struggling actor) to battle the son (Paul Williams) of their long-dead arch-foe Dr. Loveless, who is dabbing in cloning and nuclear power. Available on home video.

Cast: Robert Conrad (as James West), Ross Martin (Artemus Gordon), Paul Williams (Miguelito Loveless), Harry Morgan (Robert T. Malone), Rene Auberjonois (Capt. Sir David Edney), Jo Ann Harris (Carmelita Loveless), Trisha Noble (Penelope), Jeff Mackay (Hugo Kaufman), Susan Blu (Gabrielle), Pavla Ustinov (Nadia), Wilford Brimley (President Grover Cleveland), Robert Shields (Alan), Lorene Yarnell (Sonya), Jacqueline Hyde (Queen Victoria), Alberto Morin (Spanish King), Jeff Redford (The Kid), Ted Hartley (Russian Tsar), Skip Homeier (Joseph), John Wheeler (Henry), Mike Wagner (Manager), Joyce Jameson (Lola).

300a. More Wild Wild West. [Pilot #2]. CBS 10/7/80. 2 hours. CBS Entertainment. Director: Burt Kennedy. Executive Producer: Jay Bernstein. Producer: Robert L. Jacks. Writers: William Bowers and Tony Kayden. Creator: Michael Garrison. Music: Richard Markowitz and Jeff Alexander.

A sequel to *The Wild Wild West Revisited*, and the second attempt to revive the beloved Western starring Robert Conrad and Ross Martin as secret agents in the Old West. This time, the agents are pitted against mad scientist Jonathan Winters. Guest star Victor Buono was the bad guy in the original *Wild Wild West* pilot, and Harry Morgan and Rene Auberjonois reprise their roles from the first revival.

Cast: Robert Conrad (as James West), Ross Martin (Artemus Gordon), Harry Morgan (Robert T. Malone), Rene Auberjonois (Sir David Edney), Jonathan Winters (Professor Albert Paradine), Victor Buono (Dr. Messenger), Liz Torres (Juanita), Randi Brough (Yvonne), Candi Brough (Daphne), Emma Samms (Mirabelle), Avery Schreiber (Russian Ambassador), Dr. Joyce Brothers (Bystander), Jack LaLanne (Jack LaStrange), Hector Elias (Spanish Ambassador), Joe Alfasa (Italian Ambassador), Dave Madden (German Ambassador), Gino Conforti (French Ambassador).

BIBLIOGRAPHY

Barnouw, Erik. *Tube of Plenty: The Evolution of American Television*, rev. ed. New York: Oxford University Press, 1982

Bedell, Sally. *Up the Tube: Primetime TV and the Silverman Years*. New York: The Viking Press, 1981

Brooks, Tim, and Earle Marsh. *The Complete Directory of Primetime Network TV Shows 1946–Present*, Rev. Ed. New York: Ballantine Books, 1981

Castleman, Harry, and Walter J. Podrazik. *Watching TV: Four Decades of American Television*. New York: McGraw-Hill, 1982

Christensen, Mark, and Cameron Stauth. *The Sweeps: Behind The Scenes in Network TV.* New York: William Morrow and Company, 1984

Cole, Barry S. *Television—Selections from TV Guide Magazine*. New York: The Free Press, 1970

Eisener, Joel, and David Krinsky. *Television Comedy Series: An Episode Guide to 153 TV Sitcoms in Syndication.* Jefferson, N.C.: McFarland and Company, 1984

Feuer, Jane, and Paul Kerr and Tise Vahimagi. *MTM—Quality Television.* London: British Film Institute, 1984

Fireman, Judy. *TV Book.* New York: Workman Publishing Company, 1977

Gerani, Gary, and Paul S. Schulman. *Fantastic Television.* New York: Harmony Books, 1977

Gianakos, Larry James. *Television Drama Series Programming: A Comprehensive Chronicle, 1959–1975.* Metuchen, N.J.: Scarecrow Press, 1978

—————*Television Drama Series Programming: 1947–1959* Metuchen, N.J. Scarecrow Press, 1980

—————*Television Drama Series Programming: 1975—1980* Metuchen, N.J. Scarecrow Press, 1981

——————*Television Drama Series Programming: 1980–1982* Metuchen, N.J. Scarecrow Press, 1983

Gitlin, Todd. *Inside Primetime.* New York: Pantheon Books, 1983

Head, Sydney, with Christopher H. Sterling. *Broadcasting in America,* 4th ed. New York: Houghton Mifflin Company, 1982

Kelly, Richard. *The Andy Griffith Show,* revised and expanded edition. Winston-Salem, N.C.: John F. Blair, Publisher, 1984

Levinson, Richard, and William Link. *Stay Tuned: An Inside Look at the Making of Primetime Television.* New York: St. Martin's Press, 1981

——————*Off Camera: Conversations With the Makers of Primetime Television.* New York: American Library, 1986

Maltin, Leonard. *TV Movies and Video Guide.* 1990 Edition. New York: New American Library, 1989

Marill, Alvin H. *Movies Made for Television—The Telefeature and the Mini-Series.* New York: New York Zoetrope, 1987

McCarty, John, and Brian Kelleher. *Alfred Hitchcock Presents.* New York: St. Martin's Press, 1985

McNeil, Alex. Total Television—A Comprehensive Guide to Programming from *1948 to the Present,* 2nd ed. New York: Penguin Books, 1984

Meyers, Richard. *TV Detectives.* San Diego, Cai.: A.S. Barnes and Co., 1981

Miller, Merle, and Evan Rhodes. *Only You, Dick Daring: How to Write One Television Script and Make $50,000,000.* New York: William Sloan Associates, 1964

Mitz, Rick. *The Great TV Sitcom Book.* Expanded Edition. New York: Pedigree Books, 1983

Newcomb, Horace, and Robert S. Alley. *The Producer's Medium.* New York: Oxford University Press, 1983

Parish, James Robert. *Actors Television Credits 1950–1972.* Metuchen, N.J.: Scarecrow Press, 1973

——————, *and Mark Trost.* Actors Television Credits, Supplement I. Metuchen, N.J.: Scarecrow Press, 1978

——————, *and Vincent Terrace.* Actors Television Credits, Supplement 11: *1977–1981.* Metuchen, N.J.: Scarecrow Press, 1982

——————, *and Vincent Terrace.* Actors Television Credits, Supplement III: *1982–1985.* Metuchen, N.J.: Scarecrow Press, 1986

Perry, Jeb H. *Universal Television: The Studio and Its Programs, 1950–1980.* Metuchen, N.J.: Scarecrow Press, 1983.

Scheuer, Steven H. *The Television Annual 1978–79.* New York: Collier Books, 1979

——————, *Movies on TV.* New York: Bantam Books, 1982

Schow, David J., and Jeffrey Frentzen. *The Outer Limits: The Official Companion.* New York: Ace Science Fiction Books, 1986

Terrace, Vincent. *Encyclopedia of Television—Series, Pilots and Specials 1936–1973.* New York: New York Zoetrope, 1986

——————, *Encyclopedia of Television—Series, Pilots and Specials 1974–1984.* New York: New York Zoetrope, 1985

——————, *Encyclopedia of Television—Series, Pilots and Specials. The Index: Who's Who in Television 1937–1984.* New York: New York Zoetrope, 1986

TV Guide Roundup. New York: Holt, Rinehart and Winston, 1960

Weissman, Ginny, and Coyne Steven Sanders. *The Dick Van Dyke Show—Anatomy of a Classic.* New York: St. Martin's Press, 1983

Wicking, Christopher, and Tise Vahimagi. *The American Vein: Directors and Directions in Television.* New York: E.P. Dutton, 1979

Woolley, Lynn, and Robert W. Malsbary and Robert G. Strange, Jr. *Warner Bros. Television.* Jefferson, N.C.: McFarland and Company, 1985

Zicree, Marc Scott. *The Twilight Zone Companion.* New York: Bantam Books, 1982

ABOUT THE AUTHOR

Lee Goldberg is a two-time Edgar Award and Shamus Award nominee whose many TV writing and/or producing credits include *Martial Law, SeaQuest, Diagnosis Murder, The Cosby Mysteries, Hunter, Spenser: For Hire, Nero Wolfe, The Glades* and *Monk.* His many books include *The Walk, King City, Successful Television Writing, Watch Me Die,* the *Diagnosis Murder* and *Monk* series of original mystery novels, and the internationally bestselling Fox & O'Hare series that he co-authors with Janet Evanovich. As a TV development consultant, he's worked for production companies and broadcasters in Germany, Spain, Sweden, and the Netherlands. His other television reference books include *Unsold Television Pilots 1955-1989* and *Television Fast Forward.*

INDEX

Titles of unsold pilots (including alternate titles) are in **bold**; other titles (series, films, books, etc.) are in *italics*. Entries are cited as they appear in credits listings, and numbers are those of individual entries (not pages).